An Introduction to Ethics

An Introduction to Ethics

FIVE CENTRAL PROBLEMS OF
MORAL JUDGEMENT

Geoffrey Thomas

Published in the UK by
GERALD DUCKWORTH & CO. LTD
London

Published in North America by
HACKETT PUBLISHING COMPANY
Indianapolis / Cambridge

First published in the UK in 1993 by
Gerald Duckworth & Co. Ltd.
The Old Piano Factory
48 Hoxton Square, London N1 6PB
Tel: 071 729 5986
Fax: 071 729 0015

First published in North America in 1993 by
Hackett Publishing Company, Inc.
PO Box 44937
Indianapolis, Indiana 46244-0937

UK edition:
ISBN 0 7156 2431 8
A catalogue record for this book is available
from the British Library

Library of Congress Cataloging-in-Publication Data

Thomas, Geoffrey, 1944-
    An introduction to ethics / Geoffrey Thomas.
        p.   cm.
    Includes bibliographical references and index.
    ISBN 0-87220-185-6 (C : alk. paper). – ISBN 0-87220-184-8 (P :
alk. paper)
        1. Ethics.   I. Title.
BJ1012.T54   1993
170–dc20   93-6604
                                                       CIP

The paper used in this publication meets the minimum requirements of
American National Standard for Information Sciences–Permanence of Paper
for Printed Library Materials, ANSI Z39.48-1984.

⊗

Printed in the United States of America

Contents

Chapter 2. The Specification of Moral Judgement

Chapter 3. Moral Judgement and The Moral Standard

Chapter 4. The Justification of Moral Judgement

Chapter 5. Logic, Reasoning and Moral Judgement

Chapter 6. Moral Judgement and Moral Responsibility

Endnote

TO THE MEMORY OF
MICHAEL OAKESHOTT

Preface

I am indebted to my colleague, Dr Anthony Grayling, from whose initiative this book has its origin.

My next thanks must go to my Birkbeck students since 1988 for the welcome spur of their reaction to my presentation of ethics: to Cari Aitken, Raymond Boyce, Sarah Bruml, Don de Carle, David Coffey, Brian Curtis, Jonathan Dronsfield, John Florentin, Ramon Gonzalez, Stuart Greenstreet, Suzanne Hall, Natalia Karapanagioti, Cyril Lawson, Chris McWatters, Roger Mortimer, Paul Murfill, Titus Ogunleye, Rajendra Persaud, Bill Prothero, Horace Reid, Diana Roberts, David Rodway, Stefan Shankland, Robert Sheardown, Chris Smith, Javier Vidal, Margaret Watts, and Katie Yuill. Critical discussion, disagreement, endorsement: *in nocte consilium*. For me Birkbeck has lived up to its motto.

Robert Sheardown deserves special mention for constantly bringing up fresh problems in utilitarianism. Our weekly tutorials in 1990 were a real intellectual stimulation.

I have also received invaluable aid from Dr David Rees of Jesus College, Oxford, who read the greater part of my original typescript. I am indebted to him for many corrections and suggestions, but am entirely responsible for the faults that remain.

I am also indebted to my American publishers for their reader's report; and to Dr David Mitchell of Cambridge University for a long, reflective, and enlightening conversation in September this year.

Final acknowledgement is due to Leslie Marsh. I began as his tutor; he continues as my friend. I value his help and encouragement.

Birkbeck College, London   G.T.
6 December 1992

Key to References and Quotations

References to standard books and articles give the author's surname, followed by the date of publication and the page, part, section or chapter reference. Full details appear in the bibliography. 'Allan, 1970: 128-30', for example, refers to D.J. Allan, *Aristotle*, 2nd ed., Oxford, 1970, pages 128-30.

Central historical texts are normally referred to by capital letters from their titles:

EHU Hume, *Enquiry Concerning the Human Understanding.*
EPM Hume, *Enquiry Concerning the Principles of Morals. Enquiries concerning the Human Understanding and the Principles of Morals*, ed. L.A. Selby-Bigge, rev. P.H. Nidditch, 3rd ed., Oxford, 1975.
F   Kant, *Foundations of the Metaphysics of Morals*, tr. L.W. Beck, New York, 1969.
NE   Aristotle, *Nicomachean Ethics*, tr. Sir David Ross, Oxford, 1969.
R   Plato, *Republic*, tr. H.D.P. Lee, 2nd ed. rev., Harmondsworth, 1988.
T   Hume, *A Treatise of Human Nature*, ed. L.A. Selby-Bigge, rev. P.H. Nidditch, 2nd ed., Oxford, 1978.
U   J.S. Mill, *Utilitarianism, Essential Works of John Stuart Mill*, ed. M. Lerner, New York, 1971.

For translations I cite the translator's name: thus 'NE, I.7; Ross, 14' refers to *Nicomachean Ethics*, Book I, chapter 7, page 14 of Sir David Ross's translation.

CHAPTER 1

Introduction

1.1. ABOUT THE BOOK

This book, which is intended primarily for the first-year philosophy under-graduate beginning the study of ethics, will also (I hope) be of interest to the general reader who wants to know something of a philosophical angle on the moral life. It is an *introduction* to ethics in a double sense. It assumes no knowledge of philosophy in general or of ethics in particular; and it presumes further reading and reflection. The book's only finality is that it ends on a certain page.

It is a book which recognizes that people differ in the way they prefer to learn. I have had particularly in mind the student who does not want to be thrown in at the deep end but wants a groundplan of a new subject, a view of its structure.

I part company with the view that an introductory textbook needs a bias. This common view centres in the idea that a committed presentation, a book of one standpoint, forces problems and topics into a single, coherent perspective. And this supposedly is what the beginning student needs in order to avoid confusion in the face of complexity. I disagree: for the kind of student I have mainly in mind what is needed is a clear picture of the structure of the subject. So, quickly said, if you are looking for a refutation of utilitarianism, a vindication of Kant, or an assurance that we should go 'back to the Greeks' (which nowadays usually means Aristotle) as the proper starting point in ethics, you will not find it here. But then, if you are in quest of these things you are no recruit but a seasoned campaigner. Doubtless my own ideas about the best options in ethics will show through. But getting beginners to think likewise is no part of my plan.

Then to start. My aim in this chapter is:

- to show ethics as a branch of philosophy
- to outline the structure of ethics
- to mark off my own approach to ethics from rival approaches
- to set out a programme for the book

2.1. ETHICS AND PHILOSOPHY

There is no formula by which to capture all the things that have carried the name 'philosophy'. At one time 'philosophy' – the original Greek word, *philosophia*, just means 'love of wisdom' – included natural science, a usage that survives in the antiquated term, 'natural philosophy'. Philosophy no longer includes natural science on any reckoning.

Nor is it to be confused with other things. It is not 'homespun' wisdom, teaching ways of life and telling us how we should live. It is not psychology, the science of the mind or the scientific study of behaviour. It is not religion in general or theosophy in particular (the idea that we can understand God through deep cultivation of the inner life). I respect these things but they are not philosophy.

There are two activities which have always gone on under the name of 'philosophy' and which are central to the subject as now understood:

- conceptual analysis
- high-level theorizing of certain kinds

Conceptual analysis

'Conceptual analysis' sounds something unusual, possibly difficult or maybe just pretentious. The first question to ask is: what is a concept?

We approach the world through a mind-net of categories. We describe, classify, and explain: and the categories by which we do so are concepts. Note some of the things we say. 'The dog knocked over the vase', 'Inflation means unemployment', 'It was the barbiturate that brought about his death.' Dog, vase, inflation, death – these are all concepts.

But there are concepts – and concepts. Look at the three statements I quoted. They all assert *causal relations*. Effects are ascribed to the dog, to inflation, to the barbiturate. And the concept of *cause* is of immediate philosophical interest as a basic category in terms of which we interpret our experience. It plays a definite role in some sciences; and it plays an obvious and enormous role in everyday life.

One major part of philosophy, namely metaphysics, centres on such categories or concepts – concepts that are of extremely wide, perhaps even (in some cases) exceptionless, application in our experience. Every event occurs in space and time; everything is identical with itself; one thing causes another; two or more things can resemble one another, if both (say) are red and so 'share' a property or a universal (in philosophers' usage) which is 'present' in both of them. And so space, time, identity, cause, universal and a range of other concepts are analysed in metaphysics.

Again, we say: 'She says she knows, but she's only guessing', 'He's certain but he's wrong', 'He believes all too many things, far more than the evidence justifies.' Here is another cluster of concepts of quite general application – knowledge, certainty, belief, evidence: and the branch of philosophy that deals with them is epistemology or the theory of knowledge.

Equally we infer and argue; we say that one claim follows from or entails another; that two claims are inconsistent and so cannot both be true; that a position is self-contradictory: argument, inference, entailment, truth – more concepts and another branch of philosophy, namely the philosophy of logic.

The concepts we have been considering are all of extremely wide application. They do not apply just to particular areas of our experience but are put to work quite generally. Other concepts are specific to certain areas of experience. We call these *domain concepts*. For example, and crucially relevant to the present book, we hold people responsible for doing things of which we approve or disapprove, we accept or reject moral excuses, we recognize moral judgements as distinct from other kinds of claim: and ethics examines this cluster of concepts – responsibility, excuse, moral judgement – among many others. These concepts are central to our moral experience. How could we think of the moral life except in terms of such concepts?

Ethics is only one example of philosophy concerned with domain concepts. There is also aesthetics, which analyses domain concepts like art, beauty, sublimity; and political philosophy, which homes in on concepts such as the state, democracy, social justice, freedom. Examples could be multiplied.

So philosophy is concerned with concepts, and peculiarly basic concepts at that: concepts which are basic to the description, classification and explanation of very wide ranges of our experience (as in metaphysics) or to particular areas of it (as in ethics). Then what is this activity of philosophical 'analysis' of them? What is conceptual analysis?

Essentially, when you analyse a concept you try to draw out the conditions for its application. Let's move away from ethics for a moment to make the point clear in a different branch of philosophy. Take the concept of knowledge, and more specifically what is called propositional knowledge – knowing that something (call it 'X') is the case, where this kind of knowledge contrasts with practical knowledge or knowing how to do something. There is a claim that you know that something is the case if and only if three conditions are met:

(1) X really is the case; in other words, it is true that X
(2) You believe that X is the case
(3) You are justified by the evidence in believing that X is the case

This is often called the 'justified true belief' analysis of propositional knowledge. Suppose we accept this analysis; then here would be an example of a concept that can be pinned down by specifying necessary and sufficient conditions for its application. That is, unless these three conditions are met, then you do not know that X. So the conditions are necessary. And if the conditions are met, nothing else is required. You do know that X. The conditions are sufficient.

Whether or not the justified true belief analysis of propositional knowledge is correct, there are other concepts for which the necessary and sufficient conditions approach does not appear to work. In ethics, take the concept of blame. Harming you and doing so intentionally may be sufficient for blame (though I am not convinced even of that), but they are hardly necessary: I can still be blameworthy if I harm you and do so unintentionally but through negligent ignorance. It may not even be necessary to harm you; it may be enough that I try to do so. Perhaps the concept of blame is an example of a concept for which there are sufficient but no necessary conditions.

High-level theorizing

Philosophy has always included the analysis of concepts but has never been confined to just that. It has always included other activities, the most common of which is high-level theorizing of certain kinds. An example will best give the feel of such theorizing.

Philosophers have offered theories of knowledge. They have not settled for analysing the concept of knowledge in the way we briefly considered just above. They have made claims about (among other things) the structure and even the possibility of knowledge.

About the structure of knowledge: in the idea for instance that (to put it figuratively) knowledge must have a pyramid shape, with a base or 'foundation' of things about which it is impossible for us to be mistaken and from which everything else that we know is inferred or causally derived. A view of this foundationalist sort is to be found in Descartes. *Cogito ergo sum*; 'I think therefore I am': the primal certainty.

There are also claims about the possibility of knowledge: in the idea for instance that since there is nothing about which it is impossible for us to be mistaken (even the truth of that belief itself?) therefore the foundations of knowledge are missing and so nobody ever knows anything to be the case. This view is scepticism – or pyrrhonism as it is sometimes quaintly called (from Pyrrho, an ancient sceptic).

Examples of high-level theorizing in ethics would be the claims that moral judgements can be literally true or false and that it is irrational to act immorally.

As we work through ethics, check your reactions to see if these activities, of conceptual analysis and high-level theorizing, are adequate to all that is going on.

2.2. THE STRUCTURE OF ETHICS

To say that ethics is a branch of philosophy taken up with conceptual analysis and high-level theorizing of certain kinds concerning morality or the moral life, is fine and perfectly correct. But it is not enough; it does not disclose any of the internal complexity of the subject. In my view ethics has a five-part structure:

- the specification of moral judgement
- moral judgement and the moral standard
- the justification of moral judgement

- logic, reasoning, and moral judgement
- moral judgement and moral responsibility

2.2.1. The ambiguity of 'moral'

At present, that structure is a set of empty boxes. But we can start slipping some content into the boxes by considering two lists of claims. There is nothing special about these claims, which anyone might make:

List A

(1) Moral values have come to be distinguished from religious values only recently in human cultural history.
(2) Moral principles vary from one community to another.
(3) Shirley Lee has a painful moral dilemma.
(4) Remorse is a moral emotion.
(5) Josh has written a long essay on the moral beliefs of the ancient Greeks.

List B

(6) Mary Lou is not a very moral person.
(7) If you think that's a moral course of action, you show a corrupt mind.
(8) Don't accuse me of not having moral motives, you appalling hypocrite.
(9) To go on holiday during your wife's illness was hardly a moral decision.
(10) I cannot agree that animal experimentation is a moral practice.

The word 'moral', which occurs throughout these examples, clearly differs in sense between Lists A and B. Rather roughly, in List A 'moral' means 'relating to morality' and it contrasts with 'non-moral'. In List B the contrast is with 'immoral'. List B's sense of 'moral' is approximately that of 'morally good'.

To put the point another way, the claims in List A could all be made by someone whose reasoning excludes moral considerations, the *amoralist* of ethics textbooks who sees such considerations as having no relevance to his or her life. By contrast, the claims in List B, if we assume sincerity, are those of someone in whose outlook moral considerations play a role. The claims in List B are moral judgements.

'Moral judgement' is an ambiguous term. Roughly, it may refer to (1) the psychological act or process of drawing a conclusion; or it may mean (2) a claim, belief, statement, proposition or sentence – some mental entity or linguistic item. I say something more about this in 11.1. The general point is that I shall generally use the term in sense (2).

Evidently we can make a moral judgement without using the word 'moral' or its derivatives. 'Wrong', 'worse', 'evil', 'vicious', 'justice'. All these terms and many others regularly feature in moral judgements:

List C

(11) All lying is wrong.
(12) Some lying is worse than any killing.
(13) Bill is not mentally ill but plain evil.
(14) If pride and jealousy are vicious qualities, so is greed.
(15) Justice delayed is justice denied.

Now you may be visited with a thought. Is the relationship between the claims in Lists B and C, by virtue of which we call them all 'moral judgements' and distinguish them from the claims in List A, that of having a common property or properties?

That question slips us straight into the first part of ethics, the problem of the specification of moral judgement.

3.1. FIRST PROBLEM: THE SPECIFICATION OF MORAL JUDGEMENT

There is no lack of candidates for the common property or properties of moral judgements. According to different theories, moral judgements:

- have certain *formal features*:
  - prescriptivity
  - universalizability
- have a *particular content*:
  - relating to human welfare and harm
- are *categorical*
- involve a *specific emotion*
- are associated with *certain sanctions*
- reflect an *'all-in' point of view*

3.1.1. The general characterization of moral judgement

I shall not explain the terms 'prescriptivity', 'universalizability', and 'categorical' now: we can best clarify them when we look at the relevant theories (12.2, 14.1). All these theories offer us a *general characterization* of moral judgement. This is one topic within our first ethical problem.

3.1.2. The objects of moral judgement

Looking back at Lists B and C, we might also ask about the objects of moral judgement, whether there is a special set of objects which are the proper targets of moral judgement. This accordingly is another topic.

There is an idea, influential but seldom committed to print, that moral judgements fundamentally concern the actions of individual persons: that a moral judgement, whatever its surface form, is always reducible to, or paraphrasable by, a judgement on such actions. This idea is a version of *methodological individualism*, a general approach to social analysis (Macdonald and Pettit, 1981: ch. 3).

An opposing view is that certain moral judgements on collectivities and institutions (including 'legal' persons) are not thus reducible. Everyone remembers Marx (a bit) as distinguishing in the preface to *Capital* between the moral assessment of capitalism and the moral assessment of the actions of individual capitalists. In our own day a firmly non-marxist philosopher, John Rawls, holds that judgements of justice are primarily about institutions and only indirectly and derivatively about the actions of individual persons (Rawls, 1971). And for Onora O'Neill institutions and collectivities are agents properly attracting a wide range of moral judgements, not simply those of justice (O'Neill, 1986: 32-8, 49). See also Scruton, 1988: 73-8.

Now turn back to Lists B and C and note the ostensible objects of moral judgement there – persons, courses of action, motives, decisions, practices and the rest. The translation of some of these judgements into judgements referring only to the actions of individual persons might be rather involved. That practical point aside, do you think that reduction is possible in principle in all cases? However it strikes you, you are starting to think about a topic within the specification of moral judgement.

3.1.3. The elucidation of moral concepts

There is a further topic. We might be interested in the *range of concepts* entering into moral judgements, concepts of whose diversity we have some idea from List C – 'wrong', 'worse', 'evil', 'vicious', 'justice'. We can step outside C and extend the list greatly. At the limit the aim would be to enumerate and analyse all the relevant moral concepts, giving where possible a 'decompositional' analysis in terms of necessary and sufficient conditions: 'an action is just if and only if ....' In one sense of 'meaning' such an analysis would give the meaning of the relevant moral terms.

We might also seek to group moral concepts. Bernard Williams, for example, divides moral concepts into 'thick' and 'thin'. The 'thicker' a concept, the tighter its connection with descriptive criteria. If I say, for instance, 'Dillon did something really wrong last week', you have no concrete idea what he did. Perhaps he quit his job; perhaps he knocked his neighbour senseless; perhaps ... How can you say, unless I say more? 'Wrong' is a thin concept. Contrast 'Dillon did something really courageous last week.' In this case you know that, if I am right, Dillon did an action (whatever it was) in the face of unpleasant obstacles, painful difficulties. 'Courage' is a relatively 'thick' concept. See B. Williams, 1985: 140-5; and Gibbard, Blackburn, and Burton, 1992.

3.1.4. Summary

The problem of the specification of moral judgement splits up into the topics of:

- the general characterization of moral judgements
- the objects of moral judgement
- the elucidation of moral concepts

On this problem, this first part of the structure of ethics, I will restrict myself in this book mainly to the general characterization of moral judgements, allowing for the possibility e.g. that a general characterization may itself rest in part on a view of the objects of moral judgement.

4.1. SECOND PROBLEM: MORAL JUDGEMENT AND THE MORAL STANDARD

Lists B and C contain various claims. Your first thought will of course be that they are an unconnected heap.

4.1.1. The moral criterion

Suppose we confine ourselves to moral judgements on the actions of individual persons. We might then say, putting some order into the heap, that even if we deny the claim that moral judgements on persons, motives, decisions and so on can be *reduced* to moral judgements on the actions of individual persons, still the former take their main significance from the latter. Persons, motives, decisions and the rest are morally important mainly as sources of actions.

Ethical monism

Venturing another step we might next say that all moral judgements on the actions of individual persons are answerable to a single moral consideration. With that step we commit ourselves to ethical monism.

Ethical monism is the view that there is only one morally relevant consideration. When we make moral judgements on actions there is one principle, a single moral criterion, by which they are to be gauged. The moral criterion gives a moral standard for actions.

Ethical monism generally runs on a theory of intrinsic value. Certain states of affairs are intrinsically valuable, worthwhile for their own sake: states of affairs of just one type. For a hedonist, only states of pleasure are intrinsically valuable. On this basis, if you looked to hedonism for a moral criterion, you would hold that actions are morally assessable purely in terms of their production of pleasure. There are no competing considerations. This form of hedonism would be a type of ethical monism.

Ethical monism has no necessary connection with hedonism. You can argue that there is only one morally relevant consideration to which all actions are answerable without any commitment to this particular view of what that consideration is. I am simply offering a first view of ethical monism and using hedonism as an example to give some content to it. Our discussion of ethical monism will centre on utilitarianism, with its claim that the single moral criterion is the maximization of utility.

Ethical pluralism

Ethical pluralism presents an opposing point of view to monism. It offers a less unified account of morality. For the pluralist there is an irreducible plurality of morally relevant considerations that can pull apart in particular situations and produce moral dilemmas. One representative of ethical pluralism is Sir David Ross, with his theory of 'prima facie' duties in *The Right and the Good* (1930) and *The Foundations of Ethics* (1939).

Ross will figure in our discussions. Going against the grain of standard interpretation, I shall also take Kant as a representative of ethical pluralism. Kant is usually presented as the ethical monist *par excellence*, with his single moral criterion of consistent universalizability. The standard view is a disaster, however, which blocks the perception of Kant's full account of morality.

Ethical particularism

If pluralism contradicts monism, particularism is its complete contrary. For the particularist every moral situation is *sui generis*, unique: there are no general moral considerations, one or many. There are only situations with the requirement of moral adequacy to them. 'Situation ethics' is one alias for ethical particularism. The most thoroughgoing ethical particularist is often thought to be J.-P. Sartre in his famous discussion of the student's dilemma (Sartre, 1948: 35-7). In my own view, however, what Sartre is mainly doing is setting forth a moral ideal of personal authenticity rather than offering a moral criterion. Our guide to ethical particularism will be Jonathan Dancy.

4.1.2. The moral ideal

If theories of the moral criterion centre on the concept of action, theories of the moral ideal develop from the concept of a person. The focus is not on the question, 'What shall I do?' but on another inquiry, 'What kind of person shall I be?' or 'What kinds of person should there be?' All these questions are, of course, vague as stated; and putting the second question to oneself *may* be just a way of pondering a plan of action.

But, as the shortest reflection makes clear, if what matters is to be a certain kind of person or for a certain kind of person to exist, a whole psychic structure of perception, emotion and desire (and more besides) is embodied in this ideal. Viewed from the angle of a moral ideal, the intrinsically valuable state of affairs is the relevant psychic structure of which actions are an expression. There is no suggestion that actions have a purely instrumental significance, that (in the argot one readily uses in philosophy) they are morally assessable solely in terms of the production of states of affairs. So, for instance, Aristotle's *phronimos* or practically wise man knows what is choiceworthy. He understands the need to observe the 'mean', which he perceives in any situation for action. And his condition of character is such that his emotions and desires are correctly configured to enable him to follow the mean.

In this alternative tradition, which looks primarily not to the doings of the agent but to the mind and character of the person, we encounter not only the Aristotelian ideal but the ideals of Plato, Aristotle, the Epicureans, the Stoics, Christianity, and (in the neglected East) of Vedanta, Yoga, Buddhism, Zen: plus many other ideals in a fuller list.

4.1.3. Summary

The moral standard, our second ethical problem, divides into two topics, namely the moral criterion and the moral standard:

- the moral criterion
  - ethical monism   - ethical pluralism
  - ethical particularism
- the moral ideal
  - Plato   - Aristotle
  - Epicureanism   - Stoicism
  - Christianity   - Vedanta
  - Yoga   - Buddhism
  - Zen

For manageability I will take just one exponent of the moral ideal, Aristotle. To follow up the other options, on Plato see Crombie, 1962: ch. 6 and Norman, 1982: ch. 2. Earle, 1988, Farringdon, 1967: ch. 2 and 12, and DeWitt, 1954: ch. 12-14 are good first guides to Epicureanism. On Stoicism see Blanshard, 1961: ch. 2; K. Campbell, 1985; Long, 1974; Rist, 1969; and Stock, 1908: ch. 4. On Christianity, Vedanta, Yoga, Buddhism and Zen, see Elinde, 1987.

5.1. THIRD PROBLEM: THE JUSTIFICATION OF MORAL JUDGEMENT

Suppose, working through the first ethical problem, we have arrived at a general characterization of moral judgements; we can set them off from non-moral judgements. Suppose also that we have probed the second ethical problem and have looked at theories of the moral criterion and the moral ideal. The sceptic's raised eyebrows suggest the obvious questions. What is the status of moral judgements? Why should it matter to a rational person to make moral judgements or to consider the moral judgements made by others? What rationale (if any) can be given for the moral life, to which moral judgements belong? These questions put a crude circle round another ethical problem: the justification of moral judgements.

5.1.1. Truth

Perhaps moral realism makes the most direct response to these questions. The key word is *truth*. Some moral judgements are literally true. This is the central claim of moral realism, and the most audacious. Most of us would allow that if a judgement is true, this is a strong justification for it. But exactly what does this claim of truth on behalf of moral judgements amount to? There are varieties of moral realism, but most versions involve two claims (Sayre-McCord, 1988: 5):

(1) moral judgements can be literally true or false
(2) some moral judgements are literally true

'Realism', in the label 'moral realism', has no commendatory force. It has simply been transferred into the vocabulary of modern philosophy from the Latin label for a group of medieval views about the objectivity of universals – squareness, hardness, redness, etc. – as existing independently of our minds. (Sometimes a universal, such as squareness, was supposed to exist not merely apart from our minds but apart also from particular square things: but enough of history.)

Moral realism runs the gauntlet of certain varieties of relativism; and the argument between realism and relativism will need to be examined carefully. I will also need to add to the above two claims to get the full flavour of moral realism.

5.1.2. Rationality

Aside from the angle of truth, there are attempts to justify moral judgements on grounds of rationality. These grounds divide in two:

- consistency   • interest

Consistency

There is a tradition strongly represented by the 18th-century German philosopher, Kant, and in our own day by Thomas Nagel, that the moral life is rational because immorality involves a kind of inconsistency, and inconsistency is irrational.

We are likely to agree an element of consistency in our idea of rational belief.

Rationally, a person ought not to believe p and not-p, or p and not-q where q is a logical consequence of p. Equally a rational agent does not have inconsistent preferences; he does not prefer p to q, q to r, and r to p. But these intuitive notions of doxastic consistency (from the Greek word *doxa* = belief) and consistency of preference do not seem quite what is needed to show that immorality involves a kind of inconsistency. Is the immoral man necessarily and as such inconsistent in his beliefs or preferences? Unsurprisingly Kant has something different in mind. One of his ideas is that an immoral principle of action is self-contradictory, involves a 'contradiction in conception', in the sense that there is a kind of logical impossibility about the result if we imagine everyone acting on it.

Interest

On a different approach one might allow that immorality is not inconsistent but still try to give a rational person good reasons in terms of his or her non-moral or prudential interests for heeding the requirements of morality. In certain conditions of interpersonal choice, for example, those known as situations of prisoner's dilemma, a second-best outcome will result for all parties if they act self-interestedly without reliable cooperation through mutual trust. Trustworthiness is a moral virtue; and trustworthy agents can thus secure advantages closed to amoral self-seekers or rational egoists. So this line of argument suggests that one moral virtue at least is to be reckoned among a rational agent's assets.

But appeal to a person's interests can take a different approach. For Aristotle, there is a lawlike connection between happiness or well-being and virtue. But the connection is not of the external, instrumental kind that we have just noted. Human beings have an essential nature in terms of which their proper functioning can be defined. That functioning involves two kinds of excellence – excellences of mind and excellences of character. Briefly put, these excellences include possession and exercise of moral virtue with which happiness naturally and non-accidentally goes along.

5.1.3. Naturalism

'Ethical naturalism' is a term of many possible values. There is a view that moral 'beliefs' are not beliefs properly so-called, states of mind appropriate to truth, but rather emotion-based attitudes. An ethical naturalist may hold, by contrast, that moral beliefs really are beliefs, literally such. He might add that these beliefs concern the moral properties of objects; and that the truth of these moral beliefs follows when an object has certain descriptive, factual or 'natural' properties with which moral properties are *identical* or from which they *result*. To see moral properties as identical with other properties is reductionism; to see them as resulting in a lawlike way from other properties, is to view them as derivative. Thus one might suppose that an action's goodness just is its productiveness of pleasure, or that an action's goodness results from its productiveness of pleasure.

Rather differently, I use 'ethical naturalism' for the idea, very roughly, that morality is a natural phenomenon, something to which (within limits) we have a direct inclination. One application of this idea would be that morality has a foundation in our biological nature: that certain forms of altruism can be explained without remainder, made completely intelligible, as a genetically-based product of evolution. Under the heading of sociobiology we will need to consider some questions this approach raises. Its distinctiveness is evident.

The 18th-century Scottish philosopher, David Hume, offers a version of ethical naturalism with strong affinities to the account I have given here. Hume will be our main ethical naturalist.

5.1.4. Summary

The justification of moral judgements takes us along two lines: (1) attempts to show that some moral judgements can be known to be literally true and (2) attempts to show the rationality of moral judgements, to provide a rational agent with good reasons (reasons of consistency or interest) for heeding the requirements of morality. Ethical naturalism provides a functional account of morality on a biological basis.

6.1. FOURTH PROBLEM: LOGIC, REASONING AND MORAL JUDGEMENT

Perhaps the central concept of logic is that of the deductive validity of arguments. A good argument *implies* its conclusion; the conclusion follows from the premises. If and only if ('iff' in the standard contraction) the conclusion cannot be false when the premises are true, the argument is deductively valid or 'demonstrative' in older language. (If, as well, the premises actually are true the argument is sound.) When the premises of an argument merely provide evidence for the conclusion, the argument is inductive. An inductively strong argument is one of which the conclusion is unlikely to be false when the premises are true. I take Gil Harman's view that there is no inductive logic; induction belongs to reasoning (Harman, 1976 and 1984).

That point aside, to repeat, an argument is deductively valid iff the conclusion cannot be false when the premises are true. This is our intuitive idea of deductive validity. (I shall talk just of 'validity' from now on.) We might also say that the premises necessitate the conclusion. There are more sophisticated accounts, such as Alfred Tarski's model-theoretic definition (Guttenplan, 1991). But here we may keep to the intuitive idea.

If logic centres on the validity of arguments, its arguments are abstractly taken:

The Earth is larger than the Sun
Mercury is larger than the Earth

Mercury is larger than the Sun

That the premises necessitate the conclusion is good enough for the logician. That the conclusion is, in the light of our independent knowledge, absurd, is enough for a reasoner to reject one or more of the premises precisely because this is their conclusion. Logic abstracts from what we know or have reason to believe: and to describe logic as a set of rules for the manipulation of signs on paper is a caricature that contains an element of truth.

Reasoning is the psychological act or process of drawing a conclusion: of coming to believe or know that something is the case (theoretical reasoning) or of deciding what to do (practical reasoning). *Inference* is one name for this process. Logical implication holds between sentences; inference is done by people. '(P and Q)' implies 'P'; Sherlock Holmes infers that the burglar escaped through the skylight.

6.1.1. Is-ought gap

Now from a logical point of view a sharp question arises. Can an argument be valid in which the premises are descriptive or factual and the conclusion normative? E.g.:

She was old and lonely
He sat talking to her for hours

He did a good thing

Is this a valid argument? It hardly looks valid since the conclusion contains a term, 'good', which is missing from the premises. Again:

She is old and lonely
Her health is frail

You ought to help her

Is this a valid argument, or is it invalid for the same reasons as the first example? The second example prompts talk of an 'is-ought' gap. Here is a problem. The *locus classicus* for its statement is a passage at the end of Hume's *Treatise of Human Nature*, III.1.1, to be examined in chapter 5.

The first example is often said to illustrate the 'fact-value' distinction. How is this distinction related to the is-ought gap? A quick thought is that the gap is a special case of the distinction: 'She is old and lonely' and 'Her health is frail' are factual or descriptive, and 'You ought to help her' embodies one type of evaluation. But there are strong grounds for thinking that while the fact-value distinction would disappear if value judgements themselves were descriptive or factual (a logical possibility), this would still leave the is-ought gap wide open. 'Ought' has a complex logic which creates special problems.

6.1.2. 'Ought' implies 'can'

Few might be expected to deny the claim, normally attributed to Kant (Paton, 1947: 220) that if someone ought to do something then it must be the case that he can do it. If Lee ought to return Mark's money, he must be able to return the money. How could it be the case that somebody ought to do, as a requirement on action, what he cannot do? As the famous slogan goes, 'ought' implies 'can'. More formally:

(1) An agent, A, ought to do an action, x, at time t only if A can do x at t.

Now (1) implies:

(2) A ought to do x at t, therefore A can do x at t.

By contraposition from (2) we can deduce:

(3) A cannot do x at t, therefore it is not the case that A ought to do x at t.

But is this not just another instance of deriving a normative conclusion from factual or descriptive premises? One way of answering that objection would be to show that (3) is incompletely stated and needs to be expanded into:

(4) If someone cannot do an action at a time then it is not the case that he ought to do that action at that time.

A cannot do x at t.

It is not the case that A ought to do x at t.

This supplies an evaluative first premise from which, along with the factual or descriptive second premise, the evaluative conclusion derives. We need to look further into the possibilities. The topic is complicated by the ambiguities of 'can'.

6.1.3. Paradoxes of deontic logic

Logic uses various rules. Take, for example, the rule of or-introduction. 'Queen Victoria died in 1901' implies 'Queen Victoria died in 1901 or the moon is made of green cheese.' This disjunction is true if the original sentence is true; for the truth of a disjunction depends on the truth of at least one of its disjuncts (in this case, the original sentence). If 'x' is the case then 'x or y' is the case; for 'x or y' only says that 'x' is the case or 'y' is the case, one or the other or possibly both: and 'x' is the case, as we are given at the start.

Then, switching to moral judgements, does 'Lee ought to return Mark's money' imply 'Lee ought to return Mark's money or spend it'? There is a tangle of such problems known as the paradoxes of deontic logic.

6.1.4. Naturalistic fallacy

To approach our next topic, make an assumption for the sake of argument. Assume that:

(1) There can be property identities.

This is not an unreasonable assumption. Few would deny, for instance, that the property of being a female fox is identical to the property of being a vixen.

Assume further that:

(2) Moral properties are real properties of objects (of actions, etc.).

Finally assume that:

(3) The moral property of goodness is identical to a descriptive, factual property, e.g. the property of being pleasant or desired.

According to the early 20th-century Cambridge philosopher, G.E. Moore, anybody who made that third assumption would be guilty of a logical error – the naturalistic fallacy, so-called from Moore's use of 'naturalist' for what I have called descriptive or factual.

6.1.5. Logical form of ethical sentences

Still at the level of sentences, questions of logical form arise. If we turn back to Lists B and C we find different types of logical form. 'All lying is wrong' is of subject-predicate form, with the subject made up of a quantifier ('all') and a term ('lying'). In the language of traditional logic, this is a universal affirmative. Other sentences have different forms. 'Mary Lou is not a very moral person' is singular; 'Mary Lou' is a singular term, not a term plus a quantifier. 'Some lying is worse than any killing' is relational and it offers two quantified terms ('some lying', 'any killing'). 'If you think that's a moral course of action, you show a corrupt mind' is hypothetical, offering two sentences joined (as anyone can see) by an 'if'. And so we might continue. Plainly moral judgements, presented as ethical sentences, are candidates for this kind of logical analysis. Clearly relevant here also is the kind of reductive exercise mooted in 3.1.2.

When we discuss logical positivism (26.1.12) another issue will come briefly into view – are moral judgements 'propositional', i.e. capable of truth or falsity?

6.1.6. Action explanation: belief-desire theory

Practical reasoning, which is central to ethics, is directed towards action. Then, to make a connection, how can reasoning explain action? This is our first topic concerning reasoning.

If we keep to intentional action we might try the following formula to identify such action:

Person P did action x intentionally at time t iff:

(1) P did x at t.
(2) P knew (believed, was aware ...) at t that he was doing x at t.
(3) P wanted (or desired) at t to do x at t.

One question is whether intentional action always and necessarily requires an antecedent desire which, in the situation for action, produces or expresses itself in the desire to do x, and which in conjunction with the agent's beliefs, explains the action. If you accept this account of intentional action then you subscribe to the belief-desire theory.

An immediate point of relevance to ethics is that, if moral beliefs can be true or if there can be such a thing as moral knowledge, what if one simply lacks a desire to act morally? I lack a desire to act on many of my (putatively) true beliefs and on much of my (supposed) knowledge. You do not provide me with a desire to act morally if you show that my (or your) moral beliefs are true or that you or I possess moral knowledge.

Yes but, the objection may be expected, all this is old-fashioned psychology. The issue cannot be avoided. This is the point at which to confront the status of what has come to be called 'folk' or 'commonsense' psychology. This everyday psychology, with its idioms of 'belief', 'desire', 'intention', 'motive' and the rest, is held by some to be scientifically valueless. That is, the criticism runs, for scientific purposes of description and explanation the everyday idioms are too vague, open-textured, and burdened with extra tasks: for we use them in arguing, commanding, promising, exhorting, persuading and so forth. There is no prospect, it seems, of securing systematic identities or lawlike correlations between mental phenomena, picked out in terms of everyday psychology, and physical phenomena, e.g. brain states, picked out at a properly scientific (say, neuron) level.

There are two options: either to dispense with psychological discourse altogether, relying purely on sentences relating to brain states (eliminative materialism) or to replace everyday psychology with a 'scientific' psychology using the language of physical science and a new idiom (nonreductive physicalism). I should wish to signal just one problem in the replacement option. It is this: a marked feature of folk psychology is that its mental states are typically self-declarative, self-intimating. If I have a belief, a desire or an intention (say), then normally I know that I have it. Yet there is no guarantee that if we remap the mental, defining mental states in terms that correlate with brain states, this self-declarative character of mental states will be preserved. The implications for deliberation are drastic: under a revised psychology how can I decide what to do if my new-look mental states are not self-intimating?

My own inclination is to stop the argument before these two options are forced on us. I offer two points. One: the vagueness and so forth of everyday psychological idioms are glaringly obvious when we take terms like 'desire' abstractly. 'Desire' can cover anything from an intrinsic want or preference through an instrumental want to a mild inclination or the faintest velleity. But the inadequacies are less certain when we relativize such idioms to precise contexts of use. Two: if everyday psychology does not yield *scientifically* useful explanations and descriptions, this does not show (a) that it has no explanatory or descriptive power at all or (b) that such explanatory or descriptive power as it does possess is not adequate to everyday life.

Take a parallel from computer programming. Every programmer knows that, for technical reasons to do with computer architectures, commands in a high-level language such as Cobol or PL/1 fail to correlate in a lawlike way with states of the machine described at the level of machine code. To secure such correlations a language like Assembler has to be used. But nobody would claim that my entering a high-level command such as 'If N > 75 then return ('Great!')' does not explain adequately for programming purposes why the machine later produces an entry on a print-out.

In this example Assembler language matches the new idiom of a scientific psychology, while PL/1 represents the idiom of everyday psychology. Just as PL/1 commands have sufficient explanatory and descriptive power for programming purposes, so everyday psychological statements have sufficient explanatory and descriptive power for the workaday life with which ethics is largely concerned. For a clear initial exploration of the issues but a contrasting viewpoint, see Wilkes, 1978b. For later work see Churchland, 1981; Double, 1985; Fodor, 1985; and Stich, 1983.

6.1.7. Action explanation: cognitive model

The belief-desire theory does not have the field to itself even within everyday psychology. According to its rival, the cognitive model, knowledge or belief can suffice for motivation without antecedent desire. The cognitive model is espoused in different forms by Kant and Nagel. These theorists, who have already come into view as offering accounts of the justification of moral judgement as rational, connect those accounts with a theory of action explanation. A certain kind of belief can suffice for motivation to moral action.

6.1.8. Role of principles in moral reasoning

While we are making connections let us go back, past Kant and Nagel, to ethical monism (4.1). If you are an ethical monist and hold that there is a single, supreme principle of morality, i.e. ultimately just one morally relevant consideration, then a *deductivist* model of moral reasoning appears to be what you need. Your supreme principle figures as a universal major premise; next the specific circumstances are described in various minor premises; and finally a conclusion follows about action in the specific instance. For example:

Major premise: Utility is to be maximized
Minor premise: In the present circumstances utility will be maximized by doing action x

---

Conclusion: Action x is to be done (or: I'll do action x)

If, on the other hand, you subscribe to a version of ethical pluralism and hold that there is an irreducible plurality of morally relevant considerations, the deductivist model is less attractive. A *defeasibility* model looks more suitable. A morally relevant consideration or principle sets a presumption (say) that stealing is wrong, and from the specific circumstances there is a provisional conclusion that action x, which is an instance of stealing, is wrong. But that conclusion can always be rebutted by the introduction of extra circumstances which alter the case and defeat the presumption. It might be, for example, that doing action x is the only likely way of preventing somebody from starving.

Clearly moral principles fulfil different roles in the two models. Here we have another topic of moral reasoning.

6.1.9. Practical syllogism and weakness of will

There appears to be such a thing as weakness of will – the Greeks called it *akrasia.* This is not a single phenomenon but perhaps a central case for ethics occurs when an agent, with a choice between doing x intentionally and doing y intentionally, does y although his moral judgement is in favour of doing x.

If we recognize the phenomenon – Socrates thought there was no such thing – we plainly need a model of moral reasoning that will enable us to describe what happens in such cases. Aristotle handled the matter through his notion of a *practical syllogism* or chain of practical reasoning.

A practical syllogism might run as follows:

Sweet things are pleasant   (major premise)
This apple is sweet   (minor premise)

(Munch, I eat it)   (conclusion (action))

Aristotle's use the practical syllogism to explain how akrasia occurs has been found instructive. We will also look at an influential modern account of weakness of will, that of Donald Davidson.

Exactly what this phenomenon of weakness of will is, and how best to represent it in terms of the agent's practical reasoning, is the last main topic of moral reasoning.

6.1.10. Summary

Ethics presents a set of logical problems:

- the is/ought gap
- paradoxes of deontic logic
- the logical form of ethical sentences
- 'ought' implies 'can'
- the naturalistic fallacy

There are also problems of moral reasoning:

- action explanation
- practical syllogism and weakness of will
- role of principles

For reasons of space and relative importance I will clip the logical form of ethical sentences and the paradoxes of deontic logic from our list of logical topics for discussion, except for a short discussion of logical positivism's view of moral judgements as non-propositional.

7.1. FIFTH PROBLEM: MORAL JUDGEMENT AND MORAL RESPONSIBILITY

The term 'responsibility' is used in different senses and different contexts. 'The tornado was responsible for the destruction of the house.' 'Legally a company is responsible for the official actions of its employees.' Here the legal sense is quite close to a major sense of 'responsibility' in ethics: that of accountability or answerability.

Questions of moral responsibility typically arise when, crudely put, something has gone wrong. An action has been done or omitted which, by some moral standard (4.1), one would rather had not been done or omitted. The agent might be blamed accordingly. Let's look into the situation more closely.

7.1.1. Moral excuses

Suppose we share a moral standard by which we agree that an action that I have done is undesirable. Other things being equal, we accept that it would have been better, relative to our standard, for that action not to have been done. In this sense I have done wrong. On what conditions can I avoid blame for it? We need to talk about doing an action by accident, in ignorance, under compulsion or through coercion – teasing notions for analysis.

Can I avoid blame if, when our moral standards differ, you accept that I acted conscientiously? If so, we need to spell out the conditions for conscientious action.

The intersection of all these issues is the topic of moral excuses.

7.1.2. Free will

But now, we may have the thought: what if there is a universal moral excuse? What if it is a matter, not simply of particular agents not being blameworthy on particular occasions, but of nobody's being to blame for anything? In a word, what if *determinism* is true?

To a first approximation the thesis of determinism is that:

Every event has a cause.

The incompatibility between determinism and moral responsibility usually arises on the assumption that moral responsibility requires the following condition:

A person is morally responsible for what he has done only if he could have done otherwise.

Clearly this has some connection with the 'ought' implies 'can' principle we considered earlier (6.1.2):

An agent, A, ought to do an action, x, at time t only if A can do x at t.

The angle is different, however. The 'ought' implies 'can' principle looks to the connection between judgements of what an agent ought to do and statements of what he can do. The above condition of moral responsibility looks to the connection between blameworthiness and what the agent can do. The points are related but not the same. One thought might be, of course, that if the connection is in both cases logical, the issue of free will might be removed from here and put under the heading of moral judgement, logic and reasoning. But as a broad issue in ethics, free will takes in extra-logical considerations, e.g. about the truth of determinism, which justify its separate treatment.

How can we start from the thesis of determinism and finish by denying that necessary condition for moral responsibility? Consider the following informal deduction:

(1) Every event has a cause
(2) Human actions are events
(3) For every event, E2, there is a prior event or set of events, E1, which is causally sufficient for E1
(4) If E1 is causally sufficient for E2 then E1 necessitates E2: E2 cannot but occur
(5) If (3) and (4) then all human actions have prior events which necessitate them
(6) If (5) then it is causally impossible for a person to have done any action other than the one they did
(7) If (6) then no one is morally responsible

The idea behind premise (5) might be that we could not draw the line at the immediate mental events that caused the action. If I did the action because I chose to do it, there are prior events that necessitate my choice and these stretch back, if not to infinity, then certainly past any events over which I have control.

The above argument is only informal. More important, there are other approaches to the truth of determinism and to its implications for moral responsibility. The general topic is that of free will, so-called because it concerns a person's freedom to do otherwise than they did.

7.1.3. Punishment and forgiveness

Suppose I have done a wrong action for which I am to blame. Does it follow that I ought to be punished? Does it follow that *you* have the right to punish me? In the case of legal punishment a sanction is applied by the state when the laws it has issued are infringed; and the state's officials may, while you as a private citizen may not, apply that sanction. But who has issued 'the moral law'? And how may the idea that vice merits punishment be supported? If we hold a theory of the moral criterion, we will have to invoke the relevant criterion or criteria to answer the question, 'What shall I do?' in cases of punishment no less than in other matters. If a balance of utility is our guide, it may be our duty *not* to punish.

Again, there is the question of forgiveness. If (logically) only those injured by wrong-doing *can* forgive, then is forgiveness discretionary? Or is it answerable in the same way as punishment to a moral criterion (or ideal)?

7.1.4. Summary

Under the heading of moral responsibility we find four main topics:

- moral excuses
- punishment
- free will
- forgiveness

For reasons of space and centrality I will concentrate on the first two topics. On punishment and forgiveness, see Acton, 1969.

That completes my outline of the structure of ethics. Let me utter three words of caution and explain a standard distinction before I mark off my own approach from rival approaches. Talk of the 'structure' of ethics, with problems and topics as its 'elements', is a heuristic device. To make a start, this is a good way of looking at ethics. But, as you will see when your studies deepen, each problem and topic has so many intimate points of contact with others that it is more accurate to speak of *distinguishable aspects* of a whole than of elements or *separate parts* of a structure.

The problem sharpens when we deal with central historical texts, which attempt a connected treatment of different problems. Kant's definition of the moral criterion in chapter 3 is really continuous with his account of its justification in chapter 4. We simply see different faces of rationality. However, the structural approach is useful: a bad master but a good servant.

Secondly, philosophy has a way, disconcerting to some, of unbinding what seems securely fixed: of disturbing not only Francis Bacon's 'idols of the market-place' but, far worse, one's own results. Take a problem or topic, sort it out; you will still find that it looks different in the light of later study. Not even a structured approach can make the study of ethics smoothly incremental, with no loss of previous results.

Thirdly, I claim no finality for my five-part structure. Perhaps a deeper structure lies hidden. Certainly my articulation of the five-part structure is capable of refinement and elaboration. I claim only that from my account of the structure of ethics you can draw a thread of light through the labyrinth of more advanced study.

Finally, we need to notice a distinction without mention of which no modern textbook of ethics is complete: that between *meta-ethics* and *normative ethics*. In meta-ethics the meta comes from the Greek word for 'after'. The idea is that the moral life is ongoing while, with full neutrality, philosophical activity stands by and takes note of its conceptual and logical aspect. This task yields our first, second, fourth and fifth ethical problems. Meta-ethics thus differs from normative ethics, which aims to justify: to recommend morality and to prescribe a moral standard. Normative ethics in turn yields our third ethical problem. (In taking the moral standard for our second problem, we keep to conceptualization, leaving justification aside.)

I tend not to use the meta/normative distinction. To begin, the description 'meta-ethics' is too coarse-grained. Meta-ethics encompasses a diverse set of inquiries, and the single term does not sensitize us to variety. More than that, the distinction conceals the continuity between meta- and normative ethics. If conceptual analysis is central to meta-ethics, normative ethics itself can be a conceptual exercise.

How so? Let me take an example. Suppose we tried to vindicate the rationality of moral virtue. We might do this by attempting to show, with the aid of some highly general empirical facts or perhaps the specific empirical assumptions of a particular audience, on what conditions two concepts, namely moral virtue and rationality, can overlap – rather like circles in a diagram. One assumption might be that in interpersonal relationships there are advantages which cannot be had without mutual trust. Trustworthiness is a moral virtue. This gives us a perfectly sound interlock between two concepts: it is *rational* to act for advantage, and advantage depends on *moral virtue*. This is a quick indication of a genuinely conceptual exercise – one that has none of the associations of preaching and unargued conviction that cling to the term 'normative'.

It is on such lines that I should reply to Oakeshott's criticism that ethics, combining meta-ethics and normative ethics, the disparate tasks of analysis and justification, does not add up to a coherent intellectual discipline (Oake-shott, 1933: 334-5).

The possibility of this kind of interlock fractures the image of conceptual analysis as a rarefied activity clean cut from empirical investigation. But I will not linger upon this subject, which I have discussed elsewhere (Thomas, 1986; see also O.H. Green, 1982).

8.1. RIVAL APPROACHES

My own approach is to work systematically through the structure of ethics, assigning topics to problems. There are, however, at least three quite different approaches about which I need to say a word:

- central texts
- random question-tackling
- live issues of public debate

8.1.1. Central texts

Philosophy has its central texts. In the frame for ethics are Plato's *Republic*, Aristotle's *Nicomachean Ethics*, Hume's *Treatise of Human Nature*, Book III, and *Enquiry Concerning the Principles of Morals*, Kant's *Foundations of the Metaphysics of Morals*, and John Stuart Mill's *Utilitarianism*. Hume's *Enquiry concerning the Human Understanding* is also relevant as containing a classic discussion of free will.

These texts are central in the depth of their influence and in the force with which they confront ethical problems. One can, I did, and most students do, start ethics by studying them.

There are difficulties with this approach. To begin, the 'great, dead philosophers' tend to mix non-philosophical views and arguments with their philosophical work. Then how is the beginner to identify the philosophical portion? In terms of its addressing the philosophical problems of ethics? But the student does not know what those problems are.

Add another point: from the beginner's point of view the central texts, even in their philosophical portions, move across a fitful variety of problems and a random diversity of topics. Much time is wasted, and confusion risked, if (say) we turn from the *Nicomachean Ethics* to *Treatise*, Book III, expecting to find different angles on an identical set of problems and topics. But without a knowledge of the structure of ethics, what is the student to expect?

Again, in reading the philosophical portions of central texts, the student has more than philosophy to contend with. I refer to style. Consider Hume: the beauty of Hume's style speaks for itself. But Hume has serious defects as a writer. He often uses words loosely and even inconsistently. At times his arguments are too compressed. In some passages he obscures his meaning by a rhetorical flourish. Hume is a philosopher from whom we can never cease to learn. So often, taken too early, he is a philosopher from whom the student never begins to learn.

Or take Kant's *Foundations of the Metaphysics of Morals*, a text which, by virtue of its brevity, its plentiful use of examples, and its relative freedom from a technical philosophical vocabulary, is widely used in teaching ethics. There Kant's rationalism (his claim that the requirements of morality are, or derive from, norms of practical reason) puzzles the beginner: and rightly so, since the grounds of that position are only slightly revealed in the *Foundations*. And, worse, presentationally the text is a maze. The movement of argument within each of the three sections is hard to make out. The relation of the sections to one another is equally problematic. Of course, these are quick claims. But they are not claims about the deep structure of the *Foundations*; they are claims about the typical impact of the *Foundations* on the beginning student. Kant, a philosopher of immense greatness, is, for the beginner, a textual disaster.

In their various ways nearly all the central texts present difficulties of style. All the beginner should face are difficulties of philosophy.

Finally, there is a question of textual method. The study of past philosophical texts divides into distinct approaches:

- linguistic
- contextual
- reconstructive

The linguistic approach seeks to fix the most accurate documentary version of the text and to express most directly and least misleadingly what it says; the text is handled like glass. Or there is the 'deconstructionist' variant of this approach practised by Jacques Derrida which, fastening upon tacit assumptions, metaphors and systematic ambiguities, brings out the difference (and usually the inconsistency) between what the text shows and what it says. The contextual approach looks at what the author means. It probes the substance of his beliefs and not solely the propositional content of his sentences. It also seeks 'to determine the nexus with those of his contemporaries or predecessors who did most both to supply him with a working-stock of concepts and also to provoke new questions in his own mind, calling for new answers and therewith new concepts' (Vlastos, 1970: 415). Lines of later influence are also important. This is historians' philosophy. The reconstructive approach, with its irreverent slogan 'bother the text and bother the context', emphasizes the modern reader's experience in confronting the text. It can go two ways. We can bring out a connected piece of reasoning by varying a philosopher's order of presentation. Or we can accent a text's suggestiveness, selectively reconstituting its elements in a fresh pattern of modern interest.

The reconstructive approach tends to hold sway among philosophers: and it is an approach which I favour. Item, philosophical thought is relative to a language. Item, language is relative to a time and culture. Item, our philosophical thought is therefore relative to our own time and culture. Problem, how can we successfully relativize past philosophical texts since our very attempts to relativize are themselves relative to our own time and culture? Deep problem or sophistical conundrum? Reactions vary. I believe it is a deep problem, for all the brevity of my presentation of it here. Its foundations are laid deep in the humanistic tradition from Dilthey to the later Wittgenstein. But the reconstructive approach, taking its point of departure avowedly from our own concerns, nimbly sidesteps any such problem. This point is markedly in its favour.

My main point is this: if historical texts are to carry the main weight of introducing the student to the philosophical study of morality, this should go along with an induction in sophistication (which philosophers rarely possess or seldom exhibit) about the manner and rationale of the particular approach that is being adopted. Since I cannot properly provide that rationale here and do not expect it to be easily available from philosophers elsewhere, I prefer to take a different route into ethics. (For a closer look at textual methods, see Juhl, 1980; Mueller-Vollmer, 1986; and Olsen, 1982.)

The central texts will make their appearance, especially in chapter 3. On particular topics I aim to present and discuss their doctrines and, where suitable, to reconstruct. But the texts will not dominate my exposition or dictate the book's layout.

8.1.2. Random question-tackling

It is not uncommon for students to be introduced to ethics through random 'questions'. Take an example: 'Are we free to choose our moral principles?' When the tutorial question runs this way the student is best advised to run another. The question is spurious, no part of a genuine intellectual inquiry. It straddles at least two problems.

If, taking a formalist approach to the general characterization of moral judgement, we hold (say) that simply any principle can be a moral principle if we are prepared to act on it consistently and are willing for others to do the same, we clearly accept that morality does not have a restricted content and so in this sense we are 'free' to choose any principle as a moral principle. On the other hand, can we act otherwise than we do? Is determinism true? Are we 'free' to choose our moral principles in this further sense?

This is merely one example of the running together of separate problems in a single question, a conflation which the beginner (the kind of beginner I have particularly in view in this book) can well do without. Even when questions keep to one topic within a single problem, the topic can seem opaque, even baffling and pointless, without its context. Focusing on random questions is a good intellectual discipline, once one is familiar with the topics and problems. Random questions have their value, but not for the beginner.

8.1.3. Live issues of public debate

Another route into ethics is through live issues of public debate. On this approach the student is confronted with a range of socially significant issues such as euthanasia, abortion, surrogate motherhood, sexual harassment, positive discrimination and animal rights, and given the task of drawing out their ethical presuppositions and implications. This is 'applied ethics' in which actual moral problems are studied with the help of ethical theory.

But just count up the difficulties. A programme of study based on live issues of public debate has to arrange those issues in blocks that look natural to the student. But there is no guarantee and little likelihood that this arrangement will yield an ordered list of ethical problems and topics.

Moreover, while I am sure that ethics can illuminate the discussion and investigation of socially significant issues, it can do so only in a top-down way, enabling us (if we know enough about the subject-matter) to recognize the theoretical problems and topics that they involve. If, a quite different matter, we start the study of ethics at the level of the issues themselves, we face complex and controversial factual (often technical) data on emotionally provocative issues. I know the result. My experience of *introducing* ethics through such issues is that the philosophy is mist-hidden. We spin in a cloud of disputed factual data and pre-theoretical emotional reaction. Remember: this is not a case against applied ethics but only against its use as an introduction to ethics.

However, I must add that I think a much deeper idea than 'applied ethics' is Marx's notion of the unity of theory and practice – of *praxis*, or what Rupert Lodge calls simply 'reflective living' (Bottomore, 1975: ch. 4; Lodge, 1951: 1). Here we encounter not pre-set public issues to which philosophical tools are applied but the individual's personal engagements. The individual, at first naively immersed in projects or a lifeplan, steps back from that unreflective engagement and examines its conceptual presuppositions. As those presuppositions are scrutinized, elucidated and refined, so revised presuppositions inform a new engagement, which in turn provokes fresh conceptual scrutiny. Theory and practice, engagement and reflection, intertwine ceaselessly in the thread of praxis. Marx, of course, looked to the unity of theory and specifically revolutionary practice. But we can use Marx without being marxists.

My strictures on applied ethics do nothing to break the connection I earlier drew between conceptual analysis and empirical investigation (7.1.4). That connection assumed a task of conceptual analysis already in hand, which is not (or at least cannot be safely assumed to be) one's condition on first encounter with ethics. Cf. Gewirth, 1981.

9.1. PROGRAMME FOR THE BOOK

Ethics spreads like a map below us. We see a wide range of problems, a great many topics. Not all of these topics can be explored, though we shall look at most. With a mild resequencing of topics on moral reasoning, since the easiest order of first introduction is not always the best order of more detailed exposition, our programme is set out in the following table:

Problem	Topic
specification of moral judgement	formal features
	particular content
	categorical nature
	specific emotion
	certain sanctions
	'all-in' point of view
moral judgement and moral standard	moral criterion
	monism
	pluralism
	particularism
	moral ideal
	Aristotle
justification of moral judgement	truth
	moral realism
	moral relativism
	rationality
	consistency
	interest
	naturalism
	Hume
	sociobiology
logic, reasoning, and moral judgement	logic
	is-ought gap
	'ought' implies 'can'
	naturalistic fallacy
	reasoning
	role of principles in moral reasoning
	practical syllogism and weakness of will
	belief-desire theory of action explanation
	cognitive model of action explanation

Problem	Topic
moral judgement and	moral excuses
moral responsibility	free will

A final word. Students have their own ways of using books. Still I gently urge a point. Ethics has a structure; and the book has a structure to match. Something will be lost if the section headings are taken by skip-and-dip. I have tried to take a clear path through ethics; I suggest a consecutive journey along it. That advice offered, we are ready to look at ethics in detail.

CHAPTER 2

The Specification of Moral Judgement

10.1. INTRODUCTION

The purpose of this chapter is to take up the first ethical problem listed at the end of chapter 1:

- the specification of moral judgement.

As explained in 3.1.4, my discussion will focus on:

- the general characterization of moral judgement.

11.1. THE GENERAL CHARACTERIZATION OF MORAL JUDGEMENT

One way of confronting the general characterization of moral judgement is to put the question: 'How can we set off moral judgements from other kinds of judgement – economic, political, religious, aesthetic, etc.?' If we can fix the common and distinctive features of moral judgement we shall have found the necessary and sufficient conditions for a judgement to be a moral judgement.

Before addressing this topic, however, we need to ease our way free from two ambiguities.

The term 'moral *judgement*' is not fully determinate. 'Judgement' may refer (1) to a psychological *process* of deliberation or reasoning, (2) to the *product* of deliberation, or (3) simply to *what a person asserts or believes*, whether from deliberation or otherwise. That is the first ambiguity. Historically the term 'moral judgement', which derives from a theory of reasoning, is a carry-over from the Idealist philosophy which flourished at Oxford in the second half of the 19th century. One part of the idea behind it, evident in such works as Bradley, 1883 and Bosanquet, 1888, is that reasoning is 'holistic' in the sense that in inference we aim for conclusions that fit with our best total explanatory account of the world (6.1). In logic, by contrast, we aim merely for conclusions that cannot be false given the premises; the truth of the conclusion is irrelevant. 'Judgement' was thought to carry the right suggestion of deliberation and answerability to the best total account of the evidence in theoretical reasoning. It was a ready extension to use the expression 'moral judgement' for the conclusion of one kind of practical reasoning.

I shall keep mainly to sense (3): 'moral judgements' are what a person asserts or believes. Things asserted may or may not (according to one's philosophical logic) be identical to sentences, statements or propositions. The maze beckons. I shall not try to decide between these options. I find no majority view about them in the work of other moral philosophers; and I see no advantage in enforcing my own point of view here.

Still we run into another ambiguity. Moral assertions and beliefs are of different orders of generality. Highly general claims such as 'All lying is wrong' are often called *moral principles* while 'moral judgement' is reserved for claims like 'Bill is not mentally ill but plain evil', which are situationally far more specific.

Moral principles themselves can be of different levels of generality. 'One should not kill elderly people through euthanasia' (P2) is less general than 'One should not kill anyone' (P1): to break P2 is to break P1, but to break P1 is not necessarily to break P2 (there are other ways of killing people than by euthanasia).

So on a narrow usage, moral judgements are more specific than moral principles. On a wider usage moral judgements are simply what is morally asserted or believed. In the general characterization of moral judgement the wide usage prevails. According to different theories, moral judgements

- have certain *formal features*
- have a *particular content*
- are *categorical*
- involve a *specific emotion*
- are associated with *certain sanctions*
- reflect an *'all-in' point of view*

I shall consider the formal approach first. The theorist whose work I shall examine is R.M. Hare. Kant also has an account of the universalizability of moral judgements. But I will postpone Kant until we take our second ethical problem, that of the moral standard (22.2.1). Though Kant regards universalizability as a distinguishing mark of moral judgement, his discussion of this feature is inseparable (or only artificially removable) from his use of universalizability as a moral criterion to provide guidance, through the categorical imperative, for choices of action.

12.1. THE FORMAL APPROACH: R.M. HARE

The essentials of Hare's ethical theory are contained in two early books: *The Language of Morals* (1952) and *Freedom and Reason* (1963). Later works present interesting developments and applications. In particular I may mention his distinction between levels of moral thinking (Hare, 1981). But the heart of his ethical theory is still in the first two works.

12.2. HARE'S UNIVERSAL PRESCRIPTIVISM

Hare's ethical theory is usually called 'prescriptivism', though in fact prescriptivity is only one of its two key elements. 'Universal prescriptivism' is a better label. On Hare's account moral principles are:

- prescriptive
- universalizable

First I shall simply give an outline of Hare's ethical theory along with some comments. Criticism comes later.

Hare's theory can be stated in outline in 9 propositions:

Prescriptivity

(1) A moral judgement, e.g. 'I ought to put A into prison because he will not pay me what he owes', entails a prescription, i.e. a first-person imperative, 'Let me put A into prison.'
(2) A prescription embodies a desire, i.e. a felt disposition to action: a disposition to put A into prison, a disposition to do that intentional action.
(3) To assent to the moral judgement, 'I ought to put A into prison because he will not pay me what he owes' and fail to assent to the prescription in (2) is possible only on two conditions:
    (a) one's assent is merely verbal, i.e. insincere
    (b) one fails to understand the language one is using.
(4) The imperatives embodied in prescriptions differ from other first-person imperatives and from non-moral second-person commands because:
    (a) a prescription involves a principle, e.g. 'One ought to put in prison anyone who will not pay one what he owes'.
(5) This principle informs one's practical reasoning. It figures as a major premise which, along with a statement about factual conditions, entails the moral judgement in (1). E.g.:
Evaluative major premise: One ought to put in prison anyone who will not pay one what he owes
Factual minor premise: A will not pay me what he owes
Conclusion: I ought to put A in prison because he will not pay me what he owes.

Where Hare's agent faces a dilemma and, given his principles, is confronted by two or more equally binding claims, the only course is to make a decision of relative priority between the claims, a decision which implies a reformulation of his principles.

Universalizability

(6) Moral principles are what Hare calls U-type principles. They must involve no reference to individuals other than by general description (e.g. 'old persons'). That is to say that moral principles cannot include proper names ('Hector Senex') or singular terms (e.g. 'the old man in the corner').
(7) To assent to a moral principle is to accept that, if the principle applies to one situation in which one acts it must also apply to all relevantly similar situations; as one acts, so one must act consistently.

(8) To assent to a moral principle is to be willing for other persons to act on the same principle in relevantly similar situations. In particular:
(a) To assent to a moral principle is to be willing for other persons to act on the same principle in relevantly similar situations that involve oneself; as one acts, so one must be prepared for others to act towards oneself.

Formalism

(9) Just any principle is a moral principle if it meets the requirements of prescriptivity and universalizability. Some of Hare's own account of this can be found in Hare, 1952: 171-2 and 1963: 90-1.

It will be obvious how this account is to be expanded in order to deal with moral judgements directed to other people. But I shall on the whole keep to self-directed judgements. In second-person judgements the first-person imperative, 'Let me ... ' becomes the second-person imperative, 'Put A into prison' or 'Do put A into prison.' The rest of the account then follows with the necessary adjustments. When I direct a moral judgement to someone else Hare would see my utterance of the relevant sentence, e.g. 'You ought to put A into prison', as a 'speech-act' (in J.L. Austin's terminology (Austin, 1962)) in which my aim or intention is to advise or exhort you subject to the constraints of prescriptivity and universalizability. The terminology of 'speech-acts' is one which you will occasionally encounter in discussions of Hare.

12.2.1. Prescriptivism vs. descriptivism

A descriptivist like Philippa Foot argues that morality is conceptually tied to considerations of human welfare in such a way that certain factual or descriptive statements (e.g. 'She is old and lonely') automatically have moral relevance. Hare denies this on grounds of logic.

For Hare, factual, descriptive statements do not entail moral judgements. 'She is old and lonely, therefore one ought to help her' is not deductively valid. The factual statement ('She is old and lonely') entails a moral judgement ('One ought to help her') only if you invoke a moral principle ('One ought to help old and lonely people').

On Hare's account factual, descriptive considerations enter into morality in two ways:

(1) They supply the factual minor premises in moral reasoning.
(2) They provide one component of the meaning of moral terms.

Take the moral and general evaluative term 'good'. We typically use this word to express or recommend a preference; and this prescriptive component does not vary with the host of things to which the term 'good' is applied. But the descriptive component varies completely with context. A good car is one that runs cheaply, reliably, safely, etc.; a good knife is one which cuts efficiently, and so on. The criteria for the application of 'good' are variable and descriptive; the prescriptive force of the term, with its implication of 'Choose this!', is not.

12.2.2. A non-truth-functional deductivist model of moral reasoning

Hare clearly espouses a deductivist model of moral reasoning. But it has an unusual feature. Deductive arguments are generally regarded as truth-functional. The conclusion of a deductively valid argument cannot be false when the premises are true; the truth of the conclusion is thus a function of the truth of the premises.

But two of the sentences in (5) above are not truth-functional on Hare's account. They are action-guiding prescriptions, a kind of imperative or command on Hare's analysis. Imperatives and commands cannot be true or false. However, Harean conclusions do appear to follow from Harean premises.

12.2.3. Internalism vs. externalism

Hare insists that moral judgements entail prescriptions or imperatives. If my moral judgement concerns my own conduct, the prescription or imperative is of the 'Let me … ' kind. If it concerns the conduct of others, it will read 'Do this ….'

There is, on Hare's account, a conceptual connection or logical link between making the judgement and recognizing the prescription or imperative, on the one hand and, on the other, being motivated to act. There are, as we shall see, problems in spelling out the precise connection.

The present point is just that this kind of position is known as *internalism*. Internalism is the view that motivation is inbuilt in moral judgement. Sincere acceptance of a moral judgement necessarily has a motivational influence on action. To see the contrast, imagine an ethical position for which the connection between making a moral judgement and being motivated to act is purely contingent, reliant on the empirical fact that people making moral judgements are typically or often concerned to act on them.

12.2.4. A non-cognitive theory

By the same token Hare is a non-cognitivist. Moral judgements are not beliefs or matters of knowledge; they are not capable of truth or falsity. Hare believes that we can choose our moral principles; and that the ultimate justification for them is what he calls a complete 'way of life' of which they are a part (Hare, 1952: 69). To glance ahead, non-cognitivism is motivated by the difficulties of moral realism (26.1.7).

12.3. CRITICISMS OF HARE

I have now completed my exposition of Hare's theory. Next we move on to its assessment.

What 'controls' can we apply to Hare's theory? Two sets of controls, I think. The first applies to virtually any theory:

- clarity
- fruitfulness
- coherence
- novelty

The second set of controls is rather different. On his own account Hare is doing *meta-ethics*, not *normative ethics*. That is to say, he is not trying to persuade, advise or exhort us to adopt a moral standard: a moral criterion or ideal (4.1.1 – 4.1.2), with whatever justification (5.1.1 – 5.1.3). He is standing aside from the moral life, separating himself from morality as an institution, and trying to reach a general characterization of moral judgement.

The idea is that the meta-ethicist approaches the moral life as a mere observer in an attitude of receptive contemplation. Now Jurgen Habermas argues (Habermas, 1972) that fields of inquiry are defined within a normative frame of reference, by assumptions about what is worth investigation and capable of systematic study to an appropriate standard. So there are no 'mere observers'. Yet, consistently with Habermas, one might still study the moral life without commitment to a specific moral standard. To this extent the distinction between meta-ethics and normative ethics holds good.

For meta-ethics a proper test is whether Hare's theory matches our reactions, to real or imagined examples, of accepting or denying that a judgement is a moral judgement; and this test can be applied to the other theories in the rest of the chapter. For some further ideas for testing meta-ethics, see Attfield, 1987: 4-5.

At the limit, if Hare is successful, he will identify the property or properties that are common and peculiar to moral judgements. This will yield a set of necessary and sufficient conditions. If a judgement has the relevant properties, it is a moral judgement (if p then q: the condition is sufficient); and if it lacks the relevant property or properties then it is not a moral judgement (if not-p then not-q: the condition is necessary).

Novelty is the easiest item. Hare's theory broke new ground. Nothing quite like his particular combination of ideas had been to hand before. Fruitfulness I want to leave aside; that point is for you to decide. Coherence is a matter of the internal consistency of Hare's theory; and I think it is fair to say that, on the surface at least, there are no glaring tensions between propositions (1) – (9) above. An assessment of clarity is one for you to make when we have seen what blurs, if any, Hare's critics have shown up.

I cannot hope, in a brief discussion of Hare's universal prescriptivism, to cover all the criticisms it has attracted. For a more detailed discussion, see

Hudson, 1983: 201-48. More advanced material, with replies by Hare to his critics, can be found in Seanor and Fotion, 1988.

The best policy will be to take criticisms under each of the headings of prescriptivity, universalizability and formalism. If the criticisms go through, Hare has not identified necessary and sufficient conditions for a judgement to be a moral judgement. I will examine four criticisms. The key phrases are:

- the different types of moral judgement
- weakness of will
- the denial of Harean universalizability
- the restrictive content of moral judgements

12.4. CRITICISMS THAT HARE'S CONDITIONS ARE NOT NECESSARY

Under this heading I will consider the first three criticisms just listed.

12.4.1. Prescriptivity: different types of moral judgement

A point usually made sooner rather than later in discussions of Hare is that moral judgements are a wider class than the class of ought-judgements. Recall Lists B and C, neither of which contained an ought-judgement at all (2.2.1):

List B

Mary Lou is not a very moral person.
If you think that's a moral course of action, you show a corrupt mind.
Don't accuse me of not having moral motives, you appalling hypocrite.
To go on holiday during your wife's illness was hardly a moral decision.
I cannot agree that animal experimentation is a moral practice.

List C

All lying is wrong.
Some lying is worse than any killing.
Bill is not mentally ill but plain evil.
If pride and jealousy are vicious qualities, so is greed.
Justice delayed is justice denied.

That these judgements imply ought-judgements, if in fact they do, is nothing to the point. They are not themselves ought-judgements. Truth to tell, Hare quite recognizes the diversity of moral judgements. In Hare, 1952 he talks a fair amount about judgements containing 'good' rather than 'ought'. But he regards ought-judgements, judgements about what one ought to do, as central to morality.

One might cite Hare's former colleague, J.L. Austin:

In ethics we study, I suppose, the good and the bad, the right and the wrong, and this must be for the most part in some connection with conduct or the doing of actions (Austin, 1961: 126).

For this reason, ethics was sometimes known in the 19th century as 'the philosophy of conduct'. One of the issues here is that between the moral criterion and the moral ideal: whether one's view is that morality centres on the requirements of action or on the concept of a person (4.1.2). If one stresses the latter, then one's view is that a disposition to act is only one part of a morally significant structure of personality.

As well, the point is generally added, not all ought-judgements fit Hare's theory. Harman distinguishes no fewer than four types of ought-judgement (Harman, 1977: 59, 118-19). Harman picks out four 'oughts':

- 'ought' of expectation
- 'ought' of reasons
- 'ought' of evaluation
- moral 'ought'

By the moral 'ought' Harman appears to have in mind the kind of 'ought' that registers an overriding requirement on action – very much the imperative-entailing sense of 'ought' that drives Hare's ethical theory. I call this the 'prescriptive' ought.

Harman calls his second 'ought' *evaluative*. One might also call it an *ideal* or *desiderative* 'ought'. We meet it in judgements such as 'No child ought to die from hunger'. That judgement is, or can be, genuinely moral; that at least is my reaction. The judgement can record the view that, relative to a moral standard, it is undesirable for children to die from hunger, that in a morally better ordered world this sort of death would not occur. But, for all that, it need register no overriding requirement on action.

Again, Hare quite realizes the ambiguities of 'ought'. But he would argue for the centrality of his imperative-entailing, action-guiding (prescriptive) sense of 'ought'. He might add that even the ideal, evaluative or desiderative 'ought' requires, for sincerity, that one would be committed to relevant action in favourable circumstances.

This just means, though, that there are other kinds of moral judgement besides the prescriptive ought-judgement with which Hare is concerned. So that propositions (1) – (9) do not define necessary conditions for a judgement to be a moral judgement.

12.4.2. Prescriptivity: weakness of will

But even on his own central ground, is Hare's imperative-entailing, action-guiding 'ought' too strong?

There is thought to be a phenomenon, weakness of will or, as the Greeks called it, *akrasia*, caught in such remarks as Ovid's '*Video meliora proboque, deteriora sequor*' ('I see the better and applaud it, but I follow the worse') or St Paul's 'The good which I want to do, I fail to do.'

Recall how I characterized weakness of will in 6.1.9:

> An agent, with a choice between doing x intentionally and doing y intentionally, does y although his moral judgement is in favour of doing x.

Now, we might see the agent's subsequent regret, shame or remorse as evidence of the genuineness of his or her acceptance of a moral judgement; and explain what happened in terms of a desire to act morally but a stronger desire to follow some other course.

The point is that, according to some of his critics, this phenomenon of *akrasia* or weakness of will, or 'backsliding' as Hare quaintly calls it in 1963: ch. 5, cannot be handled by Hare's prescriptivism.

For what does Hare say? A moral judgement entails a prescription which in turn embodies a desire: and to have this desire is to be disposed to act accordingly. But the *akrates* (to use a Greek term that points to a later connection with Aristotle (31.1.2)), i.e. the morally weak agent, does not act accordingly. Therefore, on Hare's theory, he cannot have the corresponding desire; and so cannot accept the matching imperative; and so does not accept the moral judgement. The judgement is not genuine.

That is the problem Hare has to face. To see what resources he has to hand, let's consider the nature of a disposition. For what is at stake here is the idea of a disposition to action.

We make dispositional statements, such as 'Salt is water-soluble.' And we might analyse that particular statement in one of two ways. We might say (using a subjunctive conditional, which some logicians are not entirely happy about):

(1) 'Salt is water-soluble' = df. 'If salt were put in water, then salt would dissolve.'

Or we might avoid this subjunctive conditional and say something like:

(2) 'Salt is water-soluble' = df. 'For any salt, at any time, if the salt is in water at that time, then it is water-soluble if and only if it dissolves at that time.'

What the critics are saying is that, according to Hare:

(3) 'An agent accepts a moral judgement' = df. 'For any agent, at any time, and for any moral judgement, in any situation recognized as relevant, if the agent can (= has the opportunity and physical ability to) act intentionally on his or her moral judgement on that occasion, then the agent accepts a moral judgement if and only if he or she acts on it intentionally at that time.'

But this is just what the recognition of weakness of will rules out. For the agent does accept a moral judgement, and can act on it intentionally, but fails to do so.

How is Hare to handle this? I think his best course, and my own statement of his position, is as follows. Hare's dispositional analysis really needs to be stated more fully:

(4) 'An agent accepts a moral judgement' = df. 'For any agent, at any time, and for any moral judgement, in any situation recognized as relevant, if the agent has the opportunity and ability (physical *and psychological*) intentionally to do an action required by his or her moral judgement, then the agent accepts a moral judgement in that situation if and only if he or she acts on it intentionally at that time.'

I offer that only as a first, crude version of Hare's dispositional analysis. The key to Hare's position is that the morally weak agent is psychologically unable to act on his or her moral judgement. So the judgement is genuine but psychological impossibility blocks action as effectively as physical impossibility when you are paralysed or locked in a room.

It might be objected that this concession to psychological impossibility allows anyone to claim that they accept a moral judgement and fail to act on it only because they find it psychologically impossible to do so. But to suppose that this objection is anything to the point is to misunderstand Hare's theory. He is not concerned with what someone might, with specious plausibility, invoke as a moral excuse, but with the real event of someone's accepting a moral judgement and being unable to act on it. We grant that somebody might accept a moral judgement but, recognizing its relevance to their situation, fail to act on it because there is no opportunity or because they are physically unable to act appropriately. Then why not grant psychological impossibility on a par with physical impossibility? Why should a theory of moral judgement assume a fully unified personality?

Hare unfortunately says very little about his notion of psychological impossibility. This is an unclarity in his theory. I think we do recognize such a notion when we say that it is psychologically impossible for an person with an IQ of 49 to understand the theory of relativity. But that does not seem quite the relevant sense here. Perhaps a better parallel would be the psychological impossibility for a heroin addict to resist taking the next injection.

Since, however, Hare can recognize the phenomenon of weakness of will, his ought-judgement analysis survives intact. He is not claiming (3) above. He is not saying that the very characterization of moral judgement rules out weakness of will.

Still Hare is not safe yet. For, one objection runs, the case of the *morally weak agent* cannot strictly be one of psychological impossibility otherwise he would not be blameworthy. My reply is that this depends on our view of the connection between moral judgement and responsibility. If we take Schlick's view that to be morally responsible just is to be amenable to control through moral judgement, that it betokens a kind of educability, we can quite straightforwardly blame the *morally weak agent*. The impact of this moral judgement may precisely be to correct his practical attitude, to strengthen one part of his motivation, so that he acts better in future.

On Hare's account of weakness of will, see further Mortimore, 1971: part II; and Taylor, 1980.

12.4.3. Universalizability: Winch vs. Hare

About universalizability there is one thing on which we need to be clear right at the start. The universalizability criterion, as it is often called, is meant to do quite different work in different types of theory.

In Kant's ethical theory it is a substantive moral principle. If an action passes the 'categorical imperative' test of consistent universalizability, then it may be done. The action is permissible.

By contrast, in Hare's ethical theory universalizability is offered purely as a logical or conceptual criterion for distinguishing moral from non-moral judgements. This is one reason why it is unhelpful to make a parallel between Harean universalizability and the Golden Rule of doing as one would be done by. The Golden Rule is a substantive moral principle. Another reason why the parallelism breaks down is that the Golden Rule at best matches proposition (8); it has nothing to correspond to (6) or (7).

It is sometimes said that Hare only subscribes to universalizability as a logical criterion because he accepts the substantive (liberal) moral principle that one ought to apply to others whatever principles one applies to oneself, and conversely. If this is psychological speculation, it is best left to Hare's biographer.

The most celebrated critique of Harean universalizability comes in Peter Winch's 'The Universalizability of Moral Judgements' (Winch, 1972). For a proper angle on Winch's critique we need to note that Hare commits himself to a stronger version of universalizability than I have presented in (8). It is not merely that one must be prepared or willing for others to act on the same principle in relevantly similar situations. One must accept that nobody ought to fail to act on the same principle in such situations.

But who is 'one'? Hare's ethical theory is commonly thought to handle universalizability from two angles: (1) the action and (2) the situation or circumstances. The agent is a third angle to the triangle only in this way: that action and situation are specifiable quite independently of the agent. 'One' is an agent; and what the agent has to decide is whether he or she ought, and everyone else ought, to do the same action in relevantly similar situations.

Winch's point of departure is a story, *Billy Budd*, by the mid-19th-century American writer, Herman Melville, in which through a combination of provocation and accident Budd, a British sailor during the Napoleonic wars, has broken the King's regulations by causing the death of an officer. Captain Vere has to decide on Budd's pardon or punishment.

The burden of Winch's analysis of Captain Vere's predicament is that moral reasoning is conducted, not by an abstract 'agent', but by a 'person' with specific beliefs, desires, attitudes, commitments. Vere's situation is personal. It is partly defined by his self-image, by his view of himself as a career officer committed in honour to naval values in general and to the King's regulations in particular.

Acting in the situation described by Melville, he feels that the morally correct course is to sentence Budd to death. But Winch's point is that Vere can make this moral judgement without being committed to the view that every other agent, confronted with the need to decide on pardon or punishment in time of war and precarious discipline, ought to decide in the same way. For agents are persons; and a person's situation is partly set by the kind of person he takes himself to be. Someone uncommitted, or less deeply committed, to naval values could properly decide differently.

This is an interesting angle on universalizability. But it is not one that Hare neglects. For he actually speaks not of agents but of persons:

> ... the judgement that I ought in a certain situation to do a certain thing commits me to the view that no similar person in a precisely similar situation ought to fail to do the same thing (1963, 153).

On page 169 Winch himself quotes from Hare, 1963: 49:

> Since we cannot know everything about another actual person's concrete situation (including how it strikes him, which may make all the difference), it is nearly always presumptuous to suppose that another person's situation is exactly like one we have ourselves been in, or even like it in the relevant particulars.

Winch comments that this makes the universalizability criterion 'idle' (Winch, 1972: 169). The comment is hardly due. Hare keeps to universalizability as a conceptual constraint on moral judgement but includes the agent's personality in the situation to which a universalizable moral judgement relates. Inclusion of Vere's personality in his moral situation is exactly what Winch's analysis of *Billy Budd* is supposed to secure. But then, while Winch remarks with emphasis that his own personality is different and that he would decide differently from Vere, he offers precisely no argument against the universalizability of Vere's moral judgement *for persons of Vere's personality in Vere's type of situation.*

All in all, Winch does not succeed in my view in overturning Hare's requirement of universalizability. On Winch see Gaita, 1990 and 1991; Kolenda, 1975; Montague, 1974; and Stephenson, 1988.

12.5. CRITICISMS THAT HARE'S CONDITIONS ARE NOT SUFFICIENT

On Hare's theory just any principle is a moral principle if it meets the requirements of prescriptivity and universalizability. But there are objections to this formal approach.

12.5.1. Formalism: the restrictive content of moral judgements

Hare's view is that, contingently, i.e. as a matter of general fact, universalizability will set limits on the content of moral principles. Harean universalizability compels one to engage in imaginative role-reversal. 'If our situations were reversed, would I be prepared for you to act towards me as I'm proposing to act towards you?' If I adopt a principle which allows me to override your interests and desires, then I must be prepared for you to rely on the same principle – damagingly to my own interests and desires.

Hare allows, however, that he cannot conceptually rule out the possibility of a moral agent whom he calls 'the fanatic' (Hare, 1963, ch. 9) – or sometimes 'the Nazi'. The mark of a fanatic is that he or she has ideals which override the satisfaction of other people's interests and desires, with (and the rider is important) a complete willingness to suffer the loss or frustration of his or her own interests and desires if the positions were to be reversed. So, for instance, the fanatical racist has an ideal of 'racial purity' and is quite willing to be put to death if it should turn out that he or she is in fact a member of the offending race.

The point is, of course, that on Hare's theory the fanatic does sincerely accept a moral principle. That doesn't commit Hare to the view, which he clearly rejects, that the principle is a welcome moral principle, a good moral principle – only that it is a moral principle as opposed to a non-moral one.

More serious is another consideration. Any principle is a moral principle, if it meets Hare's requirements, no matter how trivial. Presumably the principle, 'Everyone should bow three times to every third black cat they encounter', could be a moral principle on Hare's account. This line of criticism, often called the charge of triviality, is particularly associated with Philippa Foot. Prescriptivity and universalizability are insufficient. Hare's formalism does not capture an intuition we have about morality: that morality is conceptually tied to a certain range of considerations, those relating to human (or sentient) good or harm.

Said another way, Hare concentrates on what it is to treat X as a moral principle. Foot requires of any attempt at a definition of morality that it identify a material element and specify a certain pre-set subject matter that moral principles necessarily have. Either way, it will be a further point to distinguish what we regard as good moral principles from what we regard as questionable or bad. This last point belongs to our second ethical problem, that of the moral standard (chapter 3).

13.1. THE CONTENT APPROACH: PHILIPPA FOOT

Foot's ethical theory is contained mainly in her book, *Virtues and Vices* (1978). For present purposes her most important papers are 'Moral Arguments', 'Moral Beliefs', and 'Goodness and Choice'.

Foot stands in polar opposition to Hare. To make clear the issue between them, let me represent Hare's theory in a slightly different way. Cast your mind back to the piece of Harean moral reasoning I set out under proposition (4) of 12.1:

Evaluative major premise: One ought to put in prison anyone who will not pay one what he owes

Factual minor premise: A will not pay me what he owes

Conclusion: I ought to put A in prison because he will not pay me what he owes

We can express this in terms of the agent's *reasons for acting* (14.1.2). In the example, these considerations account for and explain why a person acts as he does; they are *motivating* reasons. Hare is not offering them as *justifying* reasons. The agent would regard the reasons as justifying his action. But Hare himself is not saying that someone who goes through this process of reasoning is justified, by some objective or Hare-endorsed standard, in acting as he does. He is not trying to sell the moral point of view to us. He is only saying that, provided the requirements of prescriptivity and universalizability are met, this is a genuine piece of moral reasoning – irrespective of the content of the evaluative major premise, the factual minor premise, or the conclusion.

In other words, he is presenting a formalist account of moral reasons for acting. Provided such and such motivational conditions are met, just any judgement is a moral judgement.

Foot's central objection is that it is simply not the case that just any factual minor premise can be included in or excluded from moral reasoning.

In Foot's view, so far from its being the case that just any factual consideration is relevant or irrelevant, depending purely on one's moral principles, rather:

(1) Where there is a moral judgement, it must be supportable by appeal to considerations within a certain range;

and conversely

(2) Where there is a consideration within a certain range, a moral judgement follows or is appropriate.

Call these claims Theses 1 and 2. On the strength of Thesis 1 Foot is claiming that Hare has omitted a necessary condition for a judgement or principle to be a moral one: namely, that it is arguable for or against on the basis of a certain range of considerations. The range is variously specified as relating to what satisfies a person's *wants*, or as concerned with *human good and harm*. Other writers of the same school, such as Elizabeth Anscombe, talk of *human flourishing* (Anscombe, 1970: 233).

Roughly the picture is this: that without any thought of morality we can specify a range of considerations relating to human (or perhaps even sentient) welfare. Morality is an institution of which the rationale is to promote that welfare. Therefore, *pace* Hare, a certain range of factual matters is necessarily of moral relevance, namely those relating to human welfare. Moreover, no matters outside this range have any moral relevance at all; and, to complete the picture, not just any consideration can plausibly be seen as relevant to human welfare. An example of what is relevant to welfare would be freedom from physical injury. All this is put to us as simply a reflection of the intrinsic nature of morality as a social institution.

Thesis 2 commits Foot to the view that the moral features of a situation are consequential on its descriptive features. So in one sense she is an ethical naturalist (5.1.3).

Theses 1 and 2 make up Foot's general characterization of moral judgement. Thesis 1 defines a necessary, and Thesis 2 a sufficient, condition for a moral judgement.

13.2. THREE CAUTIONS

Before we examine these theses, I want to make three points to forestall misunderstanding and prevent irrelevant criticism.

(1) Foot does not see herself as having to formulate a sophisticated theory of the human good, any more than someone who claimed that the social institution of medicine is conceptually tied to matters of health may feel obliged to produce an advanced, scientific account of the nature of health. Her account of the relation between morality and the human good is neutral on whether there can be a *scientific* ethics, a theory of the human good fixed by the life sciences. Imagine biologically or psychologically filtered concepts completely structuring our understanding of human welfare. This vision (espied through many ethical naturalist telescopes) is one which Foot neither endorses nor rejects.

(2) Nor does Foot see herself, in making this supposedly conceptual point about the nature of morality, as being committed to any particular way of taking considerations of human welfare into account. Utilitarianism is a view that welfare is to be maximized. But to put forward that view is to offer a moral criterion, answering the question 'What shall I do?' (4.1). Foot actually rejects utilitarianism; and whatever the merits of her rejection she is certainly right not to feel committed to a particular moral criterion simply by virtue of a conceptual stand on the general characterization of moral judgement.

(3) Foot is clearly aware of the diversity of moral concepts. A wide range of concepts enter into moral judgements – 'wrong', 'worse', 'evil', 'vicious',

'justice' (3.1.3). If moral judgements are conceptually tied to considerations of human welfare as Foot claims, there is plainly a vast secondary task of analysis in tracing the connections between these particular moral concepts and human welfare.

13.3. FOOT'S ARGUMENTS: STATEMENT AND CRITICISM

How does Foot argue for Theses 1 and 2?

She makes basically two moves. The first, relating to Thesis 1, has to do with the 'importance' attached to moral judgements; the second, relating to Thesis 2, turns on her account of evaluative 'criteria'. Let's look first at the argument for Thesis 1.

13.3.1. Morality and importance

Foot says at one point:

> I do not know what could be meant by saying that it was someone's duty to do something, unless there was an attempt to show why it mattered if this sort of thing was not done. How can questions such as 'What does it matter?', 'What harm does it do?', 'What advantage is there in …?', 'Why is it important?' be set aside here? (Foot, 1978: 105-6).

Foot is right to stress *some* connection between morality and importance. But Hare could accept as much: moral judgements are action-guiding on Hare's account. They matter to one's own conduct and are meant to influence other people's conduct by advice and exhortation.

What Foot really needs is not merely *some* connection between morality and importance but a *quite specific* connection: namely that moral judgements matter because, and only because, they relate to an independently specifiable human welfare. Purely general considerations about the 'importance' of moral judgements are not enough to show that where there is a moral judgement it must be supportable by appeal to considerations within her favoured range.

More than that, Foot's theory is answerable to just the same controls as Hare's. Foot is offering us meta-ethics. She is standing off to one side, looking at morality, and trying to get a grip on the concept of a moral judgement. Her claims are therefore checkable against our reactions, to real or imagined examples, of accepting or denying that a judgement is a moral judgement.

Then take a judgement of integrity. Suppose that somebody (a hermit perhaps, or St Simon Stylites, stuck permanently on his pillar?) has a strong personal commitment to a way of life. In this way of life he recognizes overriding requirements on action quite unconnected, in Foot's mode, with human welfare. Such a person would still exhibit integrity if, threatened with a dire penalty, he did not yield but stood his ground, neither abandoning nor modifying his way of life. Here we should recognize a person's integrity in respect of principles which, *ex hypothesi*, were not tied to considerations of human welfare.

A defender of Foot's theory might reply that we should judge this person to have the moral virtue of integrity because *we* realize the general value to human welfare of having and keeping to strong personal commitments. But then, could the person *himself* not make judgements about what integrity requires of him where, again *ex hypothesi*, he does not connect morality in Foot's way with human welfare?

13.3.2. Morality and criteria

Foot's argument for Thesis 2 rests on an idea concerning the criteria for evaluation of kinds of thing. We will concentrate on 'good' as the most general term of evaluation.

'Good' can be used *predicatively* or *attributively*. Take a different term to make the distinction clear, the term 'attractive'. If Kylie says, 'Jason is an attractive actor', she may be using 'attractive' predicatively. She may be predicating attractiveness of Jason and saying that he has two qualities – namely, the quality of being attractive and, quite separately, the quality of being an actor. Or she might mean that he is attractive as an actor – unusual, elegant, resourceful in his interpretation and execution of roles, etc. In this case she is using 'attractive' attributively. There is reference only to one property, that of being an actor, while attractiveness is being ascribed in some way to this.

There is an argument in Geach, 1967 that in moral judgements 'good' is always attributive, never predicative. To be good is to be *a* good something or other; and there is no moral quality or property of goodness that can be ascribed to something as a bona fide property in its own right as we can ascribe squareness to tables or yellowness to tulips.

Geach also argues that, once we have determined what it is to be an X, we can automatically fix what it is to be a *good* X. We can do this, moreover, purely on the basis of factual, descriptive considerations.

In other words, the criteria of evaluation are straightforwardly factual and of a limited range. We say, for instance, that something is a good knife. On the Geach-Foot view, once we have determined what it is for a thing to be a knife we have determined also what it is for something to be a good knife. E.g., 'cuts efficiently', which is purely descriptive, has to be relevant to the evaluation of knives. Cutting efficiently is one of the qualities that enable a knife to serve its purposes. So we can go from description to evaluation. But not from just any description: 'was once held by Queen Victoria', is absolutely irrelevant to the evaluation of knives. Only a limited range of descriptions is relevant to evaluation.

This is just what Foot claims against Hare in the case of moral evaluation. But there appear to be a number of shortcomings in her position. I will mention three.

13.3.3. The criterial connection

In the first place, the criterial connection between description and evaluation works relatively smoothly for clearly functional objects like knives. If we move to other examples, the smoothness is progressively broken. What are the descriptive criteria to support evaluations like 'good food' (fit to eat, untainted, nutritious, palatable, …), 'good cat' (efficient mouse-killer, house-trained, docile, …), 'good Prime Minister'? For 'good food' and 'good cat' not only would a complete enumeration of relevant descriptive criteria be hard to produce, but the items I have included might be rejected by some evaluation.

Secondly, even if Foot's approach to evaluation worked well in general, we could not properly conclude that it therefore works for ethics. Moral judgements are a sub-class of evaluations. At best she would have produced an inductive argument. She would have offered some evidence to support the claim that what holds true of non-moral evaluations also holds true of moral evaluations. Her attempt to show that judgements of rudeness are conceptually tied, internally related, to the description, 'causes offence by indicating lack of respect', is of limited relevance. I am not sure that 'rudeness' is a moral notion. If it is, then so is 'respect': hence the criterion for a moral judgement of rudeness has not been shown to be purely descriptive.

Finally, even if Foot is correct that where there is a consideration within a certain range, a moral judgement follows or is appropriate, we need to take a quick look at the diversity of moral judgements before we draw any drastic conclusions. Recall from 12.4.1 the distinction between:

- the ideal or evaluative 'ought' • the prescriptive 'ought'

The most that Foot's criterial argument could deliver is that where there is a consideration within a certain range, an ideal ought-judgement follows or is appropriate.

The reason is this. Take a description: 'She is old, sick, and lonely.' Foot might succeed in showing that an ideal ought-judgement is an appropriate response to this. E.g., 'She ought not to be left alone and without help.' What the description could not yield is a prescriptive judgement, marking an over-riding requirement on action: 'I ought not to leave her alone and without help.' For suppose I am confronted with two such persons, to only one of whom I can give company and help. Which am I to help? My dilemma is not resolved by Foot's criterial argument.

So far I think Foot has not dislodged Hare's account. Her claim is that Hare has omitted a necessary condition for a judgement to be a moral judgement. But this claim, belonging to thesis (1) above, is (as we saw in 13.3.1) not convincingly argued for. Her further claim, set out in thesis (2), runs into the difficulties we have just noted.

I will just notice another comment that appears regularly in the literature, namely this: Foot's general position relies on a clear distinction between the moral and the non-moral. There is an independently specifiable human good; and morality is to be understood instrumentally entirely in relation to that. But there is a famous line of argument from Phillips and Mounce, 1965 that 'What is good or harmful to someone can depend on what his moral beliefs are; it is not always the other way round' (T.D. Perry, 1976: 189). The point is an interesting one, but hardly decisive in its own right. For why should Foot accept this claim, which is a denial rather than a refutation of her position?

A full-length book on Foot's ethical theory is long overdue, though Warnock, 1971 presents an ethical theory in some respects similar to Foot's. Aside from the references in the text, try Blumenfeld, 1973 and Frankena, 1974a. Foot replies to Frankena in Foot, 1975 (reprinted in Foot, 1978). Also of interest are Nathan, 1979; Valberg, 1977; and D. Wallace, 1983. For a critical discussion of Geach on attributive and predicative uses of 'good', see Hare, 1967 and Pigden, 1990.

14.1. MORAL JUDGEMENTS AS CATEGORICAL

There is a view about morality, often put forward as one of 'our' intuitions, one of the assumptions 'we' are apt to make, that moral judgements apply irrespective of inclination or desire. Certainly, most of us have had the experience of feeling that we ought to do something which we do not want to do, and *vice versa*. And in relation to other people a moral judgement such as, 'You ought not to torment that cat', does not have to be withdrawn merely if the person to whom it is addressed tells us sincerely that, sorry, but we have made a mistake: he *wants* to torment the cat.

This suggests another attempt to supply a general characterization of moral judgement: that all and only moral judgements are categorical imperatives. The term 'categorical imperative' derives from Kant, whose essential idea is that a categorical imperative is a principle binding on every rational agent as such. For now I want to put briefly to one side that particular, Kantian construction of the categorical nature of moral judgements. I shall keep for the moment to the idea that moral judgements are categorical in the sense that they apply regardless of inclination or desire.

14.1.1. Foot: categoricality not sufficient for moral judgement

Foot has criticized this characterization. Assume that moral judgements are categorical: then in her view it is not the case that only moral judgements are categorical since, for example, the rules of games, of clubs, and of etiquette, to say nothing of the laws of the land, equally apply regardless of desire or inclination. 'Gentlemen are to remove their hats indoors' or 'No member may introduce an inebriated guest' do not cease, the one to be a rule of etiquette, the other to be a rule of the club, merely because a bald man is reluctant to remove his hat or a member is inclined to lurch in with his boozy pal.

If these examples go through, as I think they do, then it is not a sufficient condition for a judgement to be a moral judgement that it applies irrespective of inclination or desire. One might also mention, to supplement these examples, certain principles of rationality which appear equally indifferent to desire or inclination. One says, for example, 'He who wills the end wills the means'. This principle, which clearly invokes something like Harman's 'ought' of reasons (12.4.1), may well be a requirement of rationality. Rationality-wise, if I may put it so, this is what the agent ought to do – will the means if he wills the end – irrespective of his inclination or desire to pay heed to it in his practical reasoning.

14.1.2. Foot: categoricality not necessary for moral judgement

Foot would also argue that, to turn from the sufficient to the necessary, so far from its being a necessary condition for a judgement to be a moral judgement that it is categorical, in fact no moral judgements are such.

The point is this. If we accept that rules of etiquette, rules of clubs and the rest are categorical in the sense of being relevant to one's situation from the viewpoint of a system of rules irrespective of inclination or desire, we do not suppose that these rules have automatic reason-giving force. They do not apply in this further sense. If I regard the whole system of etiquette as bourgeois nonsense (if nothing more sinister) and deride the club as a rest home for fossils, then in my practical reasoning I can separate myself from the system and the club. The relevant rules give me no reasons for action since I reject the institutions from which they derive.

But there is a strong tradition of ethical theorizing for which the requirements of morality are vitally different in this respect from these other rules. The tradition is strikingly clear in Kant's view (to which we now return) that moral requirements are mandatory for any rational agent. For a rational being, qua rational, the requirements of morality have, therefore (Kant holds), reason-giving force.

Reasons for action

'Reason-giving' in what sense, however? There are motivating reasons for action, and justifying reasons. 'Why did you demolish the gazebo?' 'It was unsightly and I wanted to get some exercise.' That answer gives a motivating reason; it explains (if true) why the person did what he did. 'Why should I demolish the gazebo?' 'It is unsightly and you need to get some exercise.' This answer offers a justifying reason: here are considerations, the claim is, whether you accept them or not, on which you would be well-advised to act. In the first case the agent himself would regard the motivating reason as also justificatory, but this is a harmless complication. For Kant the requirements of morality are supposed to have automatic reason-giving force in the sense of providing justifying reasons for action. Foot's arguments here aim to show that moral judgements do not have this feature.

A shift of sense

This takes us definitely beyond the sense in which judgements of etiquette or rules of a club are categorical. So, in a rather confused debate, we have the claim (which is a statement of 'intuition' about morality) that moral judgements are categorical in the sense of having relevance to one's situation, from the viewpoint of a moral standard, regardless of inclination or desire. Counter-examples to this claim, which appeal to rules of etiquette and the rest to show that categoricality is not sufficient for moral judgement, make no reference to justifying reasons for action. They do not address the claim that moral judgements apply, in the sense of having automatic reason-giving force by providing justifying reasons for action, irrespective of inclination or desire. Then, when we examine whether categoricality in this further sense is a necessary condition for a judgement to be a moral judgement, we encounter a denial that this is so: a denial that moral judgements automatically provide justifying reasons for action.

If we are clear about this shift of sense in the notion of 'applying irrespective of inclination or desire' we shall not be misled. But how does Foot try to show that moral judgements do not have automatic reason-giving force?

Justifying reasons for action

Suppose we follow Foot and tie moral judgements conceptually to considerations of human welfare. Suppose further that we relate the agent's motivating reasons for action to his desires in the manner of the belief-desire theory of action explanation (6.1.6), a theory that Foot appears to accept (Foot, 1978: ch. 10). Then realistically, justifying reasons for action must relate to desires, if only to 'criticized' desires that the agent would have if he were better informed or more rational. For clearly, if desire is requisite to motivation, there is little point in offering justifying reasons which ignore desire. But we do not provide justifying reasons for action simply by tying moral judgements conceptually to considerations of human welfare. For, to put a crude question, is there any especial reason why I should heed your welfare irrespective of desire?

This question plainly takes us far beyond the general characterization of moral judgement. It slips in the problem of moral reasoning and the theory of action explanation; and it involves us in the further problem of the justification of moral judgement and the question whether moral judgements do have automatic reason-giving force. Now perhaps it is clear why I said that ethical problems and topics are distinguishable but not separable (7.1.4). I think the strongest version of the categoricality of moral judgement that we can accept for now is the idea that moral judgements at least do not have to be withdrawn merely in face of a person's contrary desire.

I think a further point, basic to our present inquiry, is that claims or denials that moral judgements are categorical (in whatever sense) run on assumptions that moral judgement has already been characterized in some general way. Foot's characterization is already to hand. Kant has his own characterization based on a special concept of universalizability. The claims and denials we have considered make us ask whether moral judgements, having a certain general characterization, also have the feature of categoricality. The view that moral judgements are categorical can be offered as itself a general characterization of moral judgement. I have so taken it here. But I think that, on proper reflection, it needs a general characterization to be already in place.

On Foot's position here see Foot, 1978: 157-73. Holmes, 1974 is answered by Foot, 1974. See also Scheffler, 1979.

15.1. THE EMOTIVIST APPROACH

Emotivism goes our way and much further. We are interested to know what, if anything, sets off moral judgements from other kinds of judgement; and emotivism has an account to offer. Central to that account is the view that moral judgements have two functions: to express and to elicit emotion. But emotivism is distinctively the wider claim that moral judgements are nothing but expressions and attempted elicitations of emotion: that they are incapable of truth and cannot embody knowledge. The grounds and plausibility of that wider claim, the claim about what moral judgements are *not*, take us quite beyond a general characterization of what they *are*.

A first handle on emotivism's general characterization of moral judgement is as follows. Emotivism runs two theses:

(1) There are certain judgements in making which, unless the speaker uses sentences expressing his emotions and intended to elicit corresponding emotions in his hearer(s), he is not making a moral judgement.

(2) There are certain judgements in making which, if the speaker uses sentences expressing his emotions and intended to elicit corresponding emotions in his hearer(s), he is making a moral judgement.

Thesis (1) claims a necessary, and Thesis (2) a sufficient, condition for a judgement to be a moral judgement.

In this century the best-known emotivist texts are A.J. Ayer, *Language, Truth and Logic* (1936; 2nd ed., 1946) and C.L. Stevenson, *Ethics and Language* (1944) and *Facts and Values* (1963). I shall first look briefly at Stevenson's views, then (with a nod to the 18th century) turn to consider the influential emotivist position set out by David Hume.

15.1.1. Stevenson's emotivism

Every theory of moral judgement is sensitive to some particular aspect of the moral life. Hare fixes on the link between morality and action. Foot stresses the subject matter of moral judgements. The aspect to which Stevenson is most sharply attuned is that of moral disagreement. Moral disputes are widespread and are apt to be intractable. Of course, such disputes often turn on disagreements over matters of fact: recall the live issues of public debate to which I referred in 8.1.3. But in Stevenson's view it is quite possible and even common for moral disagreement to survive any amount of consensus over the facts. Our (factual) beliefs can coincide while our attitudes still differ.

When attitudes differ, persuasion or attempts at persuasion come into play. Moral judgements are a particular medium of persuasion. This is their common and distinctive feature. They contain terms such as 'good' and 'ought' that have an emotive meaning. These terms carry an emotional 'charge' and are two-way dispositional. In moral judgement a speaker is disposed to use these terms to express his emotion-based attitudes, and hearers are disposed to alter or strengthen their attitudes under the impact of the use of such terms. 'A ought to do x' does not literally but does emotively mean 'I disapprove of A's not doing x. Do so as well.' 'That is good' does not literally but does emotively mean 'I approve of this. Do so as well.' In uttering these moral judgements I express my emotion-based attitudes, I try to alter or strengthen your attitudes correspondingly, and may actually succeed in doing so. Moral judgements are functional to persuasion.

15.1.2. Criticisms of Stevenson's emotivism

Stevenson's emotivism has attracted much criticism. Beyond the predictable complaints about the obscurity of Stevenson's notion of 'emotive meaning', I think two broad directions of attack are distinguishable. Stevenson is criticized for tying moral judgement too closely to the activity of persuading; and it is said that in any case he has too narrow a conception of persuasion. I think these complaints are linked.

They meet in the point that Stevenson offers, or appears to offer, an unrelentingly causal picture. His idea of persuasion seems to be one in which one gets someone to do something; and the way in which one does this through moral judgement is by working on their feelings so that they do it. Hare is surely right in distinguishing 'advise' and 'exhort' from 'persuade' if this is what persuasion is and in stressing the role of the two former in moral judgement.

The causal aspect of Stevenson's account is perhaps connected with his assimilation of emotion to feeling. A feeling may be something like a pain or a thrill of pleasure; and if one thinks of the emotional component in attitudes on this model, there will be very little scope for advice or exhortation. I have never wasted time in trying to advise or exhort someone into or out of a feeling. But this is really a crude view of emotion, as may briefly be made clear.

Emotions are essentially directed to objects: fear must be fear *of* something, hatred must be hatred *for* something. This is the so-called Brentano intentionality thesis (after the late-19th-century Austrian philosopher-psychologist, Franz Brentano (Chisholm, 1976)). What one fears (e.g. a ghost) may not actually exist or, existing, might not have the properties by virtue of which one fears or hates it. But a belief about the object, namely that it exists and has certain properties, is internal to the emotion. Said another way, emotions are directed to objects under a description. Now this account is too quick and will not go through without refinement (for what of objectless emotions, if there are such things, or emotions directed to future objects which do not yet exist?). Nevertheless if we retreat just a fraction and take the view that emotions are typically directed to objects, there is large scope for argument when an emotion occurs: argument about the existence of the object or about its properties.

Once we move away from assimilating emotions to mere feelings and see the element of belief that is typically involved in them, we can find a place for argument, and correspondingly for advice and exhortation, in an emotivist characterization of moral judgement. This point holds good regardless of how Stevenson himself regarded the emotions.

There is no need even for the first-personal element, 'I approve of this', 'I disapprove of that', in a resourceful emotivist account. We might appeal to the emotion that would be experienced by an 'ideal observer' or 'impartial spectator'. For 'A ought not to do x' we might have something of the order: 'x is such as to be approved of by the ideal observer or impartial spectator', where approval would still be linked with an emotion-based attitude. I might aim to strengthen or arouse a matching emotion in you. Perhaps I can do this via our acceptance of a common moral standard. That acceptance in turn might be secured in a broad variety of ways. Perhaps the standard is one which we can give rational agents good reasons in terms of their own interests for internalizing. All these 'mights' and 'perhaps' are meant merely to mark out the possibilities of a resourceful emotivism.

For a sophisticated account of emotivism along 'ideal observer' lines, see M. Smith, 1986: 301ff. There are also some good remarks in Harman, 1977: ch. 4. For a sound, detailed examination of Stevenson's own views, see Urmson, 1968: ch. 4-6. On Ayer, see Foster, 1985: 81-4.

15.1.3. Hume's emotivism

I now turn to consider Hume. Hume's ethical theory is contained mainly in two works:

A Treatise of Human Nature (1739-40). Note the subtitle: 'An attempt to introduce the experimental method of reasoning into moral subjects.' 'Moral subjects' are roughly psychology and the social sciences. On the 'experimental method' see below.

Enquiry Concerning the Principles of Morals (1751). Hume mainly repeats the ethical ideas developed in the *Treatise*. There are differences of emphasis but in my view no serious differences of viewpoint between the two works.

For now I want to consider only his emotivist account of the nature of moral judgement. In the course of our full programme we will encounter Hume at three further points:

- the is/ought gap   • ethical naturalism
- free will

Hume's general characterization of moral judgement addresses three questions:

(1) In what does moral judgement consist? What is its nature?
(2) What are the objects of moral judgement? On what is moral judgement directed?
(3) What produces moral judgement? On what conditions does it arise?

The nature of moral judgement

The key phenomenon is approbation and disapprobation – 'certain peculiar sentiments of pain and pleasure' (T, 574). Hume will tell us that we experience a specific kind of pleasure or pain in certain conditions and in relation to certain objects. The relevant pleasures and pain are *sui generis*, unique items of experience irreducible to anything else. The pleasure of moral approval is unique, like the taste of lemon.

'Gilding or staining all natural objects with colours, borrowed from internal sentiment' (EPM, 294) – this is Hume's description of evaluation in general. What he has in mind in the case of morality is that, expressing the emotion of moral approval, we say e.g. that 'X is good'. We use the language of ascribing a property to an object but in fact we are projecting a reaction and speaking as if the object had a certain property.

There may be a slight problem with the colour analogy. Two things could, to observation, agree in all else but differ in their colour. It is not clear that two things could, to observation, agree in all else and differ only in our moral reactions to them.

The objects of moral judgement

The objects of moral approval and disapproval are 'qualities durable enough to affect our sentiments' (T, 575). For Hume this means that the prime focus of our feelings of moral disapproval and disapproval is character: and actions fall under moral judgement as their motives are expressive of character. For an account of Hume's view of character, see Bricke, 1974.

Hume does supply an explanation of sorts for the ethical ultimacy of character. In the first place, it is only character which is 'durable enough to affect our sentiments' (T, 575). His associationist psychology is at work here. Secondly, Hume thinks that moral responsibility is linked mainly to what is 'durable or constant' in the person. If an action is done out of character, as the phrase is, then 'as it proceeded from nothing in him, that is durable or constant, and leaves nothing of that nature behind it, 'tis impossible he can, upon its account, become the object of punishment or vengeance' (T, 411).

But in broad terms there is some difficulty in seeing why (except on Hume's say so) a single action could not arouse our feelings of moral approval or disapproval or why at any rate certain types of action, regularly recurrent in our experience, could not do so without ultimate reference to character.

Personal qualities, then, provoke 'certain peculiar sentiments of pain and pleasure' . We regard as praiseworthy such personal qualities as are useful or immediately agreeable to ourselves or to others; their opposites we condemn. So there are four types of relevant quality:

• qualities useful to others
• qualities useful to oneself
• qualities immediately agreeable to others
• qualities immediately agreeable to oneself

Hume's picture of the completely virtuous person is given in his portrait of Cleanthes (EPM, 269-70).

Note that there is no firm dividing line on this approach between specifically moral virtues (as these are now recognized) and other virtues or natural abilities such as wit, cheerfulness or decorum. A complaint is often made against Aristotle that his list of the moral virtues in *Nicomachean Ethics* includes many personal qualities which 'we' should no longer count as moral. Hume sides with Aristotle in this matter.

The conditions of moral judgement

Moral judgements express our emotional reactions under certain definite conditions. But what are those conditions?

At this point Hume's 'experimental method' comes in. He examines the circumstances in which moral judgement occurs. 'Experimental' means 'based on knowledge and observation'. Nothing else will serve in ethics in Hume's view. All our knowledge in any area is bounded by experience; and there are relevant differences between the human and the physical sciences. In the human sciences there is less experimental control and manipulation of variables. we are largely reduced to observation. 'We must therefore glean up our experiments ... from a cautious observation of human life, and take them as they appear in the common course of the world, by men's behaviour in company, in affairs, and in their pleasures' (T, xix). Against that limitation we can, however, set two points: that the moral life is a matter of everyday experience and that in the human sciences we can call introspection in aid.

Courtesy of this experimental method Hume identifies two conditions for moral judgement. Moral judgement occurs when one:

* checks all the relevant facts   * takes a general view

One has to check all the relevant facts:

> ... it is often necessary, we find, that much reasoning should precede, that nice distinctions be made, just conclusions drawn, distant comparisons formed, complicated relations examined, and general facts fixed and ascertained (EPM, 173).

Although there is no inconsistency between the two works, the *Enquiry* perhaps stresses rather more than the *Treatise* the place of reason in ethics, the scope for the cognitive in general in ascertaining the relevant facts. Hume means, not that one has to achieve or assume omniscience but that, within practical limits, in determining the utility or agreeableness of a character-trait one has considered everything relevant, taken it carefully into account, and has no sense that vital information is missing. One has done what one can to ensure that one is well-informed and well-advised.

One has also to have detached oneself from personal involvement. Take the case of someone else's action. In judging this morally I have to observe a certain personal detachment and make a general survey. Of the person making a moral judgement Hume says: 'He must ... depart from his private and particular situation, and must choose a point of view, common to himself with others' (EPM, 272). Or as Hume puts it in the *Treatise*: ' 'Tis only when a character is considered in general, without reference to our particular interest, that it causes such a feeling or sentiment, as denominates it morally good or evil' (T, 472).

What enables one to practise this detachment is sympathy: ' 'tis that principle, which takes us so far out of ourselves, as to give us the same pleasure or uneasiness in the characters of others, as if they had a tendency to our own advantage or loss' (T, 579). David Wiggins refers to Humean sympathy as 'our capacity to resonate to the feelings of others'.

To grasp the picture you have to know something about Hume's philosophy of mind. Hume recognizes two basic sorts of mental item:

* impressions   * ideas

There are a number of classifications of impressions. The distinction perhaps most relevant here is that between (1) original and (2) secondary or reflective. Roughly the distinction can be made out as follows.

Suppose you strike me in the face. I now have an impression. I feel the blow.

Original impressions are, as near as makes no matter, just sense impressions. Ideas are what these impressions cause; and in fact all ideas derive from and are copies of impressions on Hume's official empiricist view. So the next day I remember the blow; I now have an 'idea' of it. If, remembering the blow, I also resent it, the emotion I feel is a secondary or reflective impression. It comes about through the original impression and its related idea.

Sympathy is a secondary or reflective impression. Change the example: suppose now that you are experiencing pain. You engage in pain behaviour, writhing about, calling for help, and so on. I see this; I have an impression of it. And from your pain behaviour I believe that you are in pain. I have an 'idea' or belief about your condition. This belief causes me to have a secondary impression. I feel for you or, more literally, *with* you. I imagine what it would be like to go through what you are undergoing and in some way I reproduce in myself what you are experiencing.

If in these circumstances somebody rushes to your aid, then that person's character comes under my moral judgement. All the facts are in; I realize your predicament and understand what somebody is doing for you. I detach myself from purely personal concerns, such as annoyance that you are wearing pink with black, and experience a particular emotion of approval towards the other person. That person's character exemplifies in this case a quality useful to others.

15.1.4. Criticisms of Hume's emotivism

Two main difficulties have been found in Hume's account. The first concerns his projectivism, his idea that there is absolutely no cognitive component to moral judgement. We establish the facts of the case, then (quite separately) an emotion arises which we project, as a reaction, on to certain objects. That non-cognitive reaction exhausts our moral judgement for Hume, but this (the critics urge) is only one possibility. In part the plausibility of Hume's view depends on the cogency of rival accounts such as that given by moral realism. But there is also the question of what we are to make of projectivism on its own account. In chapter 4 we will consider some of the rival accounts and also probe Hume's projectivism.

The second difficulty centres on what has seemed to many a missing element from Hume's ethical theory, something which his 'experimental method' has not registered. If I fail to experience 'certain peculiar sentiments', that appears to be a brute fact. But, the point is made, this is false to moral experience. People can realize that they fail to disapprove morally of things which others condemn and that they condemn things which others morally approve: and such discrepancies can occasion a sharp bout of self-questioning. I cannot 'question myself' into feeling a pain or pleasure, however; I either feel it or I do not. So there is a vital moral phenomenon that Hume's ethical theory cannot encompass. On this, however, see 28.1.2, end paragraph.

15.1.5. Hume and modern emotivism

In a quick aside I want to say something on Hume's relation to the later emotivists.

(1) Hume takes a non-cognitive view of moral judgement. Moral judgement does not embody any genuine knowledge of an independently existing moral reality. Hume agrees with the later emotivists here.

What separates him from some forms of later emotivism is possibly two things, certainly one:

(2) Emotivists have sometimes held that moral judgements are statements of emotion. 'X is wrong' literally means 'I disapprove of X'. Hume holds that a moral judgement is (not a statement but) an expression of emotion. This is, however, a controversial point in the interpretation of Hume.

(3) What is not controversial is that, for Hume, there is a uniform human nature by virtue of which the emotions of moral approval and disapproval are directed on the same objects (ultimately certain states of character) for everyone. The only scope for moral disagreement is over factual matters. Emotivists, by contrast, typically allow disagreements in attitude in a way that Hume does not envisage. 'Human nature' does not react uniformly in the way Hume supposes. Stevenson has a useful account of this contrast between Hume and the later emotivists (Stevenson, 1944: ch. 12).

On Hume see further Falk, 1975; Foot, 1978: 74-80; and Mackie, 1980.

16.1. THE SANCTIONS APPROACH

The 'sanctions' approach to the general characterization of moral judgement is here given its own heading. This is undoubtedly right in terms of what the student may expect elsewhere. Logically it is unsatisfactory, however. For the sanctions approach really falls within the formal approach. Any judgement is a moral judgement, irrespective of its content, if it is associated with certain sanctions. This is the basic logic of the approach.

16.1.1. J.S. Mill's account of sanctions

The approach to the definition of moral judgement through the idea of sanctions – the applicability of sanctions as necessary and sufficient for a judgement to be a moral judgement – is particularly linked to the early utilitarian school of Jeremy Bentham and John Stuart Mill. Consider this passage from chapter 5 of Mill's *Utilitarianism* (1863):

> For the truth is, that the idea of penal sanction, which is the essence of law, enters not only into the conception of injustice, but in that of any kind of wrong. We do not call anything wrong, unless we mean to imply

that a person ought to be punished in some way or other for doing it; if not by law, by the opinion of his fellow creatures; if not by opinion, by the reproaches of his own conscience. This seems the real turning point between morality and simple expediency (U: 233).

One obvious comment is that Mill's remarks centre too narrowly on the idea of wrong: of that which we have a moral obligation not to do. They can be extended to cover what we have a moral obligation positively to do, if we widen sanctions to include e.g. praise. This extension is quite in line with the basic notion of a sanction – that of praise or blame, punishment or reward, as inducements to behaviour. But a vital limitation is at once apparent. Moral judgements, which include permissions, can relate to what an agent may do or omit, and not simply to actions which there is a moral obligation to do or (as the case may be) not to do. There are, however, no sanctions associated with permissions, unless (marginally) we include blame directed against those who prevent others from doing what is morally permissible.

In *Introduction to the Principles of Morals and Legislation* (1780, published 1789), ch. 3, 'Of the Four Sanctions or Sources of Pain and Pleasure', Bentham distinguished between:

- physical sanctions
- political sanctions
- moral sanctions
- religious sanctions

Physical sanctions, which are simply the 'penalties' that result from ignorance or neglect of the workings of nature, have no bearing on our present inquiry. Political sanctions are penal laws. Moral sanctions, also called 'popular' sanctions by Bentham, are social pressures such as contempt, hostility, withdrawal of co-operation or even ostracism. Religious sanctions are God's punishments and rewards for infringement or observance of his commands. See Norman, 1971: 33-4.

The view is still not uncommon that religious sanctions are a necessary basis of morality. The claim is that, except through fear of divine punishment or hope of divine reward, one cannot be relied on to act morally. A contrary belief is that if a person's motivation is thus determined by fear or hope then he is not acting morally at all but merely prudentially.

If so, does this not apply to all relevant sanctions – political, popular, and religious? We need to note carefully what is at stake here. A *judgement* might still be a moral judgement if and because particular sanctions were associated with it; if *behaviour* determined by sanctions did not count as moral (but merely prudential), this would not of itself nullify the claim about the nature of moral judgement.

16.1.2. Criticisms of the sanctions approach

In the case of permissions there can be moral judgements unassociated with sanctions. The applicability of sanctions is not necessary to moral judgement. And, for all we have learnt about the nature of sanctions, there can be sanctions unassociated with moral judgements. The kind of social pressures Bentham has in mind can be applied to somebody we merely do not like. The applicability of sanctions is not sufficient for moral judgement. The option simply to define a moral judgement as a judgement with which sanctions are associated remains open. So does the option to resist that definition short of cogent reasons to accept the stipulation.

Perhaps the strongest claim that can be made convincingly about the relation of sanctions to moral judgement comes through Mill's distinction between two kinds of sanction: internal and external. Bentham talks of four sanctions but they are all external to the agent; punishment and reward are applied by others than the agent himself, if only figuratively so in the case of physical sanctions. But Mill recognizes an internal sanction, that of 'the reproaches' of one's own 'conscience', even if it is fair to add that Mill sees conscience as a social product (U: ch. 3).

Now the claim might plausibly be made that it is a criterion of the agent's moral seriousness, of his genuine commitment to the moral point of view, that he is liable to feelings of guilt or remorse if he fails to act on his moral judgements (B. Williams, 1971; cf. Holland, 1972: 264-8). Beyond this, the sanctions view does not appear to capture the essence of what it is for a judgement to be a moral judgement.

17.1. THE 'ALL-IN' APPROACH

In this section I examine the final general characterization of moral judgement. I refer to the idea that moral judgements reflect an 'all-in' point of view.

This approach is, from one angle, a development of Hume's requirement that we check all the relevant facts (15.1.3). In Hume the 'all-in' perspective is linked with the claim that moral judgements involve a specific emotion; but it can be detached from an emotivist context. On these lines L.C. Becker is a prominent exponent of the 'all-in' view of moral judgements; and my account of this approach is indebted to him. See Becker, 1973 and 1986. I introduce Becker's ideas as follows.

One might have a thought: perhaps we are looking for the differentia of moral judgement at the wrong logical level. At the start I instanced economic, political, religious and aesthetic judgements and suggested that we needed to mark off moral judgements from these other kinds of judgement (11.1). We were looking, the idea was, for the moral point of view on the same level as, but distinct from, these other points of view.

This yields what Becker calls the *special* conception of morality, on which:

the moral point of view is just one among many that a rational agent might consider. According to this sort of conception, etiquette, egoism, altruism and so forth are all distinct points of view in terms of which one might choose to act. Morality is another. It is one which a rational agent could *in principle* reject, without self-contradiction. (Defenders of the special conception are therefore concerned to give an account of why one ought to adopt the moral point of view rather than some other.) (Becker, 1986: 17)

Against this conception Becker sets the *general* conception of morality:

The general conception of morality, in a nutshell, is this: moral judge-ments are judgements about what rational agents ought to do or not do, period. Moral acts and states of being are those that conform to moral judgments. Such judgments are not made in terms of the rules of an activity *within* our lives; they are not made in terms of an activity distinct from life itself. They are, rather, judgments made only in terms of living, period. They are judgments made, in principle, all things considered.

On the general conception the moral point of view is inclusive of all other points of view and is therefore on a different logical level from them. Said another way, the moral point of view can never conflict with another point of view as one partial viewpoint with another. The clash will always be between the all-inclusive viewpoint of morality and the partial viewpoint of politics, economics and the rest.

Remember that when we initially talked about the general characterization of moral judgement the idea was to find the common property or properties of moral judgements (3.1). On Becker's account the common and distinctive property of moral judgements is their all-inclusiveness.

Becker, 1986: 24-8 presents a series of objections and defence of this general characterization. To give some flavour of Becker's defence, consider the objection that aesthetic considerations are, as such, irrelevant to moral assess-ment. In part the objection runs:

But surely it is absurd to think that moral arguments are all-inclusive. Aesthetic considerations, for example, guide our conduct, but they are very different from moral ones. *Style* is not a moral quality. And it is just disingenuous to argue that style can be relevant to moral arguments indirectly – and therefore must be, or can be, considered in moral arguments. Of course it can be relevant. But it is not itself a moral consideration (Becker, 1986: 24).

Becker replies to this imaginary critic:

When we are deciding how to act, all things considered, style matters. We care about the grace with which things are done, the beauty of our surroundings, the fittingness of our conduct, the elegance of our writing. We care about these things directly, and not merely because caring about them may be indirectly relevant to the fulfilment of our professional responsibilities, or business dealings, or social expectations. Similarly, we care about tact, 'the done thing', and prudence (Becker, 1986: 25).

This is an unusual characterization of moral judgement. There is, of course, an ambiguity in 'all things considered', an expression that may imply either 'giving weight to' or 'taking account of'. Becker's position seems to be that there is no consideration of which a moral judgement *may not* take account – aesthetic, political or whatever. We might accept this position but want to deny that every type of consideration, so far as practicable, is to be *given weight* in every situation. Might there not be situations to which aesthetic considerations, for example, are irrelevant?

A point also arises concerning the impact of different relevant considerations on others besides the agent. If I am to give equal weight to such considerations as they affect you to considerations as they affect myself, this gives a definite slant to 'all things considered'.

I will leave Becker at this point. He has certainly given us something new to think about, a different general characterization of moral judgement from the standard run. Becker, 1986: 7-36 is the section you need to look at if you want to go further into this option.

18.1. REVIEW: TWO METHODS OF CONCEPTUAL ANALYSIS

We have now completed our survey of six approaches to the general characterization of moral judgement. We have considered these approaches in outline and looked at some of the objections levelled at them. You need to decide for yourself which approach or combination of approaches best serves to set off moral from other kinds of judgement.

Before we move on to the second general ethical problem, that of the moral standard, I want to outline an alternative method of conceptual analysis to the one used so far.

Our image of conceptual analysis so far has been that of searching for conditions for the application of a concept. At the limit, I said at the outset, Hare would identify necessary and sufficient conditions for a judgement to be a moral judgement. The truth may be that we cannot specify such conditions; for some concepts we can specify only necessary conditions, for others only sufficient conditions. The concept of a moral judgement may fall within this recalcitrant class.

But then, we might shift away from the direct search for conditions and consider instead what role the concept of a moral judgement plays in our scheme of life. Rather in the manner of William James we might ask: what *difference* does it make to describe a judgement as a moral judgement? What discriminations or emphases are embodied in our acceptances or denials that a judgement is a moral judgement? Why do we need the concept of a moral judgement at all?

These questions reflect the functional approach to conceptual analysis outlined in Craig, 1986-7: 211-12. In his article Craig is concerned with the concept of knowledge. Why do we need the concept of knowledge when we have that of true belief? If our answer turns on considerations, e.g., of providing a predictable basis for action, then we are replying 'functionally' and switching conceptual analysis to a different mode from the 'conditions for application' approach.

In my view the functional method can be generalized and used illuminatingly in ethics. If we apply it to the general characterization of moral judgement, our 'rival' approaches look rather different.

Craig's method nudges us with the suggestion that all these approaches may be functional, that they may serve to discriminate or emphasize features of our practical life to which we need to direct attention. I take just two examples. Perhaps we need both Hare's emphasis on the action-guidingness of moral judgements, and Foot's stress on the sensitiveness of moral judgements to considerations of human (or sentient) welfare. Hare certainly makes us think about the criteria for sincere acceptance of a personal commitment of the sort we regard as typical of morality. But equally, Foot reveals that side of morality which focuses on human (and not merely one's own) welfare and which can provoke a clash between the requirements of morality and self-interest.

This line of thought is not the fudge or idleness of saying that all the approaches are right. Did we not see problems they encounter? Rather, it is the acceptance that all have caught some feature of the moral life.

CHAPTER 3

Moral Judgement and the Moral Standard

19.1. INTRODUCTION

In the introductory chapter I drew a distinction between ethical theories that emphasize the requirements of *action* and theories that emphasize the condition of the *person* (4.1.2). Theories of the first kind (theories of the moral criterion) address primarily the question, 'What shall I do?'; theories of the second (theories of the moral ideal) the question, 'What kind of person shall I be?'

In this chapter we will open up these questions, which define our second ethical problem:

• the moral standard

The more specific aim is to examine theories of the moral criterion (represented by the utilitarians, Kant, W.D. Ross, and Jonathan Dancy) and one theory of the moral ideal (that of Aristotle). As we go along you may find it useful to check back to chapter 2 and consider which theories of the moral standard connect best with which general characterizations of moral judgement. We caught utilitarianism's historical link with the sanctions view; and it is worth noting that Hare espouses a form of utilitarianism in his later work (Sen and Williams, 1982: 23-38).

In a broad sense, of course, our theorists, in answering the questions, 'What shall I do?' and 'What kind of person shall I be?', are venturing ultimate or top-level moral judgements in their own right.

20.1. THE MORAL CRITERION

'What shall I do?' There are basically three responses to this question:

(1) consult just one consideration
(2) consult an irreducible plurality of considerations
(3) consult the situation alone

These responses yield:

• ethical monism   • ethical particularism
• ethical pluralism

Before we look into these options, we need to clear up an ambiguity in the talk so far about 'consulting a consideration'. The ambiguity is that between

(1) applying a consideration directly in a decision procedure for moral action; and (2) invoking it as a background 'control' (see Crisp, 1992).

'What shall I do?':

- 'Never kill anything' (principle)   • 'Never kill human beings' (rule)
- 'Do not kill your vexing neighbour' (application of rule in a situational moral judgement)

Here the basic consideration, 'never kill anything', is directly action-guiding; it is explicit in the principle, implicit in the rule which derives straight from it, and implicit in the situational moral judgement.

But now, take another list. 'What shall I do?':

- 'Maximize welfare' (principle)   • 'Keep your promises' (rule)
- 'Return Eddie K's motorbike this morning at 8 o'clock because you made that promise on the phone last Thursday' (application of rule in a situational moral judgement)

It may be that the basic consideration, 'maximize welfare', is simply a control to which the rule and the situational moral judgement are answerable. There may be no idea that, in applying the rule and making the judgement, we are to consult welfare and consider whether it will be maximized if we keep our promises in general and this promise in particular. It might even be that if we did take time out to weigh these points, this would bring a hazardous element into moral action since nobody would know how we are going to decide, with the result that welfare would not be maximized. Direct application of the principle, 'maximize welfare', would then be self-defeating (cf. Parfit, 1984: ch. 1-2).

I will generally take our 'theories of the moral criterion' to be theories about decision procedures for moral action. But we might do well to note that this distinction between decision procedure and background control is central to the issue of act- versus rule-utilitarianism (21.2.5).

21.1. ETHICAL MONISM

The best-known example of ethical monism is:

- utilitarianism

Though neither the originator of the term nor the first exponent of the ethical theory, Jeremy Bentham (1748-1832) was nevertheless the first major utilitarian theorist. In *An Introduction to the Principles of Morals and Legislation* (1780), he was the first to present a comprehensive utilitarian theory. For elements of utilitarianism in Hume, see D. Miller, 1981: 72-5, 89, 190-1; and Plamenatz, 1958: ch. 2.

Later utilitarians include:

- John Stuart Mill   • Henry Sidgwick
- Hastings Rashdall   • G.E. Moore
- J.J.C. Smart

21.2. UTILITARIANISM

Utilitarianism is a goal-based ethical theory. Hence it is often called a:

- teleological theory

from the Greek *telos* = 'end' (1) 'termination' or (2) 'motive', 'aim', 'goal'. Utilitarianism sets morality a goal, an end or purpose to which it is answerable. Actions are good or bad, right or wrong, according as they promote or go against that purpose. As accurate a brief definition of utilitarianism as I can muster is that utilitarianism bids us maximize value. To maximize value (and, as a corollary, to minimize disvalue) is to promote valuable states of affairs, e.g. states of mind such as experiences of pleasure.

21.2.1. The idea of intrinsic value

To approach the matter from another side, we have a notion of intrinsic value. We regard certain things as good in themselves or for their own sake. The contrast is with instrumental or extrinsic value. The best first step is to read C.I. Lewis, 1971, Book III, esp. ch. 12-13 and to follow this with Attfield, 1987: ch. 2.

If we accept the idea of intrinsic value, this does not commit us to the existence of objective values – of a realm of values independent of mind. I may cite the slogan: 'Value is valuing.' Something has intrinsic value *for me*, if I do not want it merely because it conduces to something else. I value it for its own sake.

Understanding welfare in terms of the intrinsically valuable, utilitarianism sets morality the task of maximizing the occurrence of intrinsically valuable states of affairs. In principle it is impersonal about this; who is to enjoy the result, or who produces it, does not essentially matter. Hence the formula that utilitarianism aims to maximize the general welfare.

21.2.2. Ethical and psychological hedonism

The early utilitarians, including Bentham, thought that there is only one intrinsically valuable state of affairs – the experience of pleasure. Pleasure was taken to be a kind of sensation or internal impression (cf. Lovibond, 1989-90: 214; and Anscombe, 1981: 27).

Bentham here makes a double claim. He says that we ought to promote the experience of pleasure (including the avoidance of pain). This is *ethical hedonism* (from the Greek *hedone* = pleasure). But he also says that we cannot but seek to maximize our own pleasure; and this is *psychological hedonism*, clearly a version of determinism.

J.S. Mill gently qualified Bentham's psychological hedonism, which utilitarianism has now almost completely abandoned; and he introduced a complication into ethical hedonism. In Bentham's view, as Mill put it, the 'quantity of pleasure being equal, push-pin is as good as poetry' (Mill, 1962: 95). (Push-pin is 'a child's game, in which each player pushes his pin with the object of crossing that of another player' (*OED*), but knowing this I am none the wiser. Bingo might be a better example now.) Mill, by contrast, thought it 'better to be a human being dissatisfied than a pig satisfied; better to be Socrates dissatisfied than a fool satisfied' (Mill, 1971: 197). We are still to promote the experience of pleasure, but we are to recognize a distinction between pleasures. Pleasures can be *higher* or *lower*. Higher pleasures are preferable, a point evidenced (Mill thinks) by the fact that those who have experienced both sorts of pleasure actually prefer higher pleasures.

Mill is clear that pleasure, hence the intrinsically good, is answerable to people's preferences. And this is the clue, I think, to a troubled passage at the start of U, ch. 4:

> The only proof capable of being given that an object is visible, is that people actually see it ... In like manner, I apprehend, the sole evidence it is possible to produce that anything is desirable, is that people do actually desire it (Mill, 1971: 221).

This is often referred to in crude terms as a 'howler'. For 'visible' and 'desirable' have a different logic. 'Visible' means 'capable of being seen' but 'desirable' does not mean 'capable of being desired' but rather 'worthy of being desired'. Yet in fact there is nothing logically amiss here.

Suppose a claim were made that in a certain room there is a visible object, x. How else could I establish this claim than by appealing to the fact that in conditions of standard illumination normal perceivers actually do see it? Mill has a particular angle here since he holds that objects are 'permanent possibilities of sensation', but I ignore this complication. Because Mill (at any rate in this part of his ethical theory) has no argument to say that certain experiences are intrinsically valuable independently of our desires, preference is the only consideration to which he can appeal. That people do prefer certain pleasures when they have an informed choice, is the only card he can play.

In the visible/desirable analogy there is no error in Mill's logic. From the standpoint of his theory of intrinsic value the cases are relevantly similar. The only ineptness is in using an example that gives hostile critics a field-day.

It is a standard topic in the history of ethics whether Mill's hedonism is consistent. In telling us to go for higher pleasures is he still applying a purely hedonistic test?

The matter is complex but one consideration is central. Higher pleasures are a subset of pleasures; they are not conjunctions of pleasures and something else. Compare the situation in which someone is told to select (1) cubes, (2) blue cubes, (3) cubes and spheres. Mill's qualitative hedonism stands to simple, Benthamite hedonism as (2) stands to (1). If higher pleasures were (3)-like, hedonism would obviously be breached. But, to resort to oddity of language to make a logical point, Mill is not telling us to pursue pleasures and, something quite different, which we can bizarrely call 'highers', as well.

If there is an inconsistency in Mill's account it lies elsewhere, in his assertion that, as we have seen, 'It is better to be a human being dissatisfied than a pig satisfied; better to be Socrates dissatisfied than a fool satisfied'.

We know already that higher pleasures are preferable to lower ones; we are now told that higher pains are also preferable to lower pleasures. But how can a hedonist, even a qualitative one, prefer pain? Perhaps Mill's point is that it is better to be Socrates dissatisfied in his lower pleasures than a pig satisfied in the same. But the text does not naturally read that way. More likely Mill is recommending, over the life of lower pleasures free from pain, the life of higher pleasure in which pain incidentally occurs. See further Donner, 1983; Gibbs, 1986; Martin, 1972; and West, 1976.

Before we leave Mill, and since we have mentioned Socrates, you might just note that at the start of *Utilitarianism* Mill invokes the shade of Socrates in support of utilitarian hedonism: 'the youth Socrates listened to the old Protagoras, and asserted ... the theory of utilitarianism against the popular morality of the so-called sophist' (Mill, 1971: 189). Mill is right that in Plato's dialogue, the *Protagoras*, Socrates does espouse hedonism in general and psychological hedonism in particular: each person acts to maximize pleasure for himself (*Protagoras*, 351B-355C). As well, Socrates adumbrates something like Bentham's calculus of pleasures and pains (357B: cf. Bentham, 1967: ch. 4). But Mill appears to be wide of the mark in parading Socrates as a utilitarian. Historical niceties aside, utilitarianism's impersonal reference is missing. Utilitarianism looks to the maximization of intrinsically valuable states of affairs, in principle irrespectively of who enjoys them. Hence the usual formula that utilitarianism addresses the maximization of the general welfare. The *Protagoras* fixes its spotlight on the agent's quest for his own pleasure.

G.E. Moore introduced a version of what is commonly known as 'ideal' utilitarianism. The label comes from his celebrated final chapter of *Principia Ethica*, 'The Ideal', in which Moore discusses that which is good in itself in a high degree:

> By far the most valuable things, which we know or can imagine, are certain states of consciousness, which may be roughly described as the pleasures of human intercourse [i.e. friendship] and the enjoyment of beautiful objects (Moore, 1903: 188; for a response, see Levi, 1961).

These items might be regarded as Millian higher pleasures. But there is a complicating factor. Moore presents a theory of 'organic wholes' according to which a whole can have 'an intrinsic value different in amount from the sum of the values of its parts' (Moore, 1903: 36). Then in Moore, 1912 we encounter the view that all intrinsic goods (1) involve feeling and some other form of consciousness and (2) are organic or complex wholes. If (2) is the case, then it seems 'as if, for instance, nothing so simple as pleasure by itself, however intense, could ever be any good' (Moore, 1912: 154). See further Baldwin, 1990: ch. 4; and Robinson, 1952: 94-102.

We are still in the realm of ethical monism. For all three theorists – Bentham, Mill, and Moore – there is ultimately only one consideration to which our actions are answerable, namely the maximization of intrinsically valuable states of affairs. Whether this is also the main consideration to apply in situationally deciding what to do – recall the distinction in 20.1 – is complicated in Mill's case. Mill may well be a rule-utilitarian (21.2.5). Bentham and Moore both hold that the maximization of intrinsically valuable states of affairs is a consideration to apply, directly and overridingly, in deciding what to do.

Utilitarianism has not stood still. In later versions of the theory, welfare is interpreted in terms of the fulfilment of uncriticized desires (actual wants and preferences), hypothetical or rational desires (desires that people would or do have under certain conditions), or needs (seen as interests independent of desire). For some analysis of the simple-seeming but really quite difficult notion of need, see Thomson, 1987; Griffin, 1986: ch. 3; and Wiggins, 1987: ch. 1. A further serious point is that the utilitarian has to make a decision about the status of adaptive and counteradaptive preferences: 'sour grapes' and 'forbidden fruit' (Elster in Sen and Williams, 1982: 219-38). And anyone with an ideological angle on society will be keen to know the processes by which preferences are formed.

I shall use the term 'welfare' as a blank to be filled in by these various candidates.

21.2.3. Utilitarianism and strict consequentialism

Actions are good or bad, right or wrong, according as they promote or hinder the maximization of intrinsically valuable states of affairs.

Does this mean that actions (and in turn the motives that produce them) have purely instrumental significance morally? Is it the case that morally we are only interested in a certain causal property an action may have, that of conducing to the maximization of intrinsically valuable states of affairs? If so, then simply any action is morally justified, depending on its consequences for the maximization of value.

Utilitarianism has usually been interpreted in this way as a version of *consequentialism* – as holding that the moral rightness of an action is to be judged by the welfare that results from it. The idea is that we can distinguish between an action and its results or consequences. In the abstract the action itself is morally insignificant; its rightness is fixed by its conduciveness to the maximization of welfare.

There is nothing in the logic of utilitarianism that commits a utilitarian to this view that an action has no worth in itself – the view called *strict consequen-tialism*. The doing of an action, or perhaps the fact of an action's having been done, might itself be an intrinsically valuable state of affairs.

Yet utilitarianism is quite consistent with strict consequentialism; and many utilitarians have been strict consequentialists. Indeed the connection can go tighter if we restrict utilitarianism to Benthamite sensation-hedonism in which pleasure is conceptually distinguishable from the action or experience it accompanies. If the only thing of intrinsic value is the experience of pleasure, then since actions are not experiences of pleasure they cannot have intrinsic value. I shall not tie my statement and analysis of utilitarianism to strict consequentialism. I shall allow for the possibility that the doing of an action, or the fact of an action's having been done, might itself be an intrinsically valuable state of affairs and therefore morally reckonable among the action's 'results'. For a theory that bids us maximize welfare, I agree that this state of affairs is unlikely to be the sole and may even be a relatively insignificant factor in the total situation.

21.2.4. Action and consequence

Utilitarianism is clearly a form of consequentialism (a term which derives from Elizabeth Anscombe), if not necessarily of strict consequentialism. Actions are instruments for the production of consequences, i.e. the consequential promo-tion of intrinsically valuable states of affairs. We are to maximize value, i.e. ensure that our actions have this maximizing result.

But how *firm* is the distinction between action and consequence? There are two worries one might have here:

(1) An action often consists in bringing about a change. Opening the window is bringing it about that the window opens. Suppose I do this by moving my arm, closing my fingers on the catch, and so on. The window's opening could be said to be a result of my action, but it is also logically necessary to my action's having occurred at all. Without *that* result I have not opened the window – have not done that action of opening the window. But there are other results which do not appear to be internal to the action in this way. If (say) in opening the window I also knocked a flower pot off the sill and caused an injury to the person sitting underneath, then *these* results are not logically requisite to my having opened the window. They are external to my action.

But some results are not; this is the point of the contrast. So the distinction between action and result or consequence is not absolutely clear-cut.

(2) But even if we take the so-called 'external' consequences there are problems. We may ask how the distinction between action and consequence is to be drawn, since an action can be redescribed to include what, under a different description, is a consequence. Joel Feinberg has given an account of 'the accordion effect' in Feinberg, 1968: 106-7. Take the description 'Smith

opened the door and startled Jones.' Here 'opening the door' identifies the action, and 'startling Jones' is the consequence. But, referring to precisely the same bodily movements, we can equally say 'Smith startled Jones', where the description of Smith's action has been extended to include what, under the earlier description, was a consequence.

Try this distinction-drawing formula:

For any action, X, of any agent, A, Y is a consequence of X if and only if ('iff' in the standard contraction) in virtue of X's occurrence 'A did Y *by* X' is true.

Does this handle Feinberg's example? Smith's startling of Jones (Y) is a consequence of Smith's opening the door (X); i.e. Smith startled Jones (Y) by opening the door (X).

It seems to work for that example. It also enables us to distinguish results that are 'internal' to the action from those that are not. So, it looks odd (because the descriptions are so similar) but just possible to say that I brought about the window's being open by opening the window, but perfectly intelligible and correct to say that I knocked the flower pot off the sill *by* opening the window.

The formula is not trivial. For example, we could not plausibly reverse action and consequence and say that Jones opened the door by startling Smith; or that I opened the window by knocking the flower pot off the sill.

We should, of course, need to complicate the formula to distinguish intended or expected consequences from unintended and unforeseen ones. But I see no difficulty of principle in refining the formula to any extent.

21.2.5. Utilitarianism: a basic model

I want now to present a simple model of what I take to be the standard utilitarian position. It will be easier to see the varieties of utilitarianism if we add them as complexities to this model.

Utilitarianism can be understood as involving six claims:
(1) *Results.* The rightness of an action is to be judged in terms of its results (consequences) for welfare.
(2) *Metricity.* Welfare can be, and is to be, measured in terms of the realization of intrinsically valuable states of affairs.
(3) *Unity.* The relevant values are either all of one kind or at least form a consistent set.
(4) *Personal decision-making.* In deciding what actions to do, the individual agent's intention should be to maximize welfare.
(5) *Aggregation.* All agents are to do likewise, and so welfare will be maximized by the whole society, so far as results match intentions.
(6) *Definition of welfare.* The single value, or consistent set of values, can be specified.

Certain questions and comments shape themselves out of all this. I organize my remarks under the numbered claims.

(1) In respect of results we clearly need to make a distinction between an action's *actual* consequences for welfare and its *intended, foreseen or foreseeable* consequences. This distinction will carry over into a different assessment (in certain situations) of the moral value of the action and the morality of the agent.

Foreseeability may be a matter of practical inevitability or of probability. Probability is present in situations of risk but not of uncertainty:

> In a problem of decision under risk, the outcome of some possible course of action is not known in advance, but the range of possible outcomes of each available course of action is known, and the probabilities of all the outcomes in each range are also known. A decision is taken under uncertainty when even less knowledge is available ... In particular, even where the possible outcomes are known in advance, the probabilities of each of these are not (Altham, 1983-4: 15).

All these distinctions serve to complicate the consideration of consequences.

(2) Metricity can allow actions themselves to have intrinsic value in the sense explained in 21.1.3 above.

A common objection attempts to halt utilitarianism at the outset on this point of metricity. Welfare and valuable states of affairs are qualitative notions (so the objection goes) to which the idea of measurement is inapplicable. Is this so, however? Suppose welfare and valuable states of affairs to be analysable (at least partly) in terms of the satisfaction of preferences. If, then, I prefer p to q, and you prefer p or q to r, is it really an unwarranted intrusion of the quantitative to say that our welfare is greater if p rather than r occurs?

(3) The requirement for value to be all of one kind is clearly breached in Moore's ideal utilitarianism. Moore is still a consequentialist, since he believes that we should act to maximize the occurrence of intrinsically valuable states of affairs, but he recognizes a plurality of such. So I have added the clause about a consistent set of values. One might still have a worry, for different kinds of intrinsically valuable states of affairs can compete for realization. So Moore's utilitarianism needs an ordering or indexing of his preferred states of affairs to handle the practicalities of decision-making. Priorities must be set.

(4) Personal decision-making requires clarification under this model. Of close relevance here is the distinction between:

- act-utilitarianism
- rule-utilitarianism

According to *act-utilitarianism* an action is right iff (if and only if) it maximizes welfare; that is, if and only if it produces more welfare than, or at least as much welfare as, any other action the agent can do. This is a situational test. In my specific situation, which action among all those open to me will maximize welfare?

Rule-utilitarianism, in contrast, looks to practices and rules of behaviour. According to rule-utilitarianism an action is right iff it follows a rule, following which produces more welfare than, or at least as much welfare as, the following of any other rule on which we can act. It is not necessary that, on every occasion on which we act, the best results are achieved *in a particular situation* by following the rule. There might be a rule of promise-keeping. Perhaps in a particular situation I could produce better results by breaking my promise; but the moral requirement is to follow the rule because following the rule, taking one occasion and situation with another, maximizes welfare. Rule-utilitarianism is sometimes called *indirect utilitarianism*, because the requirement to maximize welfare does not directly control situational decision-making. However, the converse does not follow; one can be an indirect utilitarian without being a rule-utilitarian. Perhaps welfare is maximized by following a Kantian or Aristotelian ethic; these are conceptual possibilities.

There is some evidence that John Stuart Mill was a rule-utilitarian. Certainly in his political and economic writings he invokes considerations of justice without any direct reference to utility; it is the rule of justice which is a 'social utility', utility itself is not be to directly consulted when we are deciding what to do. However, in U: ch. 5 Mill allows infringement of the rule of justice in exceptional cases when the social disbenefits of acting justly are particularly great.

Rule-utilitarianism involves some complicated questions. Are the rules on which rule-utilitarianism relies ideal rules – rules which, if everyone were to follow them, would maximize welfare? I do not necessarily maximize welfare if I follow a rule which would maximize welfare if everyone were to act on it, if in fact they do not. Again, the welfare-maximizing consequences of act-utilitarianism may depend on whether all members of a society are act-utilitarians, only some, very few, or only myself. See Emmons, 1973 and Hooker, 1990.

One motivation for preferring rule- to act-utilitarianism is the assumption of *bounded rationality* (Simon, 1979). Bounded rationality assumes that we cannot take account of all available information, cannot envisage rival courses of action exhaustively, and cannot estimate accurately the probability of outcomes. If we had *perfect rationality*, none of these limitations would apply, and each situation for action could be taken exactly on its merits. But (the thought is) given bounded rationality it is more sensible to follow rules.

(5) Under aggregation, welfare will be maximized *by* the whole society, but is there a restriction to welfare's being maximized *for* the whole society? And rationally why should I go even as far as that in my decision-making? There is a crucial problem, never fully resolved within the utilitarian tradition, of why it matters merely to maximize value, irrespective of *who benefits*.

(6) 'State of mind or state of the world.' One might crudely ask: well, *which*?

And, depending on which, *what* state of mind or state of the world? We can talk of well-being, the satisfaction of interests, the fulfilment of wants and preferences. But these items are not identical, and nor are they totally clear. So there is an amount of work to be done on utilitarianism's account of intrinsic value.

21.2.6. Appraisal of utilitarianism

I now take up the appraisal of utilitarianism, but with a reservation.

The reservation is that, at this stage, we must not let the appraisal of utilitarianism pull us into a different ethical problem, that of the justification of moral judgement. As a teleological theory utilitarianism links morality with interest or advantage (5.1.2) through assumptions about rational choice; and there are many puzzling and unresolved questions connected with this whole approach to vindicating the rationality of morals. I do not want to go into them now. Rather, my stress here is on the conceptualization of the utilitarian moral criterion, on its conceptual resources in face of certain criticisms.

Relevant criticisms of utilitarianism are of three main types:

- criticisms of indeterminateness   • criticisms of moral unacceptability
- criticisms of incoherence

The first two types of criticism are central to our concerns here. They have to do with our conceptualization, our very understanding, of utilitarianism as a theory of the moral criterion. Criticisms of moral unacceptability, however, have primarily to do with the justification of utilitarianism; and as such they belong to our third ethical problem, that of the justification of moral judgements. I shall consider them here only insofar as they bear on matters of conceptualization.

21.2.7. Criticisms of indeterminateness

Utilitarianism bids us maximize the occurrence of intrinsically valuable, and to minimize the occurrence of intrinsically disvaluable, states of affairs. Garth Hallett remarks that 'maximizing value and minimizing disvalue generally turn out to be equivalent. To maximize comfort is to minimize pain, to maximize joy is to minimize sadness' and so forth (Hallett, 1984: 106). However, we should note that according to

- negative utilitarianism

the minimization of disvalue (negative value) has priority over the maximization of (positive) value. To use a convenient quantification just to make a point: say that you are in great pain (at a disvalue of -5) while I am in a state of mild pleasure (at a positive value of +2). Our joint state is -3. If there are 6 'utils' or units of value to distribute, negative utilitarianism holds it preferable to allocate all 6 to you. That way, you finish up in a state of slight pleasure (+1) and my own state is unaltered at +2. Our joint state is now +3. The same joint state would have resulted if all 6 units had gone to me $(6 + 2 - 5 = 3)$. Put into a table for clarity:

You	Me	Joint state	
–5	+2	–3	Original position
+1	+2	+3	6 units given to you
–5	+8	+3	6 units given to me

To negative utilitarians, the reduction of negative value is more important, more urgent, than the promotion of positive value. In view of this, it is hard to see the force of Hallett's claim that the maximization of value and the minimization of disvalue 'generally turn out to be equivalent'. Some would urge, against negative utilitarianism, the general implausibility of holding that the relief of any small pain (or discomfort) outweighs the promotion of any good, however great (R.N. Smart, 1958).

It is not clear, however, that the basic utilitarian requirement to maximize the occurrence of valuable, and to minimize the occurrence of disvaluable, states of affairs is really determinate enough to decide the issue in respect of negative utilitarianism.

As well there are certain:

• formulaic problems

Suppose our single value is happiness. Does maximization then mean promoting 'the greatest happiness of the greatest number' (in the standard utilitarian formula)? It is easy to show that the two components of this formula, the greatest happiness criterion and the greatest number criterion, need not coincide in their application. Moreover the greatest happiness criterion turns out to be ambiguous between 'greatest total amount of happiness' and 'greatest average amount of happiness'. See Rawls, 1971: 161-75; M.G. Singer, 1963: 197-8; and Nielsen, 1973.

Again, it is not clear that the basic utilitarian requirement – to maximize the occurrence of valuable, and to minimize the occurrence of disvaluable, states of affairs – is determinate enough to guide us through the choices here.

21.2.8. Criticisms of incoherence

Criticisms of incoherence come under two main headings:

• the disutility of act-utilitarianism   • value incommensurability

The disutility of act-utilitarianism

In 21.2.5 I characterized act-utilitarianism as follows:

P1. An action is right iff it maximizes welfare; that is, if and only if it produces more welfare than, or at least as much welfare as, any other action the agent can do.

There is a criticism that act-utilitarianism is self-defeating, that if we follow it we produce less welfare than if we follow other principles. In other words:

Thesis 1. If people act on P1, this does not maximize welfare; that is, it produces not more but less welfare than other principles on which the agent can act.

The criticism rests essentially on the idea that certain rules of behaviour, and hence assurance of people's reliability in following them, maximize welfare. These rules are below the level of abstraction of the act-utilitarian principle itself; they are rules of promise-keeping and truth-telling (with whatever exceptions one needs to include in order to make the rules plausibly welfare-maximizing). But, the claim is, these rules count for nothing in a society of act-utilitarians because, for an act-utilitarian, every situation is to be assessed on its merits. If a situation requires me to break my promise or to lie in order to maximize welfare, that is what I must do as an act-utilitarian. That is, rules of promise-keeping and truth-telling do not apply in such a society. Therefore, in the absence of mutual trust, welfare is not maximized.

How does the criticism bear up under scrutiny? One point is clearly that it assumes the welfare-maximizing superiority of rule-utilitarianism in respect of the two rules. But why should an act-utilitarian accept this assumption in the attack on his position? Perhaps a deeper point is that if we were all act-utilitarians it would become impossibly difficult, given the specificity of their situational knowledge, to predict what others would do, and consequently to calculate what action act-utilitarianism would require one to do.

Another point about the criticism is that if we accept that the rule-utilitarian is right about these two rules, why cannot the act-utilitarian accept this too? Judging each situation on its merits, a society of act-utilitarians can decide to observe the relevant rules. This certainly does not concede the total rule-utilitarian position. An act-utilitarian need not accept that the whole moral life is adequately covered by welfare-maximizing rules. Only two rules have been put forward. See further Mackie, 1973.

Value incommensurability

My basic model (21.2.5) set out utilitarianism in terms of a single value or a consistent set of values. To many, including some of those sympathetic to utilitarianism, it has seemed implausible that value (or welfare) is a homogeneous magnitude – some single thing. Mill after all distinguished 'kinds of pleasures' and Moore believed in a plurality of types of intrinsically valuable experience.

If there are *plural* values, we can still be dealing with ethical *monism*. For the requirement is to maximize value – to maximize the occurrence of intrinsically valuable states of affairs. That consideration does not require value to be a homogeneous magnitude.

With plurality, however, comes the need for commensurability. But, it is claimed, some values are incommensurate.

Take Joseph Raz's formulation:

> A and B are incommensurate if it is neither true that one is better than the other nor true that they are of equal value (Raz, 1985-6: 117).

One might suppose that (say) health and knowledge were intrinsically desirable but deny that there are any grounds, purely in the abstract, for taking one to be better than the other or both to be of equal value. It is a matter of situational preferability, one might say; and the abstract inclusion of knowledge and health in a utilitarian calculation is a nonsense.

I cannot see any cogency in this criticism. Why should utilitarianism need to calculate in the abstract? As a moral criterion it is designed for situational decision-making. In such and such a situation I trade off knowledge against health; I decide to buy ten Edwardian philosophy books rather than pay for a health check. Incommensurability in the abstract yields to situational preference. I see no great problem, no crucial embarrassment, for utilitarianism here. See further Griffin, 1982: 359-61 and 1986: ch. 5; and Rashdall, 1924: II, ch. 2.

21.2.9 Criticisms of moral unacceptability

I consider three objections to utilitarianism under this heading:

- integrity
- justice
- special relationships

Integrity: Bernard Williams's critique

Williams's claim is that utilitarianism interferes with the individual's integrity. Integrity is a matter of commitment to particular projects – a categorical commitment which is not up for negotiation. But utilitarianism puts every particular personal project up for negotiation. It requires us to adopt the course which maximizes value; and in order to perform *that* action, the individual may have to surrender his commitment to particular projects. And to look at the matter from the other side, integrity may require one not to adopt the course which maximizes value.

The claim is illustrated in the dilemmas of Jim and the Indians (98-9) and

George the chemist (Smart and Williams, 1973: 97-8). In the first case there are twenty Indians in front of a firing squad in a South American village. The military authorities give Jim the option, as an honoured guest, of shooting one Indian himself and thus saving the lives of nineteen others, or (failing his acceptance of the guest's privilege) of allowing matters to take their standard course with the result that all twenty Indians will be shot. What is Jim to do if he is committed never to take human life? In the second case we meet George, who disapproves of chemical warfare. The big question now is – will George take a job in a laboratory doing weapons research of that kind? He has a family to support and is out of work. As well, if he refuses the job an arch-nasty will take it on with vigorous commitment.

Three comments:

(1) Williams's idea of integrity is a shade idiosyncratic. I should have said that integrity is a matter of commitment to principles from which one does not deviate under pressure of threat or inducement. Perhaps this is what Williams really has in mind; perhaps the talk of 'projects' is misleading. Jim's commitment to the project of life-saving might be rephrased in terms of his adherence to a moral principle of saving life. If we are going to talk specifically about projects, an apter term here is Josiah Royce's 'loyalty' – the 'willing and practical and thoroughgoing devotion of a person to a cause' (Royce, 1908: 17, cf. 51-2, 93). This is essentially a commitment to a way of life that is our inclusive or dominant end (24.2.6).

Hare defines integrity in a different way from Williams:

> I use the word, not in Bernard Williams's somewhat off-beat sense, in which Hitler was a paradigm of it – the sense in which someone displays integrity if he pursues his own 'projects' regardless of all other considerations – but in its usual sense of the honesty which, whether in someone's writing or in anything else that they do, one can trust absolutely (Hare, 1987: 71).

(2) I am not at all clear that utilitarianism would *have* to resolve these dilemmas as Williams suggests: 'that George should accept the job, and … that Jim should kill the Indian' (99). *Strict consequentialist act-utilitarianism* might yield this conclusion. But I see no necessary reason why act-utilitarianism, and no likely reason why rule-utilitarianism, as such, should do so. In the case of Jim and the Indians, why should not a utilitarian follow the rule that it is overall undesirable, and does not maximize value, to submit to the choices of people who engineer your situation as the Captain has engineered Jim's?

(3) It is perfectly possible for there to be a utilitarian rule that particular projects are to be treated as categorical in view of their deep importance to the individual. In other words, integrity (in Williams's sense) can be a utilitarian value.

For good discussions of Williams's examples, see Glover, 1975; Harris, 1974: 268-73; and Holland, 1980.

Justice

'Justice' is a wide notion. But essentially the concept of justice is that of treating like cases equally. Particular conceptions of justice define the relevant classes of like case. So we meet with rules such as 'to each according to their needs', 'to each according to their deserts' (see Perelman, 1963: 1-28).

The idea behind the appeal to justice as a criticism of utilitarianism is that justice is typically – or often – a backward-looking principle. It definitely is so on the substantive principle we considered above: according to the work someone has done, they are to be rewarded. Justice here looks back to what has happened and uses a past contribution as a basis for apportionment. (This is more plausible for some examples than others.) But, the point is made, utilitarianism is a forward-looking principle. It bids us maximize utility *now* for a *future* state of affairs. What has happened in the past is irrelevant.

I confess that I have nothing original to contribute on this subject; and I offer just two points. The first is that, whatever justice may be typically or often, it is not always a matter of reward or punishment, nor always backward-looking. No simple opposition between justice and forward-looking utilitarianism can be established. Secondly, rule-utilitarianism can respect backward-looking justice. If there is a rule of just-dealing, it can be one of the rules that rule-utilitarianism accepts. I have already mentioned Mill in this connection (21.2.5). The criticism has greater force against act-utilitarianism.

See further Attfield, 1987: ch. 8; Berger, 1979; Griffin, 1982: 354-7; Lyons, 1978; and Mill, U: ch. 5.

Special relationships

Utilitarianism tells us to maximize utility. It does not allow us, so the criticism runs, to allocate utility favourably to those with whom we have a special relationship. But ordinary moral views do allow this. William Godwin's graphic case of 'Archbishop Fénelon versus My Mother' is supposed to show the counter-intuitive deliverances of utilitarianism here.

In *Enquiry Concerning Political Justice* Godwin poses a dilemma: in a burning building, I can rescue either my mother or, a more general benefactor to humanity, the scholarly Archbishop. (Since Godwin was a militant atheist the example is not without its irony.) Hurl your relative into the flames, Godwin says, and save the Archbishop. Where utility requires no less, conscience should require no other. See Godwin, 1971: 70-1 and Monro, 1953: ch. 1.

Two responses are possible. The first is embodied in the blunt question, 'If there is a clash with ordinary moral views, so what?' The appeal to ordinary moral views is not decisive against a revisionary ethical theory like utilitarianism. This response takes us into the area of the justification of utilitarianism. The idea is that if utilitarianism can satisfactorily ground morality on interest and rational choice, there is no compelling need for utilitarian moral judgements to agree with the deliverances of pre-theoretical moral thought. The point is generalizable to cover criticisms on the score of integrity and justice also, and so can be read retrospectively into the above discussions. The second response is to suggest that a rule of giving extra importance in our calculations to those with whom we have a special relationship can be a utilitarian rule if it produces the best outcome overall.

That closes my discussion of utilitarianism for this chapter. The best point of contact for a deeper, more elaborate critique is Sen and Williams, 1982. See also Foot, 1985; Griffin, 1982; Hutchinson, 1982; and Stubbs, 1981.

22.1. ETHICAL PLURALISM

We now move on to the next stage of our discussion of the moral criterion:

• ethical pluralism

22.2. KANT

Unfashionably and polemically, I will take Kant as my representative ethical pluralist. Kant is generally presented as a prime example of an ethical monist: the advocate of a single 'supreme principle of morality'. It tends to be overlooked that if there is a *supreme* principle of morality there must be *other* moral principles as well (else there is nothing for the supreme principle to have supremacy *over*); and that Kant does not offer the supreme principle, that of the categorical imperative, as a complete guide to moral conduct.

Let me set the background. In Kant's view there is a *summum bonum*, a highest good (*das höchste Gut*) or best condition for us to be in, one and the same condition for everyone. This highest good has two elements: the moral good and the natural good. Kant's terminology for expressing this distinction is not entirely firm. But he tends to use *das Gut* for the moral good and *das Wohl* for the natural good.

The relation of the moral to the natural good is complicated but not hard to sort out in essentials. The moral good, embodied in the Good Will, is the only unconditional good. Put 'the Good Will' on hold for now; it is a major Kantian concept that we will examine later in the chapter. Someone exercising the moral good (enacting the Good Will) has virtue or, in a slightly contentious sense, perfection; someone enjoying the natural good has happiness (joy, contentment, or pleasure). See further Laird, 1929: ch. 8; Silber, 1982; and Ward, 1971 and 1972: ch. 6.

The moral agent aims (1) at his or her own virtue or perfection, a condition of regularly enacting the Good Will; and (2) at the happiness of others but in such a way as (3) to proportion happiness to virtue as far as possible. With respect to one's own happiness as a moral agent the aim is (4) to be worthy of it. A Kantian society of moral agents would enjoy the highest good, combining happiness and virtue, since each would embody moral virtue and accordingly enjoy happiness so far as others were able to provide it.

This is a far cry from answering the question, 'What shall I do?' with 'Consult just one consideration.'

This complexity of Kant's ethical theory is standardly ignored. For most students and many teachers of ethics Kant is the philosopher of the categorical imperative. The above remarks on virtue, perfection and happiness reveal one aspect of Kant's pluralism. Another aspect emerges when we note that, confronted with 'casuistical questions', Kant acknowledges genuine indeterminacy of decision-making in situations of risk or uncertainty where there are strong cross-plays of interpersonal interests (22.2.4).

The doctrine of the categorical imperative is set out mainly in Kant's *Grundlegung zur Metaphysik der Sitten* (1785), which has three English aliases:

- *Groundwork of the Metaphysic of Morals*
- *Foundations of the Metaphysics of Morals*
- *The Moral Law*

The Moral Law is the title of H.J. Paton's translation. The diversity of English titles can be confusing. One sympathizes with the philosopher who, drawn from his area of expertise, was asked by a colleague to explain the difference between the *Groundwork* and the *Foundations*, paused thoughtfully and replied that he had never been able to discover any significant differences of doctrine between them but that, so far as he knew, one was written before the other.

Left to myself I should not hesitate to prefer Paton's translation, which conveys some of the linguistic and intellectual style of the original. A student without German once told me, however, that he found Paton's translation marginally more difficult than the original text: reactions clearly vary. The medium of Lewis White Beck's translation is colloquial American English: a fine idiom in many contexts but one which, just here, to my mind, makes the colouring too modern. But I shall use Beck's translation: enshrined in university reading lists, it is the translation that students are most likely to encounter. A fine work of mid-Victorian scholarship, T.K. Abbott's *Kant's Critique of Practical Reason and Other Works on the Theory of Ethics* (1873; 6th ed., 1909), retains a good deal of value as an anthology of Kant's ethical writings. Copies are rare.

I shall keep mainly to the *Foundations*. My account centres on the doctrine of the categorical imperative, about which every student of ethics needs to know. Now that you are alerted to its pluralist context, that doctrine should not create a false impression of Kant's ethics as a one-principle monolith. In the space available I cannot discuss much more than the categorical imperative, and in an introductory text I can hardly discuss less.

Kant makes a major – historically influential and still significant – contribution to ethics on four topics:

- the moral criterion
- the justification of moral judgement
- action explanation
- free will

In the justification of moral judgement Kant's view is that the requirements of morality are, or derive from, norms of practical reason. On action explanation he believes that moral motivation always has reason at its source: that in respect of moral action we do not need to take desire as an equal partner to the cognitive element. On free will he strives to vindicate moral responsibility by a metaphysical appeal to our 'noumenal' freedom. For now I will fix on Kant's account of the moral criterion and reserve his contribution to the other topics for later chapters. See also Korsgaard, 1989.

22.2.1. The categorical imperative

Kant lays down a moral criterion, the categorical imperative ('CI' from now on).

Four formulations

Kant offers CI as a moral criterion. He gives four formulations of it, or five if we include a variation on the first formula (Paton, 1947: 129):

Formula 1 or the formula of universal law:
> Act only according to that maxim by which you can at the same time will that it should become a universal law (F; Beck, 44)

Formula 1a or the formula of the law of nature:
> Act as though the maxim of your action were by your will to become a universal law of nature (F; Beck, 45)

Formula 2 or the formula of the end in itself:
> Act so that you treat humanity, whether in your own person or in that of another, always as an end and never as a means only (F; Beck, 54)

Formula 3 or the formula of autonomy:
> Act only so that the will through its maxims can regard itself at the same time as universally lawgiving (F; Beck, 59, reformulated)

Formula 4 or the formula of the kingdom of ends:
> So act as if you, by your maxims, were at all times a legislative member in the universal realm of ends (F; Beck, 64, reformulated)

Terminology

What does Kant mean by a 'maxim'? It is a subjective principle of action. The idea is roughly this: that the maxim of your action is the *policy* implicit in what you are proposing to do. Say I have borrowed £5 from you. You have forgotten the debt; and it suits me to keep the money. And keep the money is just what I propose to do. In this case, Kant would say, the maxim of my action is: 'Whenever one has borrowed money and one's creditor has forgotten the debt, and the debt is one which it suits one not to repay, then one is to keep the money.'

Differences and inter-relations

Kant thinks that if I violate CI under its first formulation I am treating my noumenal self (my rational will, which = the moral will, which = the good will, which = the only thing capable of intrinsic value) as subservient to my phenomenal self. (On the 'phenomenal' see 22.2.3 on Kant's 'two-world metaphysics'.) So violation of the first formulation means violation of the second: see further N. Cooper, 1988. We can grasp Kant's point in terms of his second example. If I make a promise with no intention of fulfilling it, then I violate CI under its first formulation (since, according to Kant, my maxim is not consistently universalizable) and I use other people (specifically, the person to whom I make the promise) as a mere means to my own convenience.

Where to draw the line? If we go into the differences and interrelations very deeply we will become absorbed in the kind of mental chess that so delights Kant scholars. I offer the following quick overview of the various formulations.

Formula 1a adds nothing of substance to formula 1. Technically the difference between them turns on Kant's notion of a 'schematism'. 1a is the schematized version of 1. Very roughly, and without probing the tensions between the role of schematism here and in the *Critique of Pure Reason*, I should say that natural law in 1a is meant to serve as a symbol which brings out graphically CI's two dominant features in Kant's view. CI yields exceptionless laws (universality) independently of desire (necessity). More simply said, essentially Kant is emphasizing the lawlikeness of reason. With respect to knowledge it imposes on our experience a network of laws of nature (22.2.3). With respect to conduct it is equally lawlike in imposing on our conduct the 'law' of the categorical imperative. Formula 1a is Kant's way of bringing out that common activity of reason in knowledge and conduct.

Kant says that formula 1 gives the form of the moral law, while formula 2 gives its content. The broad connection appears to be that formula 1 embodies the way in which we express pure practical reason in our own person and so realize our intrinsic value; formula 2 bids us treat other people in such a way that they too can follow pure practical reason, embody intrinsic value, and not merely figure as means to our own 'phenomenal', sense-based ends. (Quite roughly, the 'phenomenal' is what we experience in space and time: see further on the phenomenal and also on pure practical reason in 22.2.3. below.) Formula 3 is important to Kant as expressing his idea that though a rational agent must act in conformity with law, yet this lawlike behaviour must be self-imposed (27.1.1). Formula 4 is a mix, a 'synthesis' as Kant calls it, of all the preceding formulas. It tells us to act as we should act if we belonged to a world in which everyone followed formulas 1-3.

22.2.2. First face of the categorical imperative: the good will and the moral will

In the *Foundations* CI connects upwards with a highly general notion, that of the good will, and downwards to four examples of moral situations.

To take the 'upwards' connection first: Kant claims that the only thing which we can think of that could have intrinsic value is a certain kind of motivation. He calls this the *good will*; and its value is independent of context or results.CI defines the conditions that your action has to meet if it is to issue from and express a *moral will*. Those conditions are precisely the conditions that must be fulfilled also if the good will is to have intrinsic value. So the good will is the moral will; the two coincide.

Kant's attempt to identify the good will and the moral will is elusive, not at all clear and consecutive. The steps, with some textual reconstruction, are roughly the following:

GOOD WILL _____

(a) A particular kind of motivation is the only thing capable of intrinsic value.
(b) Call this kind of motivation the 'good will'.
(c) A good will is not good by virtue of its results.
(d) A good will is a will which acts always on a maxim whereby I can at the same time will that it should become a universal law. Only this can make a will good irrespective of its results.

MORAL WILL _____

(e) An action is morally good (issues from and expresses a moral will) if and only if it is done from duty.
(f) To act from duty is purely to have a particular kind of motivation.
(g) This motivation is defined by the form of the maxim on which we act.
(h) The form of the maxim is that of conformability to universal law as such.
(i) Duty requires that I act always on a maxim whereby I can at the same time will that it should become a universal law.

GOOD WILL = MORAL WILL _____

Therefore (from (d), (e), and (i)):

(j) A good will is a moral will.

In making this equation Kant never says, and in fact explicitly denies, that the moral good is (1) the *sole or complete good*. He says that the good will, which = the moral will, is (2) the *only intrinsic good*. And he also says that the good will is (3) the *highest good*. On my ethical arithmetic (2) + (3) do not = (1).

22.2.3. Second face of the categorical imperative: two tests and four examples

To take now the 'downwards' connection. For Kant, CI satisfies our pre-theoretical moral notions. It is adequate to ordinary moral views, as is shown (he thinks) by its matching 'our' pre-theoretical reactions exactly in regard to four examples of moral situations. (On who 'we' might be, see Norman, 1983: 96.) This coincidence with ordinary moral views is important to Kant, by the way, on grounds which are internal to his philosophy. Rather roughly, they have to do with morality's being, in Kant's view, a function of reason, so that ordinary moral views are imbued with a rationality which Kant is simply, as he sees it, making explicit.

What are the four examples? Under crude headings, they are:

(1) duty to refrain from suicide (perfect duty to ourselves)
(2) duty to refrain from making false promises (perfect duty to others)
(3) duty to develop our talents (imperfect duty to ourselves)
(4) duty to help others (imperfect duty to others)

In the first example Kant imagines somebody 'who is reduced to despair by a series of evils'. To devise our own details, things are going badly for Marsham. He has a progressive disease which is incurable. His friends have deserted him. His wife has died. His only child has perished in a road accident. On top of that he has just been made redundant with no prospect of work at the age of 57. Marsham contemplates suicide. 'Now he asks himself whether the maxim of his action could become a universal law of nature. His maxim, however, is "For love of myself, I make it my principle to shorten my life when by a longer duration it threatens more evil than satisfaction. But it is questionable whether this principle could become a universal law of nature" ' (F; Beck, 45).

The second example has it that another person, Lucy Lightfoot as we may call her, is strapped for cash. Any money she receives, she will be unable to pay back. But the only way of getting money is by making a lying promise to repay. As with the potential suicide, things are bad: but, again, not bad enough to blot out moral reflection. Lucy reflects that, if she goes ahead and makes the promise, her maxim will be: 'When I believe myself to be in need of money, I will borrow money and promise to repay it, although I know I shall never do so.'

According to the third example, someone could develop a major talent but is disinclined to do so. To supply our own detail, imagine Louise, who could be a skilful surgeon but who prefers to follow a lotus-eater style of life. Her maxim (which Kant leaves implicit) is: 'I will neglect my gifts in the interests of a life of complete self-indulgence.'

In the fourth example a man, Percival Plumptre, in easy circumstances sees others, whom he could help, beset with difficulties. 'That's the way the cookie crumbles', he says in language unlike any that Kant used. 'Things have worked out well for me, but that's just the luck of the draw. I could help but why should I? Now, where's that other bottle of champagne?' Kant does not spell out the maxim explicitly for his fourth example. But presumably this person's maxim is: 'When my circumstances are better than other people's, I will not help them.'

Distinction between perfect and imperfect duties

Kant's commentators disagree considerably over what the distinction between perfect and imperfect duties precisely amounts to. See Norman, 1983: 103-4; and Harrison, 1969: 209. So far as I can make out, a perfect duty is exceptionless. It is one on which it is *requisite always to act* (e.g., you have an obligation to keep *every* promise). An imperfect duty is simply one on which it is *wrong for you never to act* (e.g., you do not have an obligation to give to every charity; the moral point is simply that it would be wrong *never* to give to charity). This distinction appears to pair off with the contrast (shortly to come into view) between *contradiction in conception* (the sphere of perfect duties) and *contradiction in the will* (the sphere of imperfect duties).

Two tests

How can the maxim of one's action fail the CI test? In one of two ways, Kant says. That is, if it involves a:

- contradiction in conception   • contradiction in the will

Kant's handling of his examples occasions a great deal of difficulty to modern readers. Let me tick off three things that go wrong.

(1) For the modern reader Kant's treatment of the first example is his weakest card. One's reaction is likely to be that 'we' simply do not share Kant's automatic assumption that suicide is morally wrong. But quite what 'automatic assumption' is this? Kant is envisaging only suicide viewed as advantageous (or attractive) to the agent – not suicide for the benefit of others. We may allow a right of suicide even in the first case. That, however, is not the point: which is rather that Kant is not saying what he readily appears to be saying, i.e. that suicide is always morally wrong.

(2) Neither the contradiction in conception nor the contradiction in the will

criteria appears at all plausibly to yield the conclusion Kant reaches. The first criterion should apply here, for on Kant's account the contradiction in conception test yields perfect duties; and the obligation to refrain from suicide is (again on Kant's account) a perfect duty.

For brevity I shall refer to 'the suicide' from now on, even though Kant leaves his unfortunate individual merely at the point of checking out his projected action.

What is the suicide's maxim? According to Kant: 'For love of myself, I make it my principle to shorten my life when by a longer duration it threatens more evil than satisfaction' (F; Beck, 45). Kant comments: 'One immediately sees a contradiction in a system of nature whose law would be to destroy life by the feeling whose special office is to impel the improvement of life' (ibid.).

But Kant appears here to confuse two quite distinct things: 'love of myself' (or more generally 'love of oneself', self-love) and self-preservation. Now, it certainly would be a contradiction in conception if the suicide's attitude were: 'In order to preserve myself I shall kill myself.' That is obviously adrift even before we try to universalize. But why should the suicide be committed to this attitude? Suppose the evil that depresses him is pain. His attitude is rather: 'In order to avoid pain I shall kill myself'. In his analysis of the suicide's situation Kant skids between (a) life = preservation and (b) life = quality of life.

(3) Kant has a set of assumptions. Ordinary moral views are comprehensive and coherent. Against these views we can test ethical theories by checking our reactions to real or imagined situations. These reactions are the final court of appeal in moral reflection. In 22.2.3 I explained why Kant feels a need to coincide with ordinary moral views. But this set of assumptions increases the gap between Kant and the modern reader.

Let us approach the suicide example from another direction, that of formula 2: 'So act as to treat humanity, whether in your own person or in that of any other, never solely as a means but always also as an end.' (This formulation has been found independently interesting. See Haezrahi, 1968; Maclagan, 1960; N. Richards, 1978; and Downie and Telfer, 1969.) Much work needs to be done on this formulation in respect of the precise distinction between treating people as ends and treating them merely as means.

We have a first handle on the notion from our use of expressions such as 'He used me!' Perhaps the idea behind this kind of remark is that one uses somebody if one affects their physical behaviour through compulsion, as in the case of sheer bodily manhandling, or their intentional action through coercion or deception.

But this does not give us quite what Kant intends. To see what he has in mind we have to mount a short metaphysical stairway.

Kant has a somewhat special concept of a person. All and only rational beings are persons. There is no conceptual necessity for a person to be a human being. Next we must note that human beings, for Kant, are metaphysical amphibians. We have a dual nature:

• noumenal   • phenomenal

This distinction is sometimes tagged as Kant's 'two-world metaphysics', alternatively as his doctrine of 'the two standpoints'. Everything which we experience, we experience relative to our cognitive apparatus; and this is no mere 'mirror of nature'. Objects of experience compose the realm of the phenomenal (from the Greek word for 'appear'). The noumenal is the realm of things-in-themselves, of things as they are independently of our knowledge of them.

Kant makes an assumption about the noumenal. Not only do objects of experience have a noumenal aspect, opaque to our cognitive apparatus (since to know things noumenally we should have to know them through our cognitive apparatus and independently of that apparatus, to know what difference the apparatus made to our experience: and this is in principle impossible). More than that, we ourselves have a noumenal aspect. And while we cannot know what our noumenal selves are like, we do know that they frame our experience in certain ways.

For instance, when our judgements are 'synthetic', about objects of experience, any assumptions of universality or necessity that we make must have their source not in our phenomenal nature but in the transcendental or noumenal self. A judgement such as 'All bodies are extended' is analytic for Kant; its truth is guaranteed by mere analysis of the concept of a body. And there is no mystery about how we can come to know its truth. By contrast, a judgement such as 'Every event has a cause' is synthetic; its truth cannot be vouchsafed simply by analysing the concept of an event. It is also a priori, whence the famous Kantian category of the synthetic a priori. We have not observed all possible events in all possible experience; and no judgement about such events and such experience can derive from finite experience itself. Therefore a judgement like 'All events have a cause' is a non-phenomenal, hence noumenal, contribution. The marks of this contribution are universality ('all events') and necessity ('have, i.e. must have, a cause').

Kant calls our capacity for seeing things in terms of universality and necessity our 'faculty of principles' (*Critique of Pure Reason*, B356; Kemp Smith, 301). These principles are generated by 'pure reason'. 'Theoretical reason' is not the same as pure reason; to use our theoretical reason is simply to identify the work of pure reason in matters of knowledge and to pick out the relevant principles. Practical reason is the exercise of pure reason in matters of conduct; we might call it, as Kant does, 'pure practical reason'. The CI is a 'deliverable' of pure practical reason which holds for all rational beings of necessity, i.e. unconditionally on desire.

Now, Kant believes that the rational will (the will that follows CI) is the moral will; and that the moral will is the good will.

By virtue of our divided nature, practical reason has to contend with sensibility – all those sense-based desires and inclinations that are counter-inducements to following CI and doing our duty. A 'holy will' is purely rational and has no impact of sensibility to contend with. We are persons, i.e. rational beings, but, by contrast, also creatures of sensibility.

In the practical sphere a rational being, qua rational, must always act so as to exercise practical reason, and so follow CI. What he must *not* do is to programme his life to serve exclusively the promptings of sense-based desire or inclination. To use reason in that purely instrumental way is to make what Kant calls a merely technically practical use of reason. This is to neglect his nature as a noumenal being. But this is precisely what – to return to our point of departure – Kant supposes the suicide to do. The suicide lets sensibility dictate to pure practical reason by using reason in a merely technically practical way.

So Kant believes; but he has a problem. Suppose formula 2 rules out even 'In order to avoid pain, I will kill myself'. If so, in the first place, this maxim does not involve a contradiction in conception; and secondly, the suicide is not committed to the maxim that really does involve a contradiction in conception, namely 'In order to preserve myself, I will kill myself.' Formulas 1 and 2 fail to coincide in their requirements.

I shall keep in reserve an idea that we have not in fact identified Kant's deeper approach to this matter: see section on 'Rigorism' below.

On the distinction between the two tests, of contradiction in conception and contradiction in the will, see O'Neill, 1989: ch. 5, esp. 96-101.

22.2.4. Criticisms of the doctrine of the categorical imperative

Kant's doctrine has been criticized on three main grounds:

- formalism
- rationalism
- rigorism

In considering these objections my main aim will be, as throughout this chapter, conceptualization. I want to use them to help make clear what Kant's moral criterion involves. The justification of Kant's ethical theory, with its essential idea that moral action is rational action, is a matter for us to examine in the next chapter.

Formalism

CI is meant to be practically useful as a guide to conduct. It defines perfect duties, which we must never omit to perform. Hence CI tells us what is mandatory or obligatory. We are forbidden to violate the requirement of consistent universalizability. But we may omit to perform imperfect duties on particular (but not all) occasions. So, as Kant sees it, the obligatory, the forbidden, and the permissible are all vouchsafed by CI.

The adequacy of this threefold classification has been criticized by J.O. Urmson, who argues that saintly and heroic action fall beyond the category of the obligatory and yet are not merely permissible. However, Urmson's argument does not refute the classification but at best shows its incompleteness. The issue is too complex to pursue here; see Urmson, 1958. (I may add, as an aside, that Urmson's account of heroic and saintly actions has also been seen as creating a problem for Hare's universal prescriptivism, since one might morally commend a saintly action (say) without taking oneself to be committed to a corresponding universal prescription.)

Urmson's complaint aside, the doctrine of the categorical imperative is often criticized as providing merely a negative test. It rules out a line of action if the relevant maxim cannot be consistently universalized. But it provides no positive guidance.

I think there are two main points to be made in response to this criticism. In the first place, specificity is secured through the fact that you are already planning to do an action, X, or are thinking about doing X, when the CI test falls due to be applied. That specificity is the positive element. You already know what you want to do; and the CI test is applied as a critical moral filter, removing the options which fail its requirements.

Another line of criticism is that there is no action which the CI test can rule out. We need only invoke an arbitrary specificity in order to let any action through the test. For instance, if my maxim is to take cheap wine to a bottle party and to drink superior wine brought by others, this maxim cannot be consistently universalized. Nobody would bring along the superior wine for the bringers of cheap wine to drink. But then, the idea is, I need only redescribe my action arbitrarily in order for its maxim to pass the CI test. E.g., 'I am a 48-year-old guest who will take cheap and drink superior wine if I know in advance that not all guests will do the same.' Now *that* maxim could be consistently universalized, for the simple reason that not all guests at a bottle party are 48 years old.

Kant's obvious answer to this move is that a deeper, inconsistently universalizable maxim is really involved. I.e., something like: 'So as to make an exception in my own favour, I will arbitrarily redescribe my action so as to make its maxim consistently universalizable.' And *that* maxim cannot be consistently universalized: in the bottle party example, everybody will similarly redescribe their actions arbitrarily and bring along cheap wine.

Rationalism

Kant is a rationalist in the sense that the basic test of the morally obligatory, forbidden, and permissible is a norm of reason: the CI. An action is morally good if and only if it is done from duty; and it is done from duty if and only if its motivation is conformability with universal law as such. We must disregard feeling, sympathy, personal affection, pleasure, and emotion; the whole sphere of what Kant calls 'the pathological' is absolutely irrelevant to moral worth. (Kant uses 'pathological' to indicate that we are passive in relation to these things. The word lacks its current associations and derives from the Greek *pathos*, in the sense of 'emotion'.)

To go into this criticism fully would take us far afield. Suffice it to say that Kant's position here rests on two premises, both of which are challengeable:

(1) The 'pathological' is a surd (irrational), fortuitous element in the human condition.
(2) The requirements of morality are categorical.

Since different people are fortuitously subject to different impacts of the 'pathological', Kant thinks that there is no possibility of basing morality, with its unconditional, categorical requirements, on emotion and the rest. But the categorical nature of morality and the fortuitousness of the 'pathological' are questionable assumptions here. (On the latter you might refer back to my remarks on Brentano and the intentionality of the emotions when we discussed Stevenson and the emotive theory of moral judgement (15.1.2).) See also Blum, 1980: esp. 1-11; Galvin, 1991; and Mackinnon, 1957: 82-6.

Rigorism

In the *Foundations* Kant applies the CI test to actions under very narrow and uncircumstantial descriptions. Just cast your mind back to the minimal characterizations of the four moral situations (22.2.3).

This is one basis for a rigorist interpretation of Kant. If an action falls under one of these descriptions, additional circumstances are irrelevant. Circumstances do not alter cases. The CI yields exceptionless moral rules under extremely narrow action-descriptions. So Kant holds on this interpretation.

Some commentators see a later liberalization, or at least a shift, in Kant's attitudes. With the apparent total ban on suicide in the *Foundations* we might contrast the suppler treatment in *The Doctrine of Virtue* (Kant, 1964: 86):

A man who had been bitten by a mad dog already felt hydrophobia, and he explained, in a letter he left, that since, so far as he knew, the disease was incurable, he killed himself lest he harm others as well in his madness, the onset of which he already felt. Did he do wrong?

Anyone who decides to be vaccinated against smallpox puts his life in danger, even though he does it *to preserve his life*; and, in so far as he himself brings on the disease that endangers his life, he is in a far more doubtful situation, so far as they law of duty is concerned, than is the sailor, who at least does not arouse the storm to which he entrusts himself. Is smallpox inoculation, then, permissible?

If these 'casuistical questions' are left open, we should at least note that they concern a radically different kind of example from that described in the *Foundations*. In the *Foundations*, to repeat 22.2.3, Kant is envisaging only suicide viewed as advantageous (or attractive) to the agent. The examples in *The Doctrine of Virtue* (those just quoted and others besides) turn on benefit to others. In this respect there is nothing in the latter work that Kant could not have accepted consistently in the former. So the case for a shift of attitude, let alone a liberalization of viewpoint, is not proven.

None the less, since Kant propounds his 'casuistical questions' without answering them we may assume that he is allowing for a greater context-dependence of the CI than is (I do not say 'present' but) apparent in the *Foundations*. It is only a mild gloss on Kant to say in modern terms that he is here concerned with situations of risk or uncertainty (21.2.5) in which there are strong cross-plays of interpersonal interests. In these conditions there is a perfectly genuine area of doubt about what an agent should do. And this introduces a pluralist indeterminacy into Kant's ethics.

22.2.5. Kant and utilitarianism

How does Kant stand in relation to utilitarianism?

(1) They both offer a theory of the moral criterion, answering the question, 'What shall I do?'

(2) Utilitarianism invokes a single criterion, that of maximizing the occurrence of intrinsically valuable states of affairs. Kant has a more complex picture. There is the CI test but also there are considerations about promoting one's own perfection and the happiness of others.

(3) Utilitarianism assigns morality a purely instrumental role. There is a non-moral good; and morality's rationale is to promote that good. For Kant, by contrast, the good will, which coincides with the moral will, is itself the highest and the only intrinsic (though not the complete) human good.

(4) By virtue of its stress on the goal of morality, utilitarianism is generally known as a *teleological* theory (21.2). The CI in Kant is, by contrast, a *deontological* notion. It requires us to test our maxims in terms of consistent universalizability; and looks for no external result that the test will secure. The CI test is self-justified as an absolute requirement of pure practical reason. I believe that Kant's ethical theory contains teleological elements as described in 22.2. Perhaps the safest contrast to urge here between Kant and the utilitarians is that Kant tells us to pursue goals within morality, while the utilitarians set morality itself a goal.

I should add that teleological theories need not see morality as merely externally related to a purpose to which it is answerable. Aristotle, for example, regards morality as answerable to well-being to which, however, it is internally related since morality itself is a form of human flourishing.

Further to shuffle the conceptual pack of cards: if we were to reckon the possession and exercise of moral *rights* as having intrinsic value, this would be in line with Kant's idea that an item within morality itself has intrinsic value, but it would differ from him over what that item is. For a rights-based morality, it would be the possession and exercise of moral rights; J.L. Mackie has explored the possibility of this kind of morality in Mackie, 1984. For Kant it would be the possession and exercise of a particular kind of motivation.

(5) Both Kant and the utilitarians use a notion of intrinsic value. Utilitarianism typically regards actions as merely instrumental to the production of intrinsically valuable states of affairs. But even if (as conceptually it may (22.2.3)) utilitarianism recognizes actions as themselves embodying intrinsic value, this still would not be Kant's position. For Kant regards not actions, but a certain kind of motivation, as having intrinsic value (22.2.2).

22.2.6. Kant and Hare

If we briefly rewind and glance back at Hare's ethical theory (12.2), a set of contrasts between the notions of universalizability in Kant and Hare quickly emerges.

In Hare's ethical theory universalizability is invoked as part of a definitional thesis about the concept of a moral principle: that unless one is prepared to act, and to have others act, on the same principle in relevantly similar circumstances, one's principle is not a moral one. For Kant, by contrast, the consistent universalizability of one's maxim is a rule of duty.

Moreover, the contradiction in conception test of consistent universalizability is a purely logical test for Kant; it relates to a property of the maxim. Harean universalizability turns rather on the agent's attitude, on how he is prepared to act and to have others act.

Furthermore, Kant derives the requirement of consistent universalizability from norms of practical reason while Hare does not claim that it is contrary to reason if we fail to respect universalizability.

22.2.7. The relevance of Kant

Very few philosophers now accept the details of Kant's ethical theory. But he remains an immensely influential theorist. People find him suggestive: to some his doctrine of CI stresses an important feature of morality (the categoricality of moral judgements (14.1)) while to others there is an attraction in his idea that immorality involves a kind of inconsistency. This latter idea has been taken up by a present-day American philosopher, Thomas Nagel, in *The Possibility of Altruism*.

23.1. ETHICAL PARTICULARISM

I have characterized ethical particularism as the view that there are no moral principles. This view is not a theory that adopts a sceptical or non-cognitive approach to morality. The point of saying that there are no moral principles is not to convey that there are no objective moral requirements, period; or that, while there may be moral principles, we lack adequate or any knowledge of them. Just what it positively is, we shall see shortly. My understanding of ethical particularism, a view also known as 'act-deontology' or (somewhat loadedly) 'unphilosophical intuitionism', is largely informed by two papers of Jonathan Dancy's (Dancy, 1981 and 1983). I cannot do full justice to Dancy's supple, sinuous and clever papers here. You should certainly read them if you want to explore ethical particularism further.

I shall introduce ethical particularism, with its crucial position that there are no universally morally relevant properties, through a consideration of Sir David Ross's ethical theory, which Dancy uses as a foil.

23.1.1. W.D. Ross and morally relevant properties: a foil for particularism

W.D. Ross, knighted as Sir David Ross for his services to Aristotelian scholarship, is a miserably underrated ethical theorist in his own right. There are signs of increased regard, but Ross's major ethical works, *The Right and the Good* and *The Foundations of Ethics*, are usually introduced to students only to be guyed as examples of crude and implausible intuitionism. Ross's intuitionism, his moral epistemology, is the weakest side of his ethical theory, though even here he has defenders (Lucas, 1971). But Ross offers a complex structure of pluralist ethical thought and his notion of prima facie duty is not without interest.

One of Ross's central views is that the moral rightness of an action depends on other properties that the action has. Can we specify the relevant range of properties? Ross thinks so: and he divides the range in two. On the one hand there are four intrinsic goods (Ross, 1930: 134-41, esp. 140):

- pleasure
- knowledge
- virtuous disposition
- the allocation of pleasure to the virtuous and pain to the vicious

On the other hand, there are properties such as keeping a promise, expressing gratitude for benefits received from others (Ross, 1930: 16-47).

The division between the lists is perhaps best seen in the following way. Ross's moral criterion is that although we are to augment the occurrence of the intrinsic goods in the first list, yet within that general aim the items in the second list have a relative stringency. It is not that they are absolute side-restraints on the realization of the first list items. Hardly so: for what is at stake with respect to the first list may suffice to outweigh the special requirements marked by the second. None the less, item for item, the second list has prior importance.

For Ross, the two lists identify properties that are morally relevant whenever they obtain. If promise-keeping is a morally relevant property possessed by one action, then it is also morally relevant that another action is one of promise-keeping. So: Ross has specified the range of morally relevant properties. Then in what way does the rightness of an action depend on these properties? Here we need to invoke Ross's notion of *prima facie duty*.

A prima facie duty is a prima facie duty to do what? To do an action with a morally relevant property in the range identified in Ross's first and second lists. And what is prima facie or provisional about a prima facie duty? That it registers a moral claim on the agent and not, as such, an overriding requirement of action. If an action had only one morally relevant property, then it would be not merely our prima facie but our actual duty. Our actual duty is to do the action with the most salient morally relevant property or properties in a given case.

For a utilitarian, salience (my term, not Ross's) would be an unproblematic notion. For there is only one morally relevant property for a utilitarian, that of maximizing the general welfare. Salience would be a matter of satisfying that description. Ross sees things differently. The various morally relevant properties yield moral principles. It is a morally relevant property that an action is one of promise-keeping. Therefore 'Keep your promises' is a moral principle that we have a prima facie duty to heed in all relevant situations. But moral principles are irreducibly plural; and we can only know intuitively which prima facie duty represents the morally most significant demand on us in a situation for action. This intuition or 'sense of our particular duty in particular circumstances ... is highly fallible, but it is the only guide we have to our duty' (Ross, 1930: 42).

On Ross see further: Bayles, 1984; Findlay, 1970: 50-6; and Snare, 1974.

23.1.3. Dancy contra Ross

The ethical particularist needs to dispose of Ross's claim that there are moral principles. To do this he must show that there are no universally relevant moral properties from which the principles derive. This is just what Dancy aims to do. In his view it is not the case that 'if a property is relevant anywhere it is relevant everywhere' (Dancy, 1983: 541). He tries to make good that denial.

Dancy's position may well look odd in terms of commonsense. 'Surely,' one might say, 'if it is at least one morally good element in a situation that someone gave pleasure to someone else, then giving pleasure to someone else must be such an element in any situation in which it occurs.' Is this so, however? You need to examine Dancy's own arguments. Here I suggest an independent line of confirmation for his position.

Suppose we think about the cause of a fire. What might have happened in a particular case is this. A person carelessly dropped a lighted match on the office floor. The match fell on to some dry, inflammable material, which duly ignited some hours later. The smoke alarm and the sprinkler system were out of action owing to a power failure; and Dozy Dave, the nonagenarian night-watchman, was snoring in an outbuilding. Soon the office was engulfed in flames.

That seems a plausible story of something that might happen. The lighted match caused the fire. But no one would suppose that a lighted match is 'causally relevant' to all fires for which the dropping of a lighted match was among a discrete series of prior events. Imagine the situation just described but with two differences. The lighted match was dropped as before but this time was doused by the sprinkler system. There was, however, elsewhere in the office a completely unrelated short-circuit, which caused a fire.

In this example a factor is causally relevant to one situation, causally irrelevant to another, in both of which it occurs. I see no reason why the same should not be true of a morally relevant property. If the parallel holds, then it is not the case that 'if a property is relevant anywhere it is relevant everywhere'. The causal parallel is particularly apt in relation to Ross, who regarded moral rightness as *resultant* from other properties: 'Rightness is always a resultant attribute – an attribute that an action has because it has another attribute' (Ross, 1939: 168; see also Dancy, 1981: 367ff.).

I must carefully stress, however, that I have supported Dancy's position with a line of argument quite different in detail from his own. If my argument fails, wrecked by the invalidity of my causal parallel, Dancy's arguments may still apply. I have omitted them here simply for their complexity. All I have tried to do is to break, or loosen, the hold of an idea that grips commonsense, the idea of 'relevant here, relevant everywhere'.

It is important not to run together this idea with that of Harean universalizability. Universalizability requires that, as I judge one situation, so I must judge all other situations relevantly similar. The denial of 'relevant here, relevant everywhere' means that the occurrence of a property morally relevant in one situation does not, as such, make another situation in which it occurs relevantly similar. Cf. Dancy, 1981: 544ff.

I have offered a defence of Dancy's position. In a fully adequate discussion we should need not merely to look at the final detail of what he says but also to consider challenges to his position from other quarters than Ross-style pluralism. The defence would need to be differently slanted to answer utilitarianism. For a utilitarian there is only one morally relevant property, as noted in 23.1.2. So there is no logical space for a property to be morally relevant in one situation but not in another. One property, and only one, is relevant in every situation for action. On Dancy, see further Gay, 1985. Dancy provides a simplified version of his views in Dancy, 1992.

24.1. THE MORAL IDEAL

Kant and the utilitarians both offer a choice-morality. 'What shall I do?' 'Choose that action whose maxim is consistently universalizable', is Kant's central and most distinctive answer. 'Choose that action which maximizes the occurrence of intrinsically desirable states of affairs', says the utilitarian. On the rival set Aristotle formulates a quite different ethical theory in his exposition and defence of a character-morality. Aristotle is primarily interested in the human good as a state or condition of the agent, and in the relation of the human good to moral virtue. With Aristotle we switch attention from the moral criterion to the moral ideal, even if (as we shall see) Aristotle's doctrine of the 'mean' can be seen as embodying a criterion.

In philosophy we are interested in theories of the moral ideal and not, at least directly, in paradigmatic individuals who embody a moral ideal. We are interested in (say) the Christian moral ideal, not in Jesus or St Francis – authentic models and examples though these historical persons are to all Christians. St Francis *shows* us what Christian moral virtue is; St Thomas Aquinas *tells* us what it is, stating and analysing the Christian moral ideal in the second part of his *Summa Theologiae*. As philosophers we keep to St Thomas, and as readers of this book, to Aristotle and a different moral ideal (even if St Thomas did read the *New Testament* through an Aristotelian lens).

24.2. ARISTOTLE

In the Aristotelian corpus, the body of writings traditionally or at some time attributed to Aristotle, there are four ethical treatises:

- *Eudemian Ethics* (EE)   • *Nicomachean Ethics* (NE)
- *Magna Moralia* (MM)   • *De Virtutibus et Vitiis* (VV)

MM and VV are no longer widely regarded as genuine. This is not to say that they are banal frauds, valueless for the study of Aristotle, even if VV (unlike MM) is several centuries later than Aristotle and combines Platonic elements with Aristotelian. Within limits MM and VV may still contain authentic reflections of Aristotle's ideas. EE and NE have a problematic relationship, not the least curious feature of which is that they have three common books (NE, V-VII, EE, IV-VI). A once influential view had it that EE is an early work, NE the product of Aristotle's mature reflection. But the existence of the common books counts against this interpretation.

C. Vicol Ionescu argues (Bodéüs, 1982) that there are no significant differences of doctrine between the books unique to NE and those unique to EE (NE, I-IV and VIII-X, EE, I-III, VII-VIII). Instead, these books give the two works a different orientation. NE is more closely attuned to practical guidance, EE is more theoretical. Certainly, on the theoretical side, Anthony Kenny has drawn renewed attention to EE as a major source for Aristotle's moral psychology. (The late D.J. Allan held that the main difference between NE and EE is that the former is more dialectical in its approach, the latter more expository, 'quasi-mathematical'.)

The relationship between NE and EE is further complicated by Ionescu's interpretation of the common books. They represent, he argues, the last phase of Aristotle's ethical reflection and embody the insights of *de Anima*, *Physics*, VIII and *Metaphysics*, ZHΘ on psychology, substance, movement and other matters.

The fragmentary *Protrepticus*, an early text which has ethical implications, is commonly supposed to belong to Aristotle's time of Platonic discipleship. (The tangled evolution of Aristotle's growth away from Plato, in ethics and beyond, was pioneeringly explored earlier in this century by Werner Jaeger, though a number of question-marks now hang over Jaeger's work.)

My own account of Aristotle's ethical theory is based mainly on NE. This simply reflects the predominance of NE in undergraduate teaching. These brief remarks alert you to a complex background.

My discussion of Aristotle will be more textual and contextual than I normally favour in philosophy (8.1.1). The position is this: Aristotle takes an appreciable amount for granted in his exposition. There is also the point that on first acquaintance the different elements of his theory often refuse to bond. One sees that there is *eudaimonia and* the 'mean' *and* moral education, say. The connectedness of Aristotle's understanding of these topics is scarcely glimpsed. We miss a great deal, however, if we fail to grasp how Aristotle understood his topics to interrelate. Text and context are needed to draw out the connections. The final coherence of Aristotle's treatment of his topics is another matter. For a conspectus, lucid as crystal, of the general philosophy of which Aristotle's ethics forms part, see J.A. Smith, 1935.

One last point. I have to square up to a problem about Greek terms. If you do not read Greek, you are likely to be distracted if the text breaks out into a rash of meaningless transliterations – *eudaimonia, arete, ergon, dikaiosyne*. So the reader has some rights in the matter, but then so too does Aristotle. He has the right to our recognition that Greek ethical terms rarely coincide precisely with their closest equivalents in English. It requires a special kind of insensitivity to translate '*eudaimonia*' as 'happiness' without qualm or qualification. My compromise is this: when I introduce a topic I will cite Aristotle's Greek term, select the nearest English equivalent, explain the gap between the two, then keep mainly (outside the section headings) to the English term.

24.2.1. Eudaimonia: the human good

Aristotle's aim is fruit as well as light. Ethics is a practical inquiry into the human good, *eudaimonia*, and its relation to moral virtue (NE, I.3, II.2; cf. Plato, R, I.352D). I aim in this first encounter with Aristotle's ethical theory to sketch an outline of his moral ideal: to list its components, to see how they are meant to fit together, and to look at some of the problems that arise. As with the utilitarians and Kant, I do not (except incidentally) touch upon the justification of Aristotle's view of the moral life. It will be enough at this stage if we can take a definite impression of what it is that Aristotle hopes to justify. We will step back and look at the larger picture of justification in chapter 4.

We need to tag some Aristotelian assumptions, the first of which is that there is a single specifiable culmination of human capacities, a state of the person which we can identify as man's ultimate end or highest good – a condition of complete and intrinsic excellence. Aristotle's phrase is *telos teleion*, 'final end', a state of the person (1) which every normal person actually does (and not merely should) regard as choiceworthy for its own sake; (2) to which every other condition is recognized as being of inferior value and opted for only as second-best (NE, I.7); and (3) a condition which is self-sufficient in the sense of being (relative to human kind) one of unimprovable excellence. We cannot enter a better condition if something is added to this one.

The name for this highest good is *eudaimonia*, generally 'happiness' in English translations, though 'well-being' is in some ways a better term (Norman, 1983: 39-40). 'Happiness' often suggests experiences (mental states) of joy, content-ment, or pleasure (for an excellent discussion see Kekes, 1982). Mill went so far as to identify happiness with pleasure:

> By happiness is intended pleasure and the absence of pain (Mill, 1971: 194).

And the mental state approach to happiness is apparently what Hobbes had in mind when, in the 17th century, gunning for Aristotle, he remarked that:

> the felicity of this life, consisteth not in the repose of a mind satisfied. For there is no such *finis ultimus*, (utmost aim), nor *summum bonum*, (greatest good), as is spoken of in the books of the old moral philosophers (Raphael, 1969: I, 32).

But *eudaimonia* is not a state of mind; it is a condition of the person which yields a state of mind. If you are '*eudaimon*', that is if you possess *eudaimonia*, then joy, contentment, and pleasure will be yours. That is not, however, what *eudaimonia* consists in.

As a translation 'well-being' has the merit, (1) of suggesting (or of allowing the suggestion of) an objective condition of flourishing and, (2) of avoiding the idea that Aristotle is talking merely about a state of feeling. This idea of an objective condition of flourishing demarcates Aristotle's ethical theory from the not uncommon utilitarian idea of well-being welfare as the satisfaction of wants and preferences. Even 'well-being' can entangle our footsteps, if we fail to remember that we have moved on from utilitarianism. I use it, however, as the best term available.

Aristotle expects readier agreement than perhaps we should anticipate that there is such a human good. But he accepts that its nature is disputed. There is agreement on name, disagreement in substance. Though every normal person regards well-being as intrinsically choiceworthy, the substantive goal of action is what *seems* intrinsically choiceworthy – pleasure, honour, wealth and so on (NE, I.1 and I.5). Only in the *spoudaios*, the man who has 'got it right', will the real and the apparent good coincide (NE, III.4).

Aristotle's positive task is to give us his own account of well-being, as clear and coherent as may be, and to convince us that this account is reasonably full and correct. He warns us, as F.H. Peters renders the passage in his graceful translation, that we 'must be content if we can attain to so much precision in our statement as the subject before us admits of; for the same degree of accuracy is no more to be expected in all kinds of reasoning than in all kinds of handicraft' (NE, I.3 Peters, 1906: 3; see further Hardie, 1980: ch. 3). This marks a strong disagreement with Plato (R, VI.504A-505A).

Aristotle's second assumption is that in specifying the human good we are to pay particular heed to two features of human beings. These features are mind and character: (1) intellectual condition and (2) condition of desire and emotion.

24.2.2. The intellectual virtues

We have a range of intellectual skills and proficiencies capable of excellence of development:

• art	skill or know-how (*techne*)
• science	demonstrative knowledge of the necessary and timeless (*episteme*)
• practical wisdom	intelligence in the conduct of life (*phronesis*)
• speculative wisdom	the union of intuitive reason and science (*sophia*)
• intuitive reason	knowledge of first principles from which science proceeds (*nous*)

These skills and proficiencies in their fully developed state of excellence make up the intellectual virtues: conditions of the person in which truth is possessed or knowledge embodied. Aristotle's phrase for 'intellectual virtue' is *arete dianoetike*. There is not space here to examine the intellectual virtues adequately. The most evident place for Aristotle's own account is NE, VI, but what he says elsewhere about theoretical knowledge in the *Posterior Analytics* and *Metaphysics*, E.1 is also relevant. The best guide is still, I think, Joachim edited by Rees (Joachim, 1955: 163-218). The main intellectual virtue for our purposes is *phronesis*, practical wisdom, which I have followed Nidditch in calling 'intelligence in the conduct of life' (Nidditch, 1970: 3).

24.2.3. Phronesis and the mean

If you possess *phronesis* or practical wisdom then you know what is choice-worthy; you understand the need to observe the mean. This intellectual excellence is also situationally specific. It expresses itself, in any situation for action, in the perception (*aisthesis*) of the *phronimos* (the man of practical wisdom) into the mean (*meson, mesotes*) (NE, II.6; see also II.9; and Woods, 1986). This doctrine of the mean clearly blocks our way into Aristotle until we have understood it.

The idea of a mean was not unique to Aristotle. We find it among the Pythagoreans. Nor in Aristotle himself is it peculiar to his ethics. It features in his medical theories, in his account of sense perception, and in his political discussions.

Very roughly what the man of practical wisdom discerns is what we should exhibit if, for the full range of emotions, (1) we were not subject to excess or defect and (2) we were free from corresponding extremes of desire. For example:

Defect	**Mean**	**Excess**
Cowardice	Courage	Foolhardiness
Insensibility	Temperance	Licentiousness
Illiberality	Liberality	Prodigality
Meanness	Magnificence	Vulgarity
Self-depreciation or irony	Truthfulness	Boastfulness
Boorishness	Wittiness	Buffoonery

The clause about corresponding desires is necessary to make items like wittiness explicable. It is hard to correlate wittiness, or readiness of wit, with an emotion. But a link with desire is easily made: the person who displays ready and decorous wit is fulfilling a desire to give intellectual pleasure by (say) deftly uniting incongruous ideas, while the boor's and the buffoon's desires are less sensitive to the rights and expectations of the audience. And where there is a desire there is an emotion which it produces or from which it derives, even if (as in the case of wittiness) we have no obvious name for this emotion.

Aristotle's full list of ethical virtues runs to eleven items (NE, III-V): (1) courage, (2) temperance, (3) liberality, (4) magnificence, (5) pride or high-mindedness, (6) no name but 'a similar virtue in smaller matters' (F.H. Peters), (7) good temper or gentleness, (8) friendliness or agreeableness, (9) truthfulness, (10) wittiness, and (11) justice. Mention is also made of a quasi-virtue, namely shame (*aidos*), 'a kind of fear of disgrace' (Peters, 1906: 133). Though the list includes items we should not regard as moral virtues, yet courage, temperance, and justice belong on anybody's list. To this extent Aristotle's ethical virtues are our moral virtues.

The man of practical wisdom sees the course of action matching a 'mean' state of emotion and desire. But, to shed misleading associations of the English word, there is nothing mediocre about the mean, which is also in a sense a peak of suitability (NE, II.6).

Since the mean is situationally specific it relates to an individual confronting a unique situation for action. There is no idea that the middle is 'arithmetically' equidistant from excess or defect, a fixed quantum that is one and the same for all agents (NE, II.6). The action that would be suitable, if (say) we felt neither excess nor defect of fear, will vary between different agents. If I am a trained soldier I may choose to attempt the rescue of my comrade – but not if I am faced by innumerable odds. If I am a defenceless civilian the question of an attempted rescue may simply not arise. (See Allan, 1970: 128-30; Field, 1932: 81-8; and Lloyd, 1968: 218-19 for useful points about the mean.)

While it is natural to suggest that the practically wise man's whole range of intellectual excellences may come into play in informing him of the exact circumstances of action, in fact we need to be careful here. On Aristotle's official account, *episteme, sophia* and *nous* have special objects, remote from the sphere of human action. Their objects are things that could not be otherwise – the 'necessary' and 'eternal' (NE, VI.3).

Yet, to slip quickly down a scholarly by-way, Aristotle's terminology is not always exactly tidy. From the text of NE it is clear that the operation of practical wisdom is that of *praktikos nous*. Aristotle talks freely of 'the intuitive reason involved in practical reasonings' (NE, VI.11; Ross, 153); and he offers a dual definition of choice (*proairesis*) as 'desiderative reason' (*orektikos nous*) or 'ratiocinative desire' (*orexis dianoetike*) (NE, VI.2; Ross, 139). None of this is of great philosophical substance; it can, however, be of major nuisance value in your later studies if no one makes clear to you the fluidity of Aristotle's philosophical vocabulary.

I have presented Aristotle as setting forth a moral ideal rather than as laying down a moral criterion. It is, however, clear enough that the doctrine of the mean is Aristotle's contribution to the theory of the moral criterion.

24.2.4. The ethical virtues

Arete ethike, or 'ethical virtue', is Aristotle's term for excellence of character. Caution is needed, however. By the word here rendered 'ethical' Aristotle does really mean just 'relating to character'. We are to see how far his 'ethical virtues' match our 'moral virtues' and not simply identify them as moral virtues courtesy of a traditional English translation.

Aristotle is concerned, then, with states of character. The ethical virtues are at least this; they must also be more than this if they are to be states of excellence of character. The extra element comes out in Aristotle's gnomic formula:

> Virtue, then, is a state of character concerned with choice, lying in a mean, i.e. the mean relative to us, this being determined by a rational

principle, and by that principle by which the man of practical wisdom would determine it (NE, II.6; Ross, 39).

The immediate point is that excellence of character is a disposition to choose the mean. At this point the two aspects of human excellence come together. Possessing practical wisdom among the intellectual virtues you perceive the mean in any situation for action, and being in the right state of character you are also disposed to act accordingly. Your desires, undistorted by excess or defect of emotion, reflect the middle state of whatever emotion is appropriate to your situation. These desires exactly incline you to do what the intelligent conduct of life independently requires. As a normal human being you have the power of choice (*proairesis*) even though your choices are necessitated by your conception of well-being. As practically wise you have the power of correct choice.

I think it is also possible to read off – I take this clue from Wayne Leys (Leys, 1952: 109) – certain goals and relative priorities of action from the possession of the several virtues. Aristotle helps us here when he talks of the considerations that will weigh with the courageous man who, for example, while having some concern for his own life will value the protection of his community and family more (NE, III.6; Ross, 64).

But the priorities are only approximate; and one corollary of this is that (in unAristotelian idiom) values are irreducibly plural. There is no single consideration that the courageous man has in view. The plurality of values carries a matching complexity into practical reasoning, which thus becomes sensitive to diverse and conflicting considerations (Nussbaum, 1986). To cross-connect our discussions, this points a firm contrast with ethical monism and makes Aristotle a (kind of) ethical pluralist.

How far the several ethical virtues are interrelated and whether they are capable of producing conflicting demands, is unclear. As Joseph says, 'Aristotle was more interested in the multiplicity of virtues than in the unity of virtue' (Joseph, 1935: 162). Plainly if the several virtues draw us towards competing considerations, the complexity of moral reasoning is correspondingly increased. I suspect, however, that Aristotle thought the different virtues coherent in their demands. When in NE, V he talks of the 'exercise of complete virtue' (NE, V.1; Ross, 108) he appears to be referring to the exercise of all the ethical virtues; and there is no hint of competition between their demands. Cf. Irwin, 1988; T.H. Green, 1899: §255; and Telfer, 1989-90.

We will touch on another feature of Aristotelian practical reasoning when, in chapter 5, we see how the correct choice of action – of action in line with the mean – operates through the so-called practical syllogism (31.1.2). And you might usefully supplement our discussion of moral responsibility in chapter 6 by considering Aristotle's list of cases in which the power to make the right choices none the less fails to produce the right action without blame to the agent (NE, II).

On the ethical virtues, see Hutchinson, 1986: ch. 4.

24.2.5. Eudaimonia and luck

Well-being, *eudaimonia*, to return to our starting point, is a condition of excellence of mind and character: a condition in which we possess and exercise the intellectual and ethical. virtues. Hence Aristotle's famous definition of well-being as 'activity of soul in accordance with virtue' (NE, I.7; Ross, 14). 'Virtue' (or better: 'excellence') renders the Greek term '*arete*'.

If there is a single fully developed state of human excellence, the condition of intellectual and ethical virtue, however, there is a broad variety of inferior states. To the *spoudaios*, the fully excellent man, there stand in contrast the *mochtheros* or *poneros* (NE, III.5), the *akolastos* (NE, VII.3) and, most famously, the *akrates*, the 'incontinent' person displaying weakness of will, who discerns the mean but lacks the character to act on it (NE, VII). The *akrates* will return to view in chapter 5. But you could probably do without the Greek. Simply said, all the types of character in states of excess or defect beyond the mean are varieties of human imperfection. 'For men are good in but one way, but bad in many' (NE, II.6; Ross, 38).

Aristotle tells us, then, what virtues of mind and character we need for well-being. The most realistic of moralists, he does not suppose that excellence of mind and character are sufficient for well-being. We have bodily needs for one thing; and certain virtues, such as liberality (NE, IV.1) and magnificence (NE, IV.2), are clearly dependent on material resources. There is also the question of people's attitudes towards us, a consideration at its most superficial in the kind of response we meet through the accidents of physical appearance. It is not necessary for well-being that I should be as good looking as Rob Lowe. It is, however, fairly important not be quite so ugly as Quasimodo (NE, I.8; Ross, 17).

In all this, Aristotle departs radically from Plato. In the *Republic* Socrates accepts Glaucon's challenge to prove that moral virtue (justice, *dikaiosyne*) is not only intrinsically choiceworthy but so choiceworthy that in all circumstances the morally virtuous man is *eudaimon*, happy, and in a preferable state to the non-virtuous (R, II; Lee, 103-8). Aristotle makes no such context-neutral claim on behalf of morality. Amid the cruellest and most degrading circumstances (and perhaps far short of these) you are not *eudaimon*, whatever your excellences of mind and character.

Matters take a deeper turn when we note that the acquisition of *phronesis*, or practical wisdom, is dependent on moral education – on training by those who have it already (NE, II.4). Aristotle's idea of the state as educator pervades NE, IV and recurs in *Politics*, VIII. The soundness of this education is particularly important in view of the fixity of developed character in Aristotle's view. Its possibility is complexly dependent on the right civic culture (NE, X.9, cf. VI.8).

When Aristotle says that man is *politikon zoon*, a social or political animal

(*Politics*, I.2; Saunders, 59), this is not a tedious banality about human gregariousness but a controversial claim about the exact conditions for human flourishing, namely the life of a citizen in a *polis* or Greek city-state. The *polis* provides not merely the inescapable conditions for the acquisition of practical wisdom but also, in the activity of law-making, its superlative sphere of exercise. See E. Abbott, 1898: 177-86. For our practical wisdom takes on an extra depth when, beyond the area of personal and family concerns, we use it to help guide the affairs of the *polis*. Practical wisdom becomes *politike* in this wider sphere (NE, VI.8).

How far the scope of morality is confined within the range of the *polis*, so that without political relationship to others one lacks moral relationship as well, is a separate question. The answer is not entirely clear, though the treatment of commercial justice in NE, V tenuously indicates a moral horizon wider than the *polis*.

24.2.6. Eudaimonia: two problems

We now have Aristotle's conception of the best way of life and of the personal qualities it requires – a statement and first analysis. The account of well-being to which all this is answerable is not unproblematic, however. I shall mention two points to which critics have drawn attention. The highlight phrases are:

- inclusive versus dominant end
- the intellectual versus the practical

Inclusive versus dominant end

There is a favourite scholarly crux about *eudaimonia* or well-being. Sometimes Aristotle says or implies that well-being is (seen by everyone as) a single inclusive end. At other times his language suggests a dominant end. These notions are clearly different. On the first conception there is a single, integrated condition that every controllable aspect of one's mind and character has to subserve. The second conception allows stray aspects so long as they do not intervene to mar one's central condition.

The very language of a 'final' or 'highest' end is infected with this ambiguity. Nor does the problem come purely from the infelicities of translation. Ambiguity stares at us in the original Greek. The best discussions of the problem are Hardie, 1968 and 1980; and Ackrill, 1975. But I have to say that in my view the problem is of scholarly rather than deeply philosophical interest. Aristotle wants to know what our best condition of mind and character is; and we have his account. I cannot see that one iota of that account would need to be revised, whichever conception – inclusive or dominant – should turn out best to fit the text or Aristotle's mind. The nearest philosophical question is the plausibility of Aristotle's assumption that there is a single specifiable culmination of human capacities (24.2.1). On this question see B. Williams, 1985: ch. 3.

The intellectual versus the practical

So far we have considered what is certainly Aristotle's main account of well-being in NE, an account to which the virtue of *phronesis* or practical wisdom and the observance of the mean in emotion, desire and action are central. The accent falls acutely on the practical. Before Aristotle ends NE, however, he takes up again the topic of well-being, and offers an apparently contrasting account. According to Book X perfect well-being (*he teleia eudaimonia*) is theoretical activity (*theoretike energeia*). And we may be visited with a suspicion that it is to prepare us for the ultimate and irremediable second-rateness of the practical that, even at the start, Aristotle's full definition of well-being runs: 'human good turns out to be activity of soul in accordance with virtue, and if there are more than one virtue, in accordance with the best and most complete' (NE, I.7; Ross, 14). So what is the best human life? Do the best life and the moral life fail to coincide? Is the best theoretical and contemplative or do emotion, desire, and action play a key role?

The issues are too complex and are laid too deep in Aristotle's metaphysics and philosophy of mind to explore adequately here. I can offer only the following points.

When Aristotle talks of *psuche*, the soul, he means what in one way or another is over and above our material components. Aristotle thinks he finds two parts in the soul, a rational part and a non-rational. The fullest development of the rational part is in the possession and exercise of the intellectual virtues. At the summit of the intellectual virtues, in the contemplation of the necessary and eternal, there is a grade and felt quality of satisfaction which quite eludes us in the practical sphere. The intellectual virtues represent the most perfect development of the best part of ourselves. In this sense the theoretical life (*bios theoretikos*) is superior to the practical. Cf. Defourny, 1977 and Rorty, 1978.

But though genuinely rational we are not purely rational; and our non-rational part, particularly the emotions and desires, needs to be regulated by practical wisdom. Such as we are, with our divided natures, we have to 'go practical'. Practically we can tip the balance in the direction of the *bios theoretikos*, of course, so organizing our lives as to maximize our contemplative activity – even if (to underline the obvious consequence) this downplays morality as linked with the practical.

But there is a further angle on the matter, connected with Aristotle's so-called 'function' argument (27.4.1). If, as we shall see, to be a good member of a kind is to do well the function of that kind, practical rationality is a uniquely human characteristic and has therefore a special claim to be the human function. Aristotle's God, best described as rather strange, is a rational but not a practical being. God is pure thought thinking about pure thought. He does nothing but think, since there is no more perfect activity; and he thinks about nothing but himself, since there is no object more perfect to think about. See Aristotle, *Metaphysics*, Λ; Norman, 1969. The function argument may tip the balance back in favour of the practical.

For a further discussion see Ackrill, 1975; J.M. Cooper, 1975; Dudley, 1982; and Gold, 1977. It is worth noting that for Kant, through his principle of the 'primacy of practical reason', this kind of tension cannot arise between the intellectual and the practical. On Kant see Warnock, 1968.

24.2.7. The doctrine of the mean: critique

The mean is probably Aristotle's most famous ethical doctrine. In its deceptive similarity to such saws of folk wisdom as 'nothing too much' it has an immediate appeal to many. It does have problems, however, some of them serious. For useful discussions see Grant, 1898: 107-8; Hardie, 1980: ch. VII; Joad, 1938: 97-104; Mure, 1964: 106ff; Ross, 1964: 193-7, 204-6; and J.A. Smith, 1911: xv-xvii. Three difficulties are especially worth mentioning. The key words are vacuity, moral gappiness, and awkwardness of fit.

I take the charge of vacuity first and will spend most time on this criticism. We are to act in accordance with the mean, i.e. as we should act if our emotions and desires were neither excessive nor deficient. What measure or test is available by which to determine deficiency or excess? The *phronimos*, the practically wise man, is a living embodiment of the test. The mean is the requirement of action discerned by the practically wise man. But how are we to identify the practically wise man? By his discernment of the mean. The reader spins in a circle, and one which Aristotle seems to recognize (without helping us to break out of it) at the start of NE, VI.

But we can break free. Aristotle's explicit account omits an assumption. The doctrine of the mean is a superstructure; the base, tacitly assumed, is what Oakeshott called 'a traditional manner of behaviour' and Wittgenstein 'a form of life' (Oakeshott, 1991: 60; Wittgenstein, 1958: §23; cf. Beehler, 1978; O'Neill, 1981; and Hare's 'way of life' in 12.2.4). Aristotle is identifying qualities in human beings which would make good Athenian citizens. This is his 'politics of morals' (Cashdollar: 1973, 145-60; Morrall, 1977: ch. IV). He fixes on certain kinds of disposition displayed in regularly recurrent types of situation – the disposition of the courageous man in battle, of the liberal man in easy circumstances, and so on – where correctness of disposition and appropriateness of action are determined by the standards of a traditional way of life. The situational relevance of these standards is what the practically wise man unmysteriously discerns (as in our own day a trained accountant, say, discerns the situational requirements of an audit under British law and commercial practice). Or if there is any mystery it is in need of illumination by cognitive psychology, not philosophy. See further Nyiri, 1988; and Baillie, 1934.

When in other contexts Aristotle tells us to consult ordinary moral views (*ta endoxa*: NE, I.4, VII.1, X.2) this is just what we should expect on the above line of interpretation. Communal *endoxa* are the voices of tradition. When the tradition is silent, or the ordinary moral views are 'vague, ambiguous, apparently contradictory' (Barnes, 1980: 492) then that is the time for an Oakeshottian 'pursuit of intimations' (Oakeshott, 1991: 66-9).

But why follow a tradition, the sceptic asks? But why not read Aristotle and realize that the question is out of place? the commentator replies. Tradition is not, on the Aristotelian view, external to well-being. The *polis*, with its traditional manner of behaviour, is an inescapable condition of human flourishing: 'of poised and proportionate living' (Babbitt, 1931: 125). This is the lost world of Aristotle.

So much for the criticism of vacuity. Next I take that of moral gappiness. The point is often made that Aristotle's list of virtues not only includes items that we should not regard as moral but equally omits several that we should expect to find. There is no mention of benevolence (which is not at all the same thing as the 'generosity' of NE, IV.1). A Christian might find Aristotelian high-mindedness (NE, IV.3) rather at odds with humility. The social context-dependence of Aristotle's ideal is nowhere plainer than in his depiction of the high-minded man, the *megalopsuchos* (see Huby, 1967: 49-50; and Krook, 1959: 69-75). Note this passage:

> ... a slow step is thought proper to the proud man, a deep voice, and a level utterance; for the man who takes few things seriously is not likely to be hurried, nor the man who thinks nothing great to be excited, while a shrill voice and a rapid gait are the results of hurry and excitement (NE, IV.3; Ross, 94).

This seems, however, merely to illustrate the perfectly general dependence of a moral ideal, an ideal of the person, on a conception of a best way of life that will normally go far beyond morality in any narrow sense. Why else will a Christian list of virtues include (say) the theological virtues of I Cor. xiii.13: faith and hope? (Omission is not the only point here for a Christian, of course. As Aquinas saw, the doctrine of the mean seems hardly to apply to the theological virtues. Does it actually make sense to suppose that we could have too much faith in God? Picture a shoulder-tapping devil, 'Nothing too much!' See Aquinas, 1892: I, 191.)

The final criticism I have awkwardly called awkwardness of fit. The point is just this: that the list of Aristotelian mean states looks remarkably artificial when we consider justice and temperance. What are the 'too much' and 'too little' between which just action is intermediate? Aristotle himself says that just action is midway between acting unjustly and being unjustly treated. This is scarcely impressive; the mean nowhere else takes us 'outside' the agent to a consideration of how the agent is treated. And if temperance is 'self-control', then as Ross points out '(t)he only thing that can be opposed to self-control is lack of self-control'. It is hard to resist Ross's comment that 'the main point to be noted here is the breakdown of the doctrine of the mean' (Ross, 1964: 207).

24.2.8. Aristotle, Kant and the utilitarians

No one should suppose that theories of the moral ideal and theories of the moral criterion can be set irreconcilably against one another in a clear line of cleavage inflexibly dividing the history of ethics. Any worthwhile theory of the moral ideal will supply a moral criterion on pain of vacuity in situations for action. We saw how the doctrine of the mean is Aristotle's offering on that score. But the broad contrast remains between two types of ethical theory.

Aristotle, Kant and the utilitarians will reappear in the next chapter: the story continues. For now, extremely briefly before we move on to chapter 4, I want to note some contrasts inexplicit or unmentioned so far. Catch, then, four quick points – tail lights glimpsed before the chapter turns the bend.

(1) In Aristotle well-being is a universal object of wish; everybody wants it. However, not all can have it since there are social and personal preconditions of the kind we noted in 24.2.5; and the availability of the highest human good shrinks even more if we take Aristotle seriously about the superiority of the theoretical life. For Kant the good will is available to the individual agent irrespective of Aristotelian preconditions.

(2) Kant excludes pleasure and the whole sphere of 'the pathological' from any positive moral relevance (22.2.4) but for Aristotle it is a mark of the fully virtuous agent that he takes pleasure in the exercise of virtue (NE, I.8 and II.3). Without too much distortion we can extract from Aristotle four necessary and sufficient conditions for virtuous action: (1) the action is voluntary and chosen by the agent (NE, III); (2) it is done for its own sake (NE, II.4); (3) it results from a firm and stable state of character; and (4) the agent takes pleasure in doing the action. These conditions give a gloss to what it is to exercise practical wisdom and the ethical virtues.

(3) On the utilitarian side the main unstated contrast is that utilitarianism invokes an explicit rule that serves as a decision procedure for ethics -standardly the formula of maximizing the general welfare. For Aristotle any statable rules, beneath the requirement to observe the mean, hold only for the most part (NE, II.7). They are rules of thumb indicating the types of action that normally embody the mean; and no such rules can capture every precise action 'adapted to the situation with a beautiful adequateness, in every detail just right, neither too little nor yet too much, like the petals of a rose' as Bosanquet put it (Bosanquet, 1912: 398). However, unless one is a very rigid rule-utilitarian, one will allow like Aristotle that rules hold only 'for the most part'.

Situationally, of course, the mean is not a rule that we apply but a 'discernible' of practical wisdom. Aristotelian unstatability also marks a contrast with Kant, since the categorical imperative is statable in formulas 1-4.

(4) A further difference between Aristotle and the utilitarians lies in Aristotle's respect for ordinary moral views as against the revisionary aspect of utilitarianism (21.2.9). This respect aligns Aristotle with Kant (22.2.3), though the routes along which they converge are highly different. And there is a non-revisionary *tendency* in Hume, Mill and Sidgwick, in different ways, to think that ordinary moral views approach the utilitarian position (see e.g. Mill, U: ch. 2). One qualification to the Kantian alignment is that Aristotle allows that the ordinary moral views can be vague, ambiguous, apparently contradictory, while Kant (at least in the *Foundations* and at least for the examples he considers) takes ordinary moral views to be clean, pristine and insulated from the troublesome features Aristotle recognizes.

On Kant and Aristotle, see also Friedman, 1981; Swindler, 1975; and Adkins, 1960: 2-3.

CHAPTER 4

The Justification of Moral Judgement

25.1. INTRODUCTION

If we can tell moral judgements apart from non-moral ones (chapter 1), and are told what to do by theories of the moral criterion or what to be by theories of the moral ideal (chapter 2), what validity do moral judgements have? How are moral judgements to be justified, if at all?

In looking at some answers to these questions we take up our third general ethical problem:

• the justification of moral judgement

Attempts to validate moral judgements follow three main routes, by appeal to:

• truth   • naturalism
• rationality

Rationality branches into:

• consistency   • interest or advantage

I examine first the route of truth.

26.1 TRUTH: MORAL REALISM

If some moral judgements are true, they have a high order of validity. Otherwise said, the connection between justification and truth is a powerful one, if we can exploit it on behalf of morality.

Moral realism is precisely a view on which moral judgements can be literally true or false, and some moral judgements are literally true – and (to add to the characterization in 5.1.1) are known to be true by virtue of an independently existing moral reality. I shall set this out in a model of moral realism shortly. For now, just note some contrasts we can already draw.

Moral realism holds, not merely that moral judgements are genuinely propositional and so can be true or false, but that some are true. J.L. Mackie, by contrast, espouses a so-called *error theory* on which moral judgements can indeed be true or false – and they are all false, because (though they are propositional or truth-claiming in logical form) there is no independently existing moral reality by virtue of which they can be true. So they are one and all false (Mackie, 1977: 35, 48-9).

Logical positivism, whether or not associated with emotivism, denies that moral judgements can be true or false. Moral judgements are non-propositional (no matter what their grammatical form) and are thus incapable of truth or falsity. They are exclamatory, optative, imperatival, expressive and elicitory of emotion, or whatever: but, whatever the case, not true or false (26.1.2).

Moral realism and ethical relativism are generally contrasted and taken to be exactly inimical. In fact, however, the relation of relativism to truth is by no means straightforward.

26.1.1. Truth and relativism

The real problem is that 'relativism' is a fuzzy term. I might make an elementary logical point and insist that *if a position is 'relativist' then it must hold that one determinate thing is relative, in some specifiable way, to another.* Where there is relativity, there must be at least a two-term relation. This point is often quite lost on users of the term. Sometimes one encounters talk of 'relativism' in the sense merely of extreme scepticism, a denial that claims in some domain can be objectively grounded.

'Relativism' is a word which covers a multitude of views, some examples of which are as follows:

(1) Truth claims are only probable on given evidence (truth claims are relative to evidence).
(2) Truth claims are specific to domains of discourse (disputes about truth claims are relative to such domains).
(3) All moral judgements contain an implicit reference to the speaker, some other person, a group or certain moral standards (the logical form of moral judgements is person-, group- or standard-relative).
(4) Doing right (being moral) consists in following the norms of one's society (doing right is relative to socially accepted norms). One version of this view is that of 'my station and its duties' (Bradley, 1927: essay 5):
(4.1) Doing right (being moral) consists in fulfilling the requirements of one's social role(s).
(5) Moral judgements are nothing but reflections of a particular economic order of society, conditioned by the mode of production (moral judgements are relative to an economic order: marxism).
(6) Moral judgements are nothing but statements of socially accepted norms of conduct (the truth of moral judgements is relative to the norms they report).
(7) Moral judgements are nothing but expressions of socially accepted norms of conduct (the appropriateness of moral judgements is relative to the norms they express).
(8) Moral judgements are nothing but statements of the feelings and attitudes

of the person making them (the truth of moral judgements is relative to the personal feelings and attitudes they report).

(9) Moral judgements are nothing but expressions of the feelings and attitudes of the person making them (the appropriateness of moral judgements is relative to personal feelings and attitudes).

(10) Accepted norms of conduct vary between societies (the incidence of norms is relative to particular societies: cultural relativism).

It is clear from this list that no simple connection holds between truth and relativism. (I refer in general simply to 'relativism', the limitation to ethical or moral relativism being understood.) Relativism does not as such disallow that judgements, including moral judgements, can be true. Only the 'nothing but' views, namely (5) – (9), necessarily run counter to moral realism with its acceptance of an independently existing moral reality by virtue of which some moral judgements are known to be true.

Relativist views are often quick claims, short on argument. Take the marxist position outlined in (5). Spinning our heads with grand social theory, we might develop this position as follows.

'It is not the consciousness of men that determines their being, but on the contrary it is their social being that determines their consciousness' (Marx, 1976: 3). The material aspect of our lives is socially the determining factor, conditioning all social phenomena from the legal system through to moral and religious beliefs. The key to this material aspect is the mode of production, which analyses out into the forces of production (technology) on the one hand and, on the other, the relations of production (patterns of ownership).

As the forms of production develop, particular patterns of ownership are established which create dominant and subordinate social classes. The dominant class at any given time tends, through its cultural grip, to select (not necessarily self-consciously) the legal arrangements, moral and religious beliefs, and so on, which are functional to its economic status.

But the forces of production develop continuously and necessitate new patterns of ownership. Forces and relations of production fall regularly out of alignment and new patterns of ownership establish themselves with new dominant classes. These recurrent tensions or 'contradictions' between forces and relations of production – the 'dialectical' element in Marx's 'historical and dialectical materialism' – are the engine of history, the key to all fundamental social change.

The logic of history is that eventually only one class will remain, namely the proletariat; and when this happens, in the communist society of the future, under a technology of abundance, economic determinism will end and the era of 'truly human history' will begin. And so we are swept breathlessly along through a theory of history and society.

Yet all that emerges from this for ethics is the bare claim that different moral beliefs are functional to different economic orders of society. Suppose we take 'functional' in this sense: that there can be a particular economic order only if there are certain moral beliefs that legitimate it, alternatively that these moral beliefs are necessary to the stability of the economic order. Beliefs about the wrongness of theft, for instance, might underpin private ownership of the forces of production.

This is not completely obscure and not completely implausible. But it is gloss, not analysis. All the real work of analysis in correlating variations of moral belief precisely with changes in the mode of production, remains to be done. Engels made a start but left a huge task unfinished (Engels, 1878: ch. 9-11). A detailed and convincing marxist sociology of morals is still to seek.

For this reason (and in no way dismissively) I will suspend (5), the marxist option. So the options for relativism, contra realism, are (6) – (9).

26.1.2. Realism contra relativism

How might these views be argued for? A standard argument rests on two considerations (Hallett, 1984: 34-8):

   • disagreement   • intractability

So we have:

(A) Moral disagreement is widespread. There is no moral judgement made by one person or society which is not questioned or rejected by another. (This is a version of view (10) above.)
(B) Moral disputes are intractable. There is no recognized decision procedure by which moral disagreements can be adjudicated.

Therefore the following disjunction or set of possibilities, C:

(C1) There is no independently existing moral reality for us to know.
(C2) If there is an independently existing moral reality it is unknowable by us.
(C3) If there is an independently existing moral reality it is unknown to us.

Therefore the following disjunction, D (a repeat of (6), (7), (8) and (9) above:

(D1) Moral judgements are nothing but statements of socially accepted norms of conduct (the truth of moral judgements is relative to the norms they report).
(D2) Moral judgements are nothing but expressions of socially accepted norms of conduct (the appropriateness of moral judgements is relative to the norms they express).
(D3) Moral judgements are nothing but statements of the feelings and attitudes of the person making them (the truth of moral judgements is relative to the personal feelings and attitudes they report).
(D4) Moral judgements are nothing but expressions of the feelings and attitudes

of the person making them (the appropriateness of moral judgements is relative to personal feelings and attitudes).

One point to pick up from this straightaway is that the argument is simply not deductively valid. There is no plausibility in the claim that the conclusion cannot be false if the premises are true. Anyone might affirm the premises but deny the conclusion without self-contradiction. The conclusion contains terms which do not even figure in the premises. I need not labour the point, which is that if we have any sort of argument here it can only be inductive. The relativist argument would have to be that it is unlikely that the conclusion is false, when the premises are true.

Hallett's response is to deny the truth of premises (A) and (B). In his view the argument against realism overrates the extent of moral disagreement and overplays the intractability of moral disputes. None the less, though he thinks it exaggerated, Hallett cannot deny what Morris Ginsberg calls 'the diversity of morals' (Ginsberg, 1956). Cf. Ladd, 1985.

26.1.3. Relativism contra realism

Let me now move another figure on the chessboard, Gil Harman, who says in effect: given the fact of disagreement and the fact of intractability, what is the inference to the best explanation (Harman, 1977: 3-10)? (You must read Harman for yourself. I am here adapting him to a context of argument different from that of his own presentation of these matters. The idea of inference to the best explanation is essentially that we have some reason to believe what would, if true, best – most simply, economically, etc. – explain a known fact. See Harman, 1965 and Mellor, 1976: 233-4.)

Hallett explains such disagreement and intractability as he recognizes. He appeals to considerations of:

- difficulty
- tied verdicts
- emotional involvement

Moral issues are difficult. They are conceptually involved and entangled with complex and controversial factual (often technical) data (8.1.3). As well, we are often too anxious to pick out a single pre-eminently best course of moral action when really there are only alternatives equally good. Finally, moral issues provoke emotional reactions which are apt to undermine adequate discussion.

How might Harman reply to this? By appeal to economy of explanation. True, he might say, if we *assume* an independently existing moral reality, then disagreement and intractability can be explained. But why make that assumption in the first place? If we start off with disagreement and intractability, the simplest explanation for them is that moral judgements derive from:

- socially accepted norms
- psychological sets

The inference to the best explanation of socially accepted norms and psychological sets in clearly a further problem. But it is clearly open to Harman to suggest that we can explain norms and sets satisfactorily enough without assuming that they are cognitive, i.e. that they embody knowledge of an independently existing moral reality.

Harman's whole approach can be seen as an application of *Occam's Razor: entia non sunt multiplicanda praeter necessitatem*, entities are not to be multiplied unnecessarily. Crudely: do not assume more than you absolutely have to in order to explain something.

But Hallett might counter that when moral judgements are the product of socially accepted norms or psychological sets, we are here presented with irrational ways of 'fixing belief'. He might direct us to C.S. Peirce's classic paper, 'The Fixation of Belief' (Peirce, 1934), with its polemic against (among other things) the methods of:

- tenacity (dogged adherence to congenial beliefs)
- authority (acceptance of established beliefs)

26.1.4. A model of moral realism

This seesaw debate has no obvious end. The attempt to circumvent moral realism by a relativistic appeal to considerations such as disagreement, intractability and simplicity of explanation seems unlikely to clinch the issue.

So the issue of moral realism (the validity of its distinctive claim that some moral judgements are true, and are known to be so, by virtue of an independently existing moral reality) has to be faced directly at some stage. See further Attfield, 1979.

Let us set out the realist position provisionally in a model. Moral realism holds that:

(1) Moral judgements can be literally true or false.
(2) Some moral judgements are literally true.
(3) There is an independently existing moral reality by virtue of which true moral judgements are true.
(4) We can and do know the literal truth of some moral judgements.

The clause concerning 'an independently existing moral reality' indicates that realism is uninterested in attempts to invoke analyticity or meaning-rules, so that e.g. a judgement like 'That is wrong' just means 'I disapprove of that'. In a short morning's work anyone might thus vindicate the truth of moral judgements. Realism is looking for something more ambitious. It is possible that 'ethical absolutism', a term that vaguely floats in ethical discourse, is another name for moral realism. But 'absolutism' can also cover rigorism (22.2.4) and the idea that an action can be *malum in se*, evil in and of itself (33.1.5). A term so willowy is best discarded.

26.1.5. Idealism, anti-realism, realism

Before we examine the model further, I want to tidy up some labels. It is easy to get caught in the toils of a set of oppositions between:

- idealism
- anti-realism
- realism

Realism contrasts with and is to be opposed to both idealism and anti-realism; but the intelligibility of realism is befogged by the unclarity of the contrasting terms.

Idealism

Idealism is primarily a metaphysical thesis about the general character of reality. There are a variety of idealist positions. John Foster usefully distinguishes three (Foster, 1982: 3):

(1) Ultimate reality is wholly mental.
(2) Ultimate reality is wholly non-physical.
(3) The physical world is the logical product of facts about human sense-experience.

Foster himself, for reasons that do not concern us, refers to 'contingent reality' in his formulations of (1) and (2). If (1) is the theory that only my mind exists, then we have solipsism. The standard name for (3) is phenomenalism. And so one might go on.

Anti-realism

Anti-realism is primarily a theory of meaning. Bede Rundle indicates:

> two sharply opposed accounts of meaning. On the one side we have the view that the meaning of a statement, a form of words which can be true or false, must be specifiable in terms not simply of conditions which determine when the statement is true and when it is false, but conditions which we can recognize as obtaining when they do obtain. On the other side is the position which sees no necessity for insisting upon any such connection with knowledge: we specify the meaning of a statement by specifying its truth-conditions, but we must allow the possibility that these truth-conditions should be conceived of independently of what we know or what we can come to know; to know the meaning of P is to know what it is for P to be the case, but whether P is in fact true or not is a matter which might well transcend any human knowledge (Rundle, 1972: 2).

Rundle associates the first position, that of anti-realism, with the contemporary Oxford logician Michael Dummett. The second position, usually attributed to the 19th-century German logician Frege, is realism. The key point here is realism's recognition-transcendence idea of truth; the meaning of a sentence is fixed by its truth-conditions, and those conditions are evidence-transcendent. Anti-realism, by contrast, uses an evidence-relative idea of truth, something quite close to the old idea of warranted assertibility. A side-issue is whether, in contrast to anti-realism, realism has to hold the principle of bivalence that every sentence is determinately either true or false.

Realism

Thus explained by Rundle, realism is a theory of meaning. But it is also, like idealism, a metaphysical position. In its metaphysical aspect it has been well (if briefly) expressed by Edo Pivcevic:

> There is something that exists independently of whether it is thought or talked about (Pivcevic, 1986: 248).

26.1.6. Objections to realism in general

Two attempts may be made to scupper moral realism at the outset. The first is the move that denies coherence to realism as a philosophical theory. If realism is incoherent, *a fortiori* moral realism cannot be valid. The second is the move to tie moral realism to a particular theory of truth, the correspondence theory, and to urge that since the correspondence theory of truth is inadequate, moral realism is vitiated.

I here forego either attempt. I am not persuaded that realism is incoherent. I am not ready to reject the correspondence theory of truth. I do not accept that realism is tied conceptually to the correspondence theory. These are large matters and I must be brief.

On the issue of realism's incoherence I need only point to the immense mass of literature in which the matter is eagerly and acutely debated. Personal views aside, there is no consensus or even a majority view. And if that seems too democratic an angle on a philosophical matter, the following is not: I assume realism's coherence and fix on problems that arise for it on that assumption. If realism should turn out to be incoherent, this would be the final nail in moral realism's coffin. But it would not invalidate the specific critique of moral realism to be examined here. (On the possible incoherence of realism, see Grayling, 1987 and 1991-2.)

26.1.7. Problems of moral realism

According to the correspondence theory, a sentence, statement, proposition or belief (all possible 'truth-bearers') is true if and only if (on different formulations) it corresponds to a fact, to the facts, to a state of affairs, to how the world is, or to reality (all possible truth-makers). The theory attracts two standard objections.

The first is that the only way we have of identifying facts is through the use of sentences or statements: e.g. statements are true if they correspond to the facts but facts can only be identified by means of true statements. The other objection is that the crucial relationship of 'correspondence' is vague. Is there to be a structural correspondence by which the components of a statement relate to the components of a state of affairs? (On Wittgenstein's early 'picture theory' of meaning a sentence has a diagram- or map-like relationship to the facts which it represents.) If not, how is the relationship of correspondence to be understood?

It is not clear how far these objections rely on particular versions of the correspondence theory. But there is at least a strong case for regarding Tarski's theory of truth as a correspondence theory (Jennings, 1987); and it appears to escape the above objections. There is little risk in saying that Tarski's theory is of reputable current standing.

Tarski's theory of truth runs into great technicality (see Platts, 1979: ch. 1, itself only a simplified statement). The quick version is as follows. Sentences (which are linguistic entities) have parts or elements; and the semantic value, the meaning, of the sentence is fixed by the semantic values of these elements together with their structure within the sentence. The truth of the sentence depends on its satisfaction by a sequence (of non-linguistic entities). A sequence is an ordered set of objects. Take the sentence, 'x is black', represented by 'Bx″', along with the sequence:

<Nelson's Column, the pencil in my hand, Alpha Centauri ...>

The superscript in 'Bx″' indicates that 'x' is to be paired with the second object in the sequence, namely the pencil in my hand. In this case 'Bx″' is true if and only if the pencil in my hand satisfies the description, 'is black'.

The problem for some versions of the correspondence theory, of being able to specify facts only via sentences or statements of which the truth is assumed, does not here arise. Facts are not invoked; sequences are simply ordered sets of objects.

Equally, addressing the other problem found in the correspondence theory, there is an explicit structural relation between the elements of a sentence or statement and the order of objects in a sequence.

I see no reason why moral realism cannot run on Tarski's theory; and no reason to reject Tarski's theory as obviously inadequate for a theory of truth (but cf. O'Connor, 1975). There are, as well, other theories of truth besides the correspondence theory: the coherence theory, for instance, for which truth is a relation of coherence (i.e. consistency plus mutual entailment) within a system of sentences, statements, etc. On the coherence theory see Joachim, 1906; Rescher, 1973; and Haack, 1975. If the correspondence theory should prove finally untenable, moral realism might yet find a theory on which to base itself.

In the assessment of moral realism there are many points we could consider. I settle for three major headings of comment:

- the metaphysics of moral realism
- the moral psychology of moral realism
- the epistemology of moral realism

I shall take Platts, 1979: ch. 10 (reprinted in Sayre-McCord, 1988: 282-300) as a model for moral realism. But I need to add a word of justification. Platts wrote in 1979 and moral realism has been much discussed since then. Crudely put, the debate has moved on. Yet Platts' work has a certain classic status. Not only is it widely referred to, but also it represents a specially full-bodied version of moral realism.

Granted: if we pare down moral realism to the two claims in 5.1.1 that moral judgements can be literally true or false and that some moral judgements are literally true, we are not thereby committed to the view that true moral judgements are true by virtue of an independently existing moral reality. Free from that commitment, moral realism can unzip new possibilities. Many of these are explored in Sayre-McCord, 1988: see also Scaltsas, 1989. In my view, however, it is Platts' kind of position, the 'full-bodied' position as I call it, for which 'moral realism' has traditionally stood. On this basis I keep to Platts; in your further reading you should ignore any such restriction.

26.1.8. The metaphysics of moral realism

Under this heading I will examine:

- supervenience

Supervenience

Tarski gives moral realism a respectable theory of truth. But can moral realism make convincing use of it? Take the following moral judgement:

'Kim's action was unfair.'

Tarksi-wise an object, Kim's action, satisfies the description 'is unfair', if and only if that object, Kim's action, is unfair. Truth, as we know, requires satisfaction by a sequence. Say:

<Nelson's Column, Kim's action, Alpha Centauri ...>

If the relevant object in the sequence, here the second object, Kim's action, satisfies the description, i.e. has the moral property of unfairness, then the judgement 'Kim's action was unfair' is true. For convenience I omit exact time-references, multiple Kims in the world, and so on, which affect nothing of principle.

Nothing appears to block the possibility of literal truth. But there are real problems in attributing moral properties to objects. One of these concerns supervenience, our present topic.

Kim's action cannot have barely the moral property of being unfair. It cannot have literally that one property and no other. Then in what relation does that property stand to the other properties which his action also has – e.g., of being done on 9 July, of taking place at 14.40 hours, etc.? Call these other properties non-moral, descriptive or (with G.E. Moore) natural. 'Supervenience' is the usual term for the relation of moral properties to other properties.

Suppose the following claims are true:

(1) Moral (and all evaluative) properties are supervenient on non-moral, descriptive or natural properties. (I will talk of 'descriptive' properties for short.)
(2) No two things (persons, actions, institutions, practices, policies or whatever) exactly similar in all their descriptive properties can differ solely in their moral properties.
(3) Moral properties are not identical with descriptive properties.
(4) In moral knowledge we do not (which I think means 'cannot') infer the presence of moral properties from the presence of descriptive properties.

(1) and (2) appear to be incontrovertible. For realism, moral properties are autonomous in respects (3) and (4) (Platts, 1979: 244-5). In regard to (4) Platts cites the aesthetic parallel of seeing a face in a collection of dots; we do not and, I guess, in any sense relevant to aesthetic perception, cannot, infer the presence of the face.

Blackburn, 1971 argues for the incompatibility of (2) and (4). The tension arises as follows. If, according to (4), the unjustness of Kim's action is not inferable from its descriptive properties, then something's having particular moral properties is not entailed by its having certain descriptive properties. So why can Kim's action not have the same descriptive properties as Kieran's but with the moral difference that Kieran's action is fair? But that possibility, derived from (4), clashes with (2).

Ian McFetridge offers probably the most sophisticated discussion of Blackburn's paper (McFetridge, 1985, but see also Klagge, 1984). Another view stems from J.L. Mackie. On this view an autonomous moral property which (a) cannot exist without descriptive properties, with which (b) it is not identical, and (c) whose presence is not inferable from the presence of descriptive properties, is a metaphysical oddity. See J.L. Mackie, 1977: 38 on 'the argument from queerness'. So far as I know, however, queerness has never prevented anything from existing. So perhaps Mackie's argument is not conclusive.

26.1.9. The moral psychology of moral realism

There are two topics to consider under this heading:

- dilemmas
- action

Dilemmas

What is a moral dilemma and why should the occurrence of moral dilemmas pose a problem for realism? A moral dilemma is an unresolved matter internal to a person. Unlike a moral dispute it does not occur between people. Guttenplan, 1979-80: 75-6 offers a provisional four-part typology of moral dilemmas:

- the resoluble
- the resoluble with remainder
- the uncertain
- the tragic

In the first case, Spiro has (to use my own examples) made two promises of which he cannot keep both. He thinks his situation through and decides that one promise is trivial, the other more serious, and so he resolves without further qualms to keep the serious promise.

In the second case, Spiro again (obviously a martyr of the moral life) has a problem. He is sure that his employer, the wily Kim, is exploiting a monopoly position in the local labour market and paying him an unfairly low rate. Spiro is unsure, however, whether it would be morally correct to compensate himself by practising a gentle degree of fraud.

In the third, Spiro has made two serious promises. He is clear that one is marginally more important than the other. But in failing to keep the less important promise he is visited with compunction. He feels that the situation would be very much better if he could keep both promises and had not to choose between them. Keeping the more important promise, which he has definitely decided to do, still produces a moral loss or disvalue to which he remains sensitive.

In the final case, Spiro is pulled diversely by two dire and equal considerations. He must satisfy one consideration or the other to avoid total moral calamity. But he can detect no relevant difference of moral importance between them and he sees major moral disvalue in what is lost whatever he does.

All these cases are examples of moral dilemmas and of logically distinct types of dilemma. But why should the occurrence of dilemmas pose a problem for moral realism?

The argument is that realism's assumption that moral judgements are (purely) cognitive runs foul of our experience of moral dilemmas: that the 'phenomenology' of moral dilemmas is not as it would be if moral judgements were cognitive.

The point goes that moral dilemmas are asymmetrical to belief conflicts.

The two phenomena fail to mesh in the right way; that is, they do not match as they would match if moral judgements were cognitive. The line of argument is mainly associated with Bernard Williams, 1965 (reprinted in Sayre-McCord, 1988: 41-58).

The kind of failure of fit that Williams has in mind is this. If we start from (non-moral) beliefs, I believe (say) p, q, and r. On reflection, I realize that p and q cannot both be true if r is true. I believe, say, that (p) Harold Wilson was prime minister from 1964 to 1972. I also believe that (q) Harold Wilson and Ted Heath were not prime ministers at the same time. But I further believe that (r) Ted Heath was prime minister in 1971.

Worse belief conflicts can befall middle-aged gentlemen looking back. I check my memories carefully, consult a reference book, write to friends, ring up a radio phone-in programme, and eventually surrender belief (p) for belief (p1) that Harold Wilson was prime minister from 1964 to 1970.

Now, this is not always how belief conflict is resolved. For of course it may be a matter of probability with a lingering doubt about the provisionally rejected belief. But I keep to the sort of case most favourable to Williams' argument.

Belief (p) is now eliminated. Cognitively I simply lose it, whatever subterranean existence it may lead among the mazy penetralia of the subconscious. But in a moral dilemma matters are different. In cases of the resoluble with remainder and the tragic, I accept that there cannot be an overriding requirement of action to do two incompatible things. But, opting for one, I yet regret being unable to do both. I still wish I could have fulfilled the other option too. How can there be this extra feature of regret if moral judgements are (purely) cognitive? There is nothing to match regret in the Wilson/Heath example above.

How troublesome is this argument for the moral realist? No more than a marginal diversion, I should say: for there are different types of moral judgement. What one acts on are practical, prescriptive judgements; what one leaves undone is covered by ideal, desiderative or evaluative judgements. All such judgements may be true; and what one regrets is simply that one is not in a situation in which the dilemma either did not arise or could have been resolved without remainder. What might match in the Wilson/Heath example is irritation that one had to take time out to resolve the belief conflict or sadness at the decay of a once reliable memory.

Action

For realism, moral judgements are (purely) cognitive. They are (and are nothing but) judgements of knowledge or belief about an independently existing moral reality. On just this point there is an argument against it which relies on the assumption that moral judgements necessarily have a motivational influence on our actions. The argument can be set out as follows (adapting Snare, 1975):

(1) Of necessity no (purely) cognitive judgement has any motivational influence on action.

(2) Of necessity all moral judgements have a motivational influence on action.

Therefore:

(3) No moral judgement is (purely) cognitive.

One drawback to this argument is that premise (2) seems no more plausible, in advance of considerable argument, than moral realism itself. It is a strong version of internalism (12.2.3). But then, suppose we relax premise (2). Suppose we say:

(2.1) Contingently all moral judgements have a motivational influence on action.

or

(2.2) Contingently some moral judgements have a motivational influence on action.

Then in response to (2.1) the moral realist can say that its strength in the argument depends on premise (1) and that there is no reason why he should accept premise (1). Again, premise (1) cannot be simply appealed to, but requires strong supportive argument. If we keep premise (1) and add premise (2.2) the realist can reply that true moral judgements, qua cognitive, fall in the class of moral judgements that do not as such have a motivational influence on action but (if we accept the belief-desire model of action explanation) require the extra element of desire. Desire is the relevant contingency.

On the relation of moral realism to action, see Platts, 1979: 255ff.

26.1.10. The epistemology of moral realism

The knowledge relevant to moral realism appears to be propositional knowledge, knowledge-that rather than knowledge-how (in Ryle's celebrated distinction: Ryle, 1949; cf. B. Smith, 1988). Contrast the difference between knowing that a granny knot is a reef-knot crossed the wrong way, which cannot be untied when it is jammed (and knowing precisely what this means, which I do not) and knowing how to tie such a knot. The practical expertise is not guaranteed by the theoretical knowledge.

An aside: Socrates and 'Virtue is Knowledge'

The Socratic slogan, 'Virtue is Knowledge', involves both kinds of knowledge. If you know what justice is then you can formulate the essence of justice in a definition: you know that justice is such-and-such. You have *episteme* or knowledge. Conversely if you cannot formulate the essence of justice then you do not know what justice is and so cannot be just. But Socrates also thinks of the virtues as skills (*technai*). The virtuous person has a moral ability, a skill like that of a doctor, navigator, general, shepherd, shoemaker (the examples vary). Virtue emerges as a master- or supreme *techne*, as directive, and not merely as one skill among others. Plato finally rejected the analogy in *Republic*, Book V. But there are similarities and differences between virtues and skills marked off in earlier dialogues. The crucial differences are that:

(1) the skilful practitioner of an art excels only in a specific activity or set of connected activities, while moral expertise covers all activities; and
(2) virtue can only be used for good ends, but skills can be put to good or bad uses.

This view of the virtues always hesitated between the idea that virtue itself is really and truly and literally a skill and the idea that it is merely like, analogous to, a skill. I have wittingly allowed the hesitation to infect my own language above.

To return: if moral knowledge for moral realism is propositional knowledge, knowledge-that, we require from it an account of the possession of this knowledge.

There are ethical theories for which problems of moral epistemology do not arise. If you hold, on the one hand, that moral judgements serve purely to express and elicit emotion, or that they are imperatives, commands in some way, then what is there to be known? Knowledge is tied to truth; and while an expression of emotion can be authentic it can hardly be true, and the truth or otherwise of a command is a nonsensical notion.

So not every ethical theory needs an epistemology; and, on the other hand, not every theory, needing an epistemology, needs specifically a moral epistemology. If, for instance, you identify moral with descriptive, empirical properties (so that, for example, to be good just is to produce pleasure), well you certainly need an epistemology. You need to know what will produce pleasure. There is no specifically moral knowledge involved and no need in that sense for a moral epistemology.

Questions of moral epistemology became particularly important in ethics when, in the 17th and 18th centuries, epistemology itself, the theory of knowledge, moved centre-stage in philosophy. To encompass the history of ethical justification in one sweep is too crude. But it is not entirely crass to see the central thrust of earlier justification in an attempt to deduce a moral standard – a moral criterion or a moral ideal – from a metaphysical scheme. How can we evaluate morally with metaphysical validity? Ethics went 'transcendental', if I may put it so, and looked to the nature of the universe (Plato, Aristotle, the Stoics) or to the will of God as the ground on which to base morality.

In fact the 'will of God' approach subdivided (see Windelband, 1893: 332). For Aquinas God wills and commands the good because it is good; the good is not good because God wills and commands it. Duns Scotus and William of Occam, by contrast, held that the good is so only because God wills and commands it. Ockham went so far as to say that the moral good might even have been the exact opposite to what it is. The problem is a variant of the so-called Euthyphro dilemma in Plato (*Euthyphro*, esp. 9E-11B; see Mackinnon, 1972). The divergence of viewpoint has implications for moral epistemology:

> Thomas [Aquinas] teaches that God commands the good because it is good, and is recognised as good by his wisdom. For Thomas, therefore, goodness is the necessary consequence and manifestation of the divine wisdom ... [M]orals is a philosophical discipline whose principles are to be known by the 'natural light'. ... With Scotus and Occam, on the contrary, the good cannot be an object of natural knowledge, for it might have been otherwise than it is; it is determined not by reason, but by groundless will (Windelband, 1893: 332-3).

Aquinas has a long account of the use of reason as a road to moral knowledge. But even for him the epistemological question was not centrally important; there was always revelation as well as reason. The epistemological question seized the limelight with the general rise of epistemology in the 17th and 18th centuries.

There are three main epistemological possibilities. If there is moral knowledge, knowledge of the truth of moral judgements, this can be by way of:

- moral sense   • nothing exceptional
- intuition

Moral sense

How are we to know what is morally right or wrong – the truth of principles or the requirements of particular cases? By what sounds like a faculty, namely a 'moral sense', said Lord Shaftesbury and Francis Hutcheson. Hutcheson, for instance, tells us that 'by a superior sense, which I will call a moral one, we approve the actions of others' (Raphael, 1969, I: 263).

When we encounter somebody doing or contemplate ourselves doing a certain action, say then pleasure or pain of a particular kind is aroused, a pleasurable or painful emotion of a specific sort. That emotion correlates with and is caused by the moral property of the action. The occurrence of the emotion reveals the presence of an independently existing moral property by which it is caused and with which it is correlated in a lawlike way. The action is not good or bad because it arouses a particular kind of emotion; rather it arouses a particular kind of emotion because it is good or bad. The parallel is with a litmus test: a substance is not an acid because it turns litmus red. The litmus goes red because the substance is an acid.

This moral correlation is relevant, by the way, to the problem of action for moral realism as set out above (26.1.9). The moral sense theory causally connects knowledge and emotion (and hence desire). The occurrence of knowledge or belief without desire is therefore forestalled.

None the less the theory of moral sense has its critics and its problems – not always quite the same thing. For instance one criticism is really no problem for the theory at all: this is the criticism which, taking the theory to assume literally a moral faculty, pursues the embarrassing consequences of this with glee. If we have a faculty of sight, its organ is the eye. Then do we have a moral eye or perhaps even a moral nose somewhere in our non-physical innards? As noted, to have a moral sense is simply to be susceptible to a particular kind of emotion about which a specific causal story is to be told. A serious point, a genuine problem, lies perhaps elsewhere. The causal correlation on which the theory relies, between an action's have a moral property and its triggering a particular emotion, needs independent verification. Our only knowledge of the alleged cause (the presence of the moral property) is through the supposed effect (the occurrence of the emotion).

I should mention, as a point of historical alert, that Hume appeals to the notion of a moral sense without, in my view, any notion of an objective correlate of the sort that Shaftesbury and Hutcheson assume. But the ambiguity of labels should be a familiar matter by now.

Intuition

For any serious appeal to intuition in ethics we need to know:

(1) What is the differentia of intuitive knowledge; i.e. what is distinctive about this kind of knowledge that marks it off from other kinds?
(2) What types of thing can be intuitively known?
(3) What particular things actually are intuitively known?
(4) How are we to tell genuine cases of intuitive knowledge from cases of mere subjective assurance?

Ethics briefly aside, intuitive knowledge is characterized negatively, indirectly, or metaphorically. Intuition, we are told, is 'non-inferential'; and when we know something intuitively it is 'as if' we were seeing it. Or perhaps in intuition we 'see with the mind's eye'.

To characterize intuition more substantively we have to appeal, I think, (a) to the conceptually self-evident and (b) to the presentationally non-observational. The terms will become plainer if we go to the second and third questions and consider what types of thing can be and what particular things actually are intuitively known (if there are any such). If I were an intuitionist I might claim as self-evident that two parallel lines cannot enclose a Euclidean space.

Or I might claim to have non-observational knowledge that it now seems to me as if I am typing on a word processor: I do not observe this mental state (as I might observe the machine itself) but simply have it. For these particular things intuitively known, the relevant types of thing are geometrical truths and certain mental states.

If we now move back to ethics, I think the main idea of intuition has been that of self-evidence after the manner of mathematical and logical truths. We certainly find an appeal to mathematics in Samuel Clarke (1675-1729). For Clarke certain moral principles are vouchsafed to intuition; they are self-evident just as are certain mathematical principles. In *A Discourse of Natural Religion* Clarke is clear:

> that from the different relations of different persons to one another, there necessarily arises a fitness or unfitness of certain manners of behaviour of some persons towards others: is as manifest, as that the properties which flow from the essences of different mathematical figures, have different congruities or incongruities between themselves (Raphael, 1969, I: 192).

Clarke offers particular moral principles that are 'manifest' in this way. They include endeavouring to promote 'the universal good and welfare of all' and the principles of justice and equity (Raphael, ibid.).

But what have Clarke and similar thinkers to say to our fourth question: how to distinguish genuine cases of intuitive knowledge from cases of mere subjective assurance? If we assume (itself a problematic matter) that there can be intuitive knowledge in general, how are we to know when there is moral intuitive knowledge in particular? Prima facie the appeal to interpersonal assent fails in the moral sphere in the face of the pervasiveness of moral disagreements and the intractability of moral disputes. At best the intuitionist will be hard pressed to come up with a criterion to distinguish genuine intuition from subjective assurance. At worst disagreement and intractability will drive him back into the tussle between Hallett and Harman in which, short of extra considerations, the very existence of moral knowledge, intuitive or other, is in doubt.

On Clarke see Sidgwick, 1967: 179-84 and on intuitionism in general, W.D. Hudson, 1967 and Lucas, 1971. Note that Ross's ethical pluralism (23.1.1) rests on an appeal to intuitive knowledge for which our apprehension of the axioms of Euclidean geometry is supposed to provide a parallel (Ross, 1930: ch. 2 and 1939: ch. 4). For the views of another 18th-century intuitionist besides Clarke, see Bishop Butler (Butler, 1967; Sidgwick, 1967: 191-200 and Sturgeon, 1976).

There is a variant of the intuitionist approach in John Locke. Locke rejected innate ideas but recognized intuition (which occurs in realizing 'the agreement or disagreement of two ideas immediately by themselves, without the intervention of any other'). Demonstration is a special kind of intuition to be found in the passage of thought between the premises and conclusion of a deductively valid argument. The Locke few people know is the Locke who in his *Essay concerning Human Understanding* (1690), the first classic of modern empiricism, projected the ideal of a demonstrative ethics along these lines: *Essay*, III.11.16 and IV.1-3. See also Mattern, 1980: 33-8.

Nothing exceptional

Platts rather misleadingly calls his epistemological position intuitionist (Platts, 1979: 243-7). He is not an intuitionist in Clarke's way. He dons the intuitionist mantle simply to deny that moral knowledge is inferential. Platts believes that we recognize the presence of moral properties directly. How so? The main burden of his discussion is that we arrive at moral knowledge in a perfectly standard empirical manner. 'We detect moral aspects in the same way we detect (nearly all) other aspects: by looking and seeing' (Platts, 1979: 247). He elsewhere says that attention, perception and reflection are the routes to moral no less than to other kinds of empirical knowledge (Platts, 1980: 76).

This is nothing if not a combative attitude. I offer two brief comments. First, if the claim is that moral knowledge is observational, Platts has just the same problem that Hallett faces against Harman. Why does the inference to the best explanation lead us to conclude that we observe independently existing moral properties rather than that we project psychological sets or socially accepted norms (26.1.3)?

Secondly, it is unclear whether Platts assumes a causal theory of moral knowledge on which, if I know that (say) action x is morally wrong, my true belief is caused by x's being morally wrong, or whether some non-causal explanation is assumed. If the account is to be non-causal, Platts needs to be careful in his choice. Perhaps, for instance, my belief that x is morally wrong is 'properly evidenced' by other beliefs, as on Armstrong's reliability theory of knowledge (Armstrong, 1973). But, of course, knowledge involving properly evidenced belief is inferential; and Platts has rejected an inferential account of moral knowledge.

26.1.11. Semi-realism

Moral realism and relativism of the 'nothing but' variety (26.1.1) are opposites. I may just briefly mention, however, an intermediate possibility on which David Wiggins has worked in recent years. Between the poles of a sheer independent moral reality and the bare projection of sets and norms, there is room for a view on which moral properties are real but are not such that they exist quite independently of our feelings and responses. They can be present whether or not any particular person is aware of them, though not independently of all human contribution. As Wiggins puts the point:

It is almost impossible to conceive how human engagement could survive extinction of the idea of values as something that in some serious sense we discover (out there, so to say) in the world. But for the idea of ... discovery ... to subsist it is not necessary that the perception of values should be utterly independent of what human beings are like (Wiggins, 1980: 186).

On these lines a parallel is sometimes drawn between moral and secondary properties (cf. McDowell, 1988 and Wright, 1988). No one supposes that an object is black, independently of human response. But the experience of seeing black is not to be explained in terms of mere personal reaction or social practice. If the objectivity of moral properties could be vindicated on interpersonal grounds as strong as those on which we ascribe secondary properties, many would welcome the result. That there is greater convergence in the ascription of secondary than in that of moral properties might handled on Hallett-style lines. For a look at the possibilities of a valid parallelism between secondary and moral properties, see Wiggins, 1987: 106-7.

Oddly enough, Platts' illustration of seeing a face in a collection of dots (Platts, 1979: 244) is exactly right for just this sort of intermediate position, not for the ambitious realism he in fact espouses.

There is not the space, unfortunately, to examine this third option in greater detail. Wiggins' own account of his developing position, which he tends to label 'cognitivism', can be found in Wiggins, 1987 and 1990-1. Wiggins' work can be hard for a beginner to penetrate: one, because he uses sophistications from the philosophy of language to make his points and, two, because his precise statement of his views is often attuned to professional debates with which the beginner is unfamiliar. Reviews may help to open up Wiggins' work: try Charlton, 1988a and Depaul, 1990.

26.1.12. Logical positivism and ethics

Before we quit moral realism I want to take up one matter which is still apt to find its way into discussions – the idea of a non-propositional ethics.

We have allowed moral realism its assumption that moral judgements can be true or false. They are genuine assertions. If we deny that there is an independently existing moral reality, we can still accept that moral judgements are assertions. The point is just that none of them is true, for there is nothing for these assertions to be true of.

Logical positivism, which found classic expression in A.J. Ayer's *Language, Truth and Logic* (1936: 'LTL' for the rest of this section) was unwilling to allow so much. For logical positivism there is a distinction between grammatical and logical form. Clearly 'Lee should have returned to Sally' has the grammatical form of an assertion. But is it a proposition, where a proposition is something that can be true or false? A proposition can be analytic or synthetic. Roughly, that is, it can be verified in one of two ways. Either we can determine its truth by reference to the definition of its terms ('A vixen is a female fox'), or we need empirical evidence, a basis of observation ('Jim is picking tulips').

Whatever is neither analytic nor synthetic is neither true nor false; and what is neither true nor false is meaningless. It was a short step from this to conclude that moral and aesthetic judgements as well as theological and metaphysical statements were, in the famous slogan, 'neither true nor false but meaningless'. For they appeared neither to answer to observation nor to be true by virtue of the definition of their terms.

Plainly logical positivism has a rather special notion of meaninglessness. Moral judgements are not meaningless in the way that gibberish is; nor are they nonsensical in the manner of 'green quadrilaterals dream furiously'. Some form of emotivism was brought into play to explain what moral judgements positively are if they are neither true nor false, though emotivism can be defended without reference to the verificationist theory of meaning (as in Stevenson, 1944).

Logical positivism is no longer the force it was. Once it sought to relegate other philosophical approaches to history; now logical positivism itself belongs to history. Ayer revised his position; and much of the apparatus on which the theory relied has come under critical scrutiny. Quine is famous for his denial of a tenable distinction between the analytic and the synthetic (Quine, 1953: 20-46); and there are well-known difficulties about the status of the claims of logical positivism itself, many of which seem to be neither analytic nor synthetic.

Logical positivism was nothing absolutely new; it was clearly prefigured in Hume. Hume, EHU, II matches LTL, ch. 1; the analytic/synthetic distinction of LTL, ch. 4 is foreshadowed in Hume, T, I.3.1 and EHU, IV.1. Even the emotivist account of moral judgements in LTL, ch. 6 is anticipated in T, III.1.1. But in the sharpness of its polemical pronouncements logical positivism packed together a diversity of elements in a particularly pungent form; and its impact on ethics was considerable. One way of reading Hare's ethical theory, for instance, is to see it as an attempt to produce a significant ethical theory free from emotivism and the verificationist theory of meaning.

On logical positivism see Foster, 1985: 73-84; Harrison, 1989; Joad, 1950; and Kolakowski, 1972: 203-40.

27.1. RATIONALITY

We continue to discuss possible justifications of morality. But now we take a different angle, that of rationality. This is not to suggest that the concepts of truth and rationality are unrelated; one aspect of rationality is that one resolves 'cognitive dissonance' and does not retain two contradictory beliefs, which cannot both be true. None the less we can talk of practical consistency ('he helped Lee, then he helped Mark in just the same circumstances') or of means-end rationality ('she knew what she wanted and went for it with poise and determination') without invoking the concept of truth.

I take consistency first. I want to consider two attempts to show that immorality – failure to observe the requirements of morality – is irrational because it involves a kind of inconsistency. These attempts belong to:

- Kant
- Nagel

27.1.1. Consistency: Kant

We left Kant in the last chapter when we had examined his doctrine of the categorical imperative. To recap: the good will is the only thing of intrinsic value, and the good will is the moral will. A moral will is a will that acts on the categorical imperative, a principle requiring us (roughly put) to act on consistently universalizable maxims.

The principle of morality is the categorical imperative, the principle of consistent universalizability in the maxims of one's actions is spelt out in Formula 1 and expanded in Formulas 1a-4 (22.2.1). How is the principle of morality to be connected with rational agency?

In what follows I offer a reconstruction of Kant's argument to capture the essential play of his ideas. I shall sit loose to Kant's exact text in the *Foundations* and the *Critique of Practical Reason* so as to describe his basic, distinctive position (as I see it) rapidly with some clarity. For textually more sensitive discussions, see O'Neill, 1989 and Wood, 1976.

(1) A rational agent must be free.
(2) A rational agent must act on a principle determining action for every possible situation.
(3) The principle in (2) must be one on which all rational agents are to act.
(4) Only if an agent is subject to a self-imposed principle can he be free.
(5) Under requirements (2) and (3), the principle of morality is the only possible self-imposed principle for a rational being as such.

What is the pattern of ideas behind this argument? As usual there are a number of assumptions at work. Suppose that determinism is true and that we act of necessity under the causal impact of our beliefs and desires. Kant says that in this case we could give no application to the idea of rational agency; a rational agent would be no different from any other agent. Choice would be subject to external causality under laws of nature for all agents alike.

But (Kant also says) we can make no sense of the idea of rational agency operating independently of law. The rational is the lawlike. Rational agency must act in conformity with law; but for rational agency to be free, as it must be, this lawlike behaviour cannot be imposed on it, else we are back in the grip of external determination which nullifies rational agency.

So we must think of a self-imposed law; the rational agent is self-determining. Then take the rational agent simply as such, i.e. independently of desires and inclinations which vary between different rational agents. The only law that any rational agent, simply as such, will give to himself is the law of acting in a lawlike way. And what is it to act in a lawlike way but to follow the categorical imperative?

There are broadly two manners of positive response to the argument. We might, in the first place, take the coarse structure of the argument as presented and refine it with sub-premises and definitions until no gap remained in our understanding. Alternatively we might take the argument as workably intelligible and go back to Kant's text with the hope of illumination from the reconstructed argument.

What I shall do here, however, is to pose a challenge to Kant on the basis of the argument in hand. For it seems to me (a) that Kant assumes and nowhere proves premise (3) and (b) that even if we grant premise (3) we cannot deduce the principle of morality from it.

I take these points in order. It is clear that Formula 1a of the categorical imperative satisfies premise (3). But it is not at all clear that the premise is one to which a rational agent must subscribe. We have a notion of means-end rationality; it is rational for an agent to take effective means towards his ends. Suppose that (in a society of self-seekers) all agents were to adopt this policy irrespective of the interests of others, it would be collectively self-defeating. Everyone's ends would be more efficiently served if this policy were not universally adopted. This gives a rational agent no reason for abandoning the policy if others abandon it. He continues to get the benefit of pursuing his ends irrespective of the interests of others, without the self-defeatingness that results when everyone else does the same. On this basis it is rational for him to reject premise (3).

So much on point (a). Point (b) is that even if we grant premise (3) we cannot deduce the principle of morality from it. In other words we can imagine all rational agents acting on the same principle without the principle's being the categorical imperative.

Let me start off with an example that Kant might welcome. It is essentially a gloss on the society of self-seekers described just above. Suppose a society of egoists, where an egoist is 'a person who on every occasion and in every respect acts to bring about as much as possible of what he values' (Gauthier, 1974: 442). There are ways of characterizing the behaviour of such a society that produce a Kantian contradiction in the will.

Two members of this society, Ian and Lee, are in a situation of prisoner's dilemma (cf. Gauthier, 1986: 79-80). They have jointly done a crime and have been arrested. Unfortunately for the police, the evidence against them is not conclusive. Confession would be extremely convenient. Accordingly the two prisoners are offered a choice. 'If you confess', the chief inspector says to each of them, 'and the other does not, then you will get one year's imprisonment and he will get ten. If you both confess, you it will be five years for both of you.

If, however, he confesses and you do not, then he will get one year and you'll go down for ten. If neither of you confesses, you will get two years each.'

In a game theory matrix:

		Lee	
		confesses	does not confess
Ian	confesses	5 years each	10 years for Lee 1 year for Ian
	does not confess	10 years for Ian 1 year for Lee	2 years each

On a minimal interpretation an egoist is an agent who goes for (what he or she takes to be) the best option, the most beneficial outcome to himself or herself. A fuller characterization is given in 28.1. What primarily calls for emphasis now is that Ian and Lee certainly are not, on any characterization, *rational* egoists. For the rational agent is one who follows 'the situational logic' (Popper, 1945: II, 97), which here includes for each agent a recognition of the strategy open to the other. Each acts irrespective of the strategy open to the other, and the result is collectively self-defeating. Ian and Lee both opt for the policy of confession since this yields, *in abstracto*, the best possible outcome. The all too concrete result is that they both get five years imprisonment when a better result was available. Kant might chime in with the comment that no rational agent could will the universalization of this policy for obvious reasons.

But (to repeat) Ian and Lee, so far from being rational egoists, are dim self-seekers. (For those of a literary turn, the logic of their strategies is deftly dissected in Montesquieu's parable of the Troglodytes (L.10 of *Persian Letters*, 1721).) Rational egoists plainly opt for joint non-confession (on the simplifying assumption that each knows that the same options are available to the other). A rational egoist does not consider the interests of other people unless the promotion of their interests is included in what he values. There is no need for rational egoists, acting on a consistently universalizable maxim in situations of prisoner's dilemma, the principle of co-operating for mutual advantage, to observe the principle of morality in its second formulation: 'Treat humanity whether in your own person or in that of another always as an end and never as means merely.'

Clearly this challenge to Kant relies on using both Formula 1 and Formula 2 for the principle of morality. You may want to try uncoupling the two formulas and running Kant's argument on only one formula. For a different approach, see Walker, 1988.

27.2.1. Consistency: Nagel

Kant aims to show that a rational agent must accept the principle of morality as defined by the categorical imperative. There is an inconsistency between being rational and acting immorally. The present-day American philosopher, Thomas Nagel, argues in *The Possibility of Altruism* (1970) for a different inconsistency. Take the principle that all reasons for acting are reasons for promoting objectively valuable states of affairs, states of affairs valuable for everyone. This marks a constraint of rationality; it is a rational principle. It also marks a constraint of morality. For it holds that my reasons for promoting certain states of affairs are no less reasons for promoting them if you are the beneficiary than if I am. Since morality requires me to consider the interests of others, judged in terms of states of affairs valuable for them, the principle is also a moral principle. So we have a new link between rationality and morality; and Nagel's claim is that we can deny his principle only on pain of *practical solipsism*, a denial that each of us is merely one person among others equally real. Since we (presumably) do recognize that each of us is merely one person among others equally real, it is inconsistent not to accept the principle.

This is a large claim, which has attracted sharp critical discussion. It is also a claim which is encased in a set of technical terms. These have to be explained before we can get a proper grip on Nagel's argument.

Nagel's basic distinction is between *subjective* and *objective reasons* for acting. A reason for acting can be explained in terms of 'a predicate R, such that for all persons p and events A, if R is true of A, then p has prima facie reason to promote A' (Nagel, 1970: 90). More simply, part of what it is to have a reason for acting is to have a reason for promoting some event or state of affairs. A reason for acting is subjective is its specification refers back to the speaker. This occurs in, for example, the practical judgement 'I have a reason to promote A', 'A is what I want'. Objective reasons are person-neutral in respect of the speaker: e.g. 'A will be to somebody's advantage', or 'A will help Geoffrey Thomas'. You might make that last practical judgement, or I might. The standpoint is impersonal.

Practical judgements from a personal standpoint, those involving subjective reasons for action, have *motivational content*. This means roughly the following. If my practical judgement is (say) 'I have a reason to do A', then my very acceptance of that judgement is sufficient to explain my doing the action or desiring to do it and to justify the action or desire from a personal standpoint, to make it valuable for me.

Nagel's argument proceeds in three steps:

(1) Any practical judgement assertable from a personal standpoint must be assertable, with the same content, from an impersonal standpoint. In other words, all reasons are objective reasons since subjective reasons are assertable from an impersonal standpoint.

(2) Practical judgements from a personal standpoint have motivational content.

---

(3) Practical judgements from an impersonal standpoint have motivational content.

Otherwise said, if I accept a personal practical judgement, 'I have a reason to do A', this is assertable with identical content (according to (1)) in an impersonal practical judgement, 'Geoffrey Thomas has a reason to do A'. Since the personal practical judgement (according to (2)) has motivational content for me, the impersonal practical judgement 'Geoffrey Thomas has a reason to do A' must equally have motivational content for you. And 'you' are indefinitely pluralizable; that impersonal practical judgement must have motivational content for everyone. (In this sense my doing A is a state of affairs valuable for everyone.)

According to Nagel, since (3) follows from (1) and (2), the only way to resist (3) is by denying (1) or (2). But Nagel takes (2) to be incontrovertible, as informing our very understanding of the kind of thing a subjective reason is; while to deny (1) is to commit oneself to practical solipsism. And Nagel would be right if (in the example) you denied (1) inconsistently: that is, if you were to allow that your own personal practical judgements are assertable with identical content from an impersonal standpoint but do not allow the same for my personal practical judgements. For in that case you would hold that you possess a feature which I lack, the feature that your personal practical judgements are, but mine are not, assertable with identical content from an impersonal standpoint.

A clarification is due before we continue. When Nagel says that personal and impersonal practical judgements must have motivational content he does not mean that these judgements must have equal influence (Sturgeon, 1974: 382). His point is simply that they must equally have influence.

In exploring Nagel further you will get most help from Darwall, 1974 and 1983, and Sturgeon, 1974.

My own view is that (3) fails. It does not follow from (1) and (2). For me to make a personal practical judgement, with motivational content, is to regard myself as having a justifying reason for doing A. Impersonally this simply goes across as 'Someone regards himself as justified in doing A, so that doing A is valuable for him in the sense of being valued by him.' I am not committed to his being justified. I may even regard the doing of A-type actions as unjustifiable by my own moral values and moral standard.

27.3.1. Interest: utilitarianism

We have now to move on to consider a further attempt to justify moral judgements by appeal to rationality, but an appeal not to *consistency* but to *interest or advantage*. Several such approaches are available. My discussion will centre on just two of these:

- utilitarianism   • Aristotle

These two approaches are not merely different in detail; they are of logically distinct types. I consider utilitarianism first; Aristotle will be taken up in 27.4.1.

The utilitarian justification of morality is through means-end rationality. Morality is a piece of social technology to promote the occurrence of intrinsically valuable states of affairs.

We readily see how this picture emerges. Utilitarianism starts off from an *axiological*, not an ethical position. Axiology is the theory of value; and utilitarianism assumes that there are intrinsically valuable states of affairs – states of the world or states of mind. Experiences of pleasure were the early candidates for these states (Bentham, J.S. Mill: recall Mill on higher and lower pleasures (21.2.2)).

With this axiological position in place, morality is then brought into the picture. Utilitarianism is a *teleological* ethical theory; it sets morality a goal. That goal is to maximize the occurrence of intrinsically valuable states of affairs. And by relation to this single consideration we can assess actions morally as permissible, obligatory or forbidden.

27.3.2. Assessment of utilitarianism

Utilitarianism has attracted huge attention since its first systematic exposition by Bentham; and the theory itself has changed significantly over time (21.2.2). But there are three areas of recurrent comment:

- axiological foundations of the moral criterion
- utilitarianism's 'economic' model of the moral life
- dualism of practical reason

Axiological foundations of the moral criterion

One immediately pressing question is the following. Utilitarianism invokes means-end or 'technical' rationality: morality is the means, the end is the promotion of intrinsically valuable states of affairs. What is the rational status of the end? Can the relevant intrinsic values be known or otherwise rationally believed in? Is there an independently existing *axiological reality* to match the kind of moral reality that moral realism assumes? Along this line we encounter counterparts in the theory of value to the metaphysical and epistemological problems we met with in moral realism.

Does a belief in intrinsic values have to presuppose such a reality? No, because there is a subjective approach on which 'value is valuing'. On this approach something has intrinsic value for a person at a time if, at that time, that person desires that thing in itself and for its own sake, not as a means to anything else. That is a perfectly workable idea of intrinsic value as long as we know that it is a subjective theory which is on offer.

To deviate briefly, there is no reason why, on this subjectivist approach, a loopback cannot occur between ethics and axiology. Once there is an institution of morality, this can inform our intrinsic values. I can come to value morality intrinsically. J.S. Mill saw just such a possibility in U, ch. 4:

> Whatever may be the opinion of utilitarian moralists as to the original conditions by which virtue is made virtue; however they may believe (as they do) that actions and dispositions are only virtuous because they promote another end than virtue; yet this being granted, and it having been decided, from considerations of this description, what *is* virtuous, they not only place virtue at the very head of the things which are good as means to the ultimate end, but they also recognize as a psychological fact the possibility of its being, to the individual, a good in itself, without looking to any end beyond it; and hold, that the mind is not in a right state, not in a state conformable to Utility, not in the state most conducive to the general happiness, unless it does love virtue in this manner – as a thing desirable in itself, even although, in the individual instance, it should not produce those other desirable consequences which it tends to produce, and on account of which it is held to be virtue (Mill, 1971: 221-2).

But to return: a utilitarian might hold that, *faute de mieux*, his theory is to run on subjective valuings. 'One man's meat is another man's poison'; 'There is no accounting for tastes.' Everyone values certain things intrinsically; and the aim is, through social action, to maximize the realization of precisely such things. What more cogent idea do we have of the human good than one that recognizes what people intrinsically value? We have no grounds for appealing beyond that idea and no better task to set morality than that of promoting the human good so taken. How thoroughly is the subjective view to be pressed, though?

A subjective approach can still find room for something like Mill's distinction between higher and lower pleasures – higher and lower intrinsic valuings – as long as this does not exceed the claim that the 'higher' valuings will be preferred if they are experienced; there can be no appeal to preferability independent of people's responses.

A more serious matter is utilitarianism's apparent indifference to the processes by which valuations are formed (Brooks, 1987-8). These processes may be of interest from an ideological angle; a marxist will tell a story about the part played by social mystification in the causation of preferences, desires, actions and attitudes. But there are other considerations too, which centre on the broad notion of rational desire.

As tricky as that notion is, we might give sense to the idea of irrational desire in terms of desires which rest on errors of calculation or reasoning or in terms of desires which we would disavow if we considered them carefully in the light of all relevant propositions of which the truth is known to us (see Shope, 1978). How might these possibilities apply to intrinsic desires?

Perhaps the question can be reset usefully as follows. When we have an intrinsic desire we 'just want' something in itself and for its own sake. But we cannot 'just want' something in another sense. There must be some description under which we want it. We must be able to offer a 'desirability characterization', in Anscombe's phrase (Anscombe, 1957: 66ff.). Then the question is: if errors of the above two sorts enter into the process by which a desirability characterization is formed, does that automatically reduce the relevant desire to instrumental status? I should say not, unless all such errors are of a means-end kind. But not all errors of reasoning, say, are of this kind. I conclude tentatively that the possibility of these errors yields an intelligible notion of irrational intrinsic desire.

If questions of irrational desire worry you, then you may also be worried by utilitarianism's seeming indifference to them. There could be a general utilitarian case for rationality – that the general welfare is not maximized unless we are rational. But it is not clear what utilitarian implications that consideration holds for the satisfaction of given irrational desires, 'here and now' irrational desires that people actually have.

Utilitarianism's 'economic' model of the moral life

Utilitarianism seems to many to have a consumption-based view of morality. So far as possible I am to produce or promote, and you are to consume, intrinsically valuable states of affairs, and vice versa. This seems a highly transactional, impersonal view. Against this 'economic' style of ethics a contrast is often made with:

> a much older tradition, going back to Aristotle and finding its most powerful expression in the writings of the young Marx, according to which creative, productive, rational *activity* is the good for men. Consumption is essential to life; its gratifications form a component of the good life when properly integrated into a healthy and well-ordered psyche. But consumption is not, and cannot be, the end for man. For Marx ... labour of the right sort is an indispensable element of the good life (R.P. Wolff, quoted by Watt, 1988: 6).

This sounds deep and *is* interesting. I am not myself sure how fair this criticism is, however. I do not think it raises any objection of principle to utilitarianism since, as we noted in our first discussion, utilitarianism can allow actions and, by extension here, forms of activity to have intrinsic value. It should also be pointed out that this theory assumes an objective theory of the human good, as is clear from such laden terms as 'healthy and well-ordered', whereas we are currently running utilitarianism on a more subjective basis. To change that basis you need to consider how far you want to depart from it. By recognizing a notion of irrational desire? By espousing an objective theory of the human good, testable by what criteria? See further: Goodman, 1975: Part I.

Dualism of practical reason

For utilitarianism morality is social technology. It is an institution whose rationale is to maximize the general welfare, however construed. The problem is to see how moral considerations, so taken, give the rational individual good reasons for acting morally. For there is no benign and simple general relationship between general and individual welfare. Along these lines the 19th-century utilitarian, Henry Sidgwick, spoke of the 'Dualism of Practical Reason' (Sidgwick, 1907: 404).

There is a rational force of self-interest:

> ... it is surely the business of Ethical Philosophy to find and make explicit the rational ground of such action [the subordination of Self-Interest to Duty]. I therefore set myself to examine methodically the relation of Interest to Duty ... This investigation led me to feel very strongly this opposition ... I put to [Mill] in my mind the dilemma: Either it is for my own happiness or it is not. If not, why [should I do it]? (Sidgwick, 1907: xvi).

But there is also the rational force of an impersonal point of view. Sidgwick thought it self-evident, that we knew by intuition, that pleasure is the sole intrinsic good. He thought it also self-evident, but a separate point, that we should promote that good. He thought finally that if pleasure is self-evidently good it is equally self-evident that there should be fairness in its distribution. If pleasure is intrinsically good then the experience of pleasure is to be promoted irrespective of whose pleasure it is. These 'shoulds' are not moral 'shoulds' – they represent rational requirements on action. If pleasure is an intrinsic good it logically cannot matter, Sidgwick might say, whose good it is.

This is the dualism of practical reason. On the side of 'Interest' there is a connection between rationality and self-interest; it is never irrational to act from self-interest. But on the side of 'Duty' an impersonal standpoint is also rational. There is no apparent necessity for these two standpoints to coincide in their requirements for action. See further Frankena, 1974b.

The problem haunted Sidgwick, who even (agnostic though he was) pursued the possibilities of an afterlife in which 'Duty' would be rewarded and so 'Interest' be satisfied after all. Bentham had glimpsed the problem but had handled it more robustly. Of course the general and the individual interest can in principle conflict; and the task of the legislator is to apply 'sanctions' so that in practice the individual's interest is to promote the general interest.

For utilitarianism Sidgwick's problem survives his particular account of it. If we go back to the subjective utilitarianism with which we started, there is no obvious ground on which your valuings give me a reason for acting. Why should I value your valuings being satisfied? But utilitarian morality as a social institution requires us precisely to value one another's valuings in such a way as to promote the general welfare.

I may add that one can read Derek Parfit's brilliant *Reasons and Persons* (Parfit, 1984) as a defence of utilitarianism which, through a particular account of personal identity, slackens the connection between rationality and self-interest. It is perhaps significant that Parfit is a close student of Sidgwick's work. Two other approaches are worth mentioning. First, one might appeal to a Nagelian impersonal standpoint to render rational the promotion of other people's interests (27.2.1). Or, secondly, in a different direction, one might follow Gauthier. In *Morals by Agreement* (1986) Gauthier makes a subtle, elaborate and profound attempt to derive morality, in the form of altruistic behaviour, from (non-moral) premises of rational choice. The promotion of individual interest, he tries to show, is most efficiently served by the acceptance of constraints that yield altruistic behaviour. The austere rigour and relative technicality of Gauthier's impressive book can prove daunting, however; and the easiest access to his ideas is perhaps through a short, early piece: Gauthier, 1970. You might also try Kavka, 1987.

27.4.1. Interest: Aristotle

Aristotle's approach to the justification of morality appeals neither to Kantian consistency nor to utilitarian means-end rationality. Like the utilitarians, Aristotle links morality with interest or advantage but in his view morality is itself a *component* of the human good, of what is good for a human being, not merely a means to it. Morality is an embodiment of reason, and rationality is the human *ergon* or function. (Cf. Gomez-Lobo, 1989.)

Two things are necessary before we can do justice to this view of morality. In the first place we have to set out Aristotle's connected position; secondly we have to steer our way clear of misunderstanding of his function-talk.

We can reconstruct Aristotle's position, setting out its key points, as follows:

(1) The good-for a member of a kind is to be a good-member-of its kind.
(2) To be a good member of a kind is to do well the function of that kind.
(3) The function of human beings is to exercise reason.
(4) Reason is embodied, but not exclusively, (a) in the exercise of phronesis or practical wisdom and (b) in the exercise of the ethical virtues.
(5) To exercise practical wisdom and the ethical virtues is to be a *good man* (a good member of humankind).
(6) To exercise practical wisdom and the ethical virtues is *good for a man*, i.e. is a component of the good for a human being (from (1) – (5)).
(7) That is, to rephrase it in our original terms, to exercise *phronesis* and the ethical virtues is one component of the human good.

This position is developed against a broad backdrop of assumptions. In the animate world Aristotle believes that we can pick out four capacities or functions: to reproduce and consume, to perceive, to move, and to think (*De Anima*, I.1, II.4, III.9). One kind of living thing, X, is lower than another, Y, iff normal members of X lack a capacity or function possessed by normal members of Y. A capacity is distinctive of a kind iff every normal member of that kind and no normal members of any lower kind have it (*De Anima*, II.2, III.12). On this basis reproduction and consumption are the functions of plants, perception is the function of animals, and thought or 'an activity of soul which follows or implies a rational principle' (NE, I.7; Ross, 13) is that of human beings.

Aristotle's term for capacity or function is *ergon*, which literally means 'work'. One danger in translating ergon by 'function' is that it invites an obvious anti-Aristotelian move. Bodily organs have functions; we speak of the function of the eye or the heart. Artefacts have functions; a clock has a function, so has a spade. Under role-descriptions, 'carpenter', 'tanner' (say), particular human beings have functions. But what plausibility is there, short of theological assumptions, in speaking of a human function *simpliciter*? Aristotle himself encourages the idea that he is thinking along the lines of a human function, in the sense of these examples, when he suggests that it would be strange if the carpenter and tanner had functions but 'man' had none (NE, I.7; Ross, 13. However, Aristotle's basic claim is that human beings have distinctive capacities. Human beings are a natural kind with features that mark them off from other natural kinds. The 'function argument' needs this interpretative gloss. See further Hardie, 1980: 23-4; Hutchinson, 1986: ch. 3; Joachim, 1955: 48-50; and Lloyd, 1968: 212-13.

27.4.2. Assessment of Aristotle

Indefinitely many points of assessment could be taken from a vast critical literature. I will take two points that seem central:

- rationality of emotion and desire   • duty versus interest

Rationality of emotion and desire

Aristotle's view of the rationality of morals clearly depends on his account of practical wisdom and the ethical virtues. An excellence of mind, namely practical wisdom, discerns the mean in situations for action; and excellence of character disposes one to act on one's discernment of the mean. The ethical virtues include at least some of our own moral virtues. So the good man exercises the moral virtues. But is Aristotle's claim that the mean embodies a requirement of *reason* tenable?

A correct condition of emotion and desire is central to Aristotle's account of excellence of character. Can we make sense of the idea of rational emotion or desire? I think we can only on the lines of 27.1.1: irrational emotions and desires are those which rest on errors of calculation or reasoning, alternatively those which we would disavow if we considered them carefully in the light of all relevant propositions of which the truth is known to us. But it is clear enough that Aristotle has something more positive in mind, in thinking of rationality of emotion and desire, than merely that emotion and desire should *not* be irrational in these ways.

I think Richard Norman has it right. Aristotle's positive idea is that emotion and desire can be 'more or less appropriate to the situation' (Norman, 1983: 52). But appropriate by what standard? In the end we have to go back to my idea of a tradition. There is a traditional manner of behaviour the situational requirements of which the *phronimos*, the man of practical wisdom, recognizes. In Aristotle's picture the *phronimos* is also the man of excellent character whose emotions and desires enable him to act accordingly.

Aristotle offers a complex and sophisticated view of morality in these terms but its grounding precisely in *rationality* seems far to seek.

Duty versus interest

In general terms we can quite see how for Aristotle there can be a conflict between *duty* and *inclination*. If (say) justice requires me to act in a certain way, and I discern this through practical wisdom, still I may lack sufficient inclination to act accordingly. If so I exhibit *akrasia* or weakness of will. It is much less clear that Aristotle can accommodate what has seemed to many a permanent feature of morality – the possibility of a clash between the requirements of morality ('*duty*', for short) and my own *interest* or well-being. This takes us back to Sidgwick's 'dualism of practical reason' (27.3.2). Persons whose 'moral' activity always ties in with their own interest are unlikely to be seen as saints or heroes of the moral life. Morality at times surely requires self-sacrifice?

In my view Aristotle tries to allow the possibility of self-sacrifice. Courage figures in his list of virtues; and self-sacrifice is something for which courage may plainly call (NE, III.6-9). But now we run straight into a problem – a paradox, no less. The exercise of moral virtue is a proper part of human well-being. But this exercise can literally kill us. Where is the human good in being dead? At the very least morality, like smoking, can seriously damage your health.

We may put the problem in terms of (1) – (7) above. The good man, in the sense of the man who is a good member of humankind, exercises the moral virtues. But where is the necessary match between the *good man* in this sense and the *good for man*? The good for man is hardly served by the loss of life that the good man incurs.

I am not fully clear on the best way for Aristotle to handle this problem, which is clearly a crux for him. I suggest the following strategy. Exercise of the moral virtues is a part of the human good; we cannot flourish without the moral virtues. But flourishing, though preferable, is not absolutely safe. Human flourishing is not the central aim of the universe; and we simply have to accept as a surd element in human life the practical paradox of risky flourishing. Given our cosmic environment the very characteristics by which we normally flourish can occasionally defeat us. Courageous death exactly illustrates this general and ineluctable truth.

For a good discussion on different lines, see Wilkes, 1978a.

28.1. NATURALISM

There is a standard sense of 'moral' in which to act morally is to act with some regard to the interests of others. Moral action cannot be egoistic action. When I act egoistically, i.e. solely from self-interest, I:

(a) go for (what I take to be) the best option, the most beneficial outcome to myself, and
(b) ignore any benefit to others or omit all consideration of their interests, or
(c) foresee merely accidental benefit to them, or
(d) aim to benefit others purely instrumentally to my own advantage

So egoism is (a) plus (b), or – since (b) excludes both (c) and (d) – (a) plus (c) or (d).

By contrast, to the extent to which I act altruistically, benefit to another is essential to what I intend, not accidental; and intrinsic to what I intend, not instrumental. There is no necessary incompatibility between the requirements of self-interest and those of altruism. To act self-interestedly is to act non-accidentally and non-instrumentally for one's own advantage, and my motivation can be both self-interested and altruistic since one and the same state of affairs might beckon to benefit non-accidentally and non-instrumentally both myself and others. But in their formal relationship to one's own and others' benefit there is a clear difference of kind between egoistic, solely self-interested and altruistic motivation. 'Moral' action is altruistic action.

Naturalism may here be taken as the view that we have a direct inclination to some forms of altruistic action; and equally that other forms of altruistic action, to which we do not have a direct inclination, are yet functional to direct inclinations that we do have.

28.1.1. Naturalism: Hume

Both views are present in Hume. In holding that we have a direct inclination to certain forms of altruistic action he parts company with some influential views of his own day. In *The Fable of the Bees*, to the scandal of contemporaries, Bernard de Mandeville presented morality as an artificial institution grafted on to social life by the cunning of politicians. See Mandeville, 1988; cf. Sidgwick, 1967: 191.

Hume's distinctive move is to interpret the direct inclination view in a particular way. It is not simply, one might say, that we have a direct inclination to moral action. Rather, certain direct inclinations that we have are moral. This is the sphere of the *natural virtues*.

The natural virtues

In 15.1.3 we noted that for Hume the objects of moral judgement are 'qualities durable enough to affect our sentiments' (T, III.3.1; 575). We morally approve or disapprove of character-traits; and, just to complete the outline picture, our moral judgements are emotional reactions that occur on certain conditions.

Hume thinks that we have a direct inclination to certain actions because their corresponding character-traits are inbuilt in human nature. He picks out the following:

- generosity (in the sense of liberality)
- charity (helping people e.g. in Good Samaritan situations)
- meekness (by which he probably means not being over-inclined to make demands on other people)
- beneficence
- clemency
- equity

Hume does not suppose that these traits are natural in the sense that one could exercise them independently of all social context. The traits are evidently other-regarding in a double sense. Animals aside, the objects of their exercise are other people. More than that, in the exercise of these traits we regard the interests of others essentially and intrinsically, not accidentally or instrumentally to our own advantage. Hume believes that people simply are such that, within limits, independently of any particular social context, such traits will show up. The limits are set by the springs of action, the sources of human motivation, which for Hume are selfishness and limited generosity (T, III.2.2). Generosity is limited by degree of sympathy, which itself is limited by degree of propinquity (T, II.1.11; III.2.1). We Humeanly 'sympathize' most when our kin are involved or when, say, 'the needs of strangers' (Ignatieff) are thrust on us with special vividness. This is no universalist ethics in which all human beings are to be treated as ends (Kant) or in which everybody is to count for one and nobody for more than one (Bentham).

Hume's particular examples of the natural virtues are not vitally important. It is enough for his purpose, and for the naturalist style of ethics which he represents, if there are kinds of action to which we have a direct inclination and these kinds of actions (and the character-traits they express) attract moral approval. For our purposes it is enough if these actions are altruistic in the sense explained in 28.1.

The artificial virtues

Hume is quite clear, however, that there are kinds of action receiving moral approval to which we do not have a direct inclination from character-traits inbuilt in human nature. For one thing, certain social *institutions* are presupposed to their possibility. Justice, which Hume understands chiefly in terms of returning what one has borrowed and not taking what does not belong to one, evidently presupposes the contingent social institution of property. Again, there are qualities one reveals in one's dealings with others beyond the circle of one's own kin. Loyalty, allegiance, veracity, all attract moral approval yet these are not inbuilt character-traits; and, respecting the world at large, one has no direct inclination to the corresponding actions.

Such traits belong to the sphere of the *artificial virtues*. The natural virtues embody and reflect our limited generosity; and Hume tells us that they are advantageous on every occasion of their exercise (T, III.3.1). The artificial virtues are grounded in self-interest. Justice, for instance, serves our self-interest in maintaining the institution of property, an institution from which, taking one occasion with another, we all benefit. The artificial virtues are functional to our direct inclination towards self-interest.

28.1.2. Assessment of Hume

Hume's ethical theory in all its aspects is one of the most widely discussed in recent philosophy. For this part of his theory I will fix on three areas of difficulty. The first is in the relation of anthropology and ethics; the second, in the projectivist view of moral judgement to which Hume is committed; the third is in the theory's lack of a moral standard.

Ethics and anthropology

Hume offers us a speculative anthropology to explain the moral life. Three questions sharply arise on the Humean account. (1) If the natural virtues are a matter of direct inclination, wherein lies their morality? (2) If the artificial virtues serve self-interest, wherein again lies our moral approval? (3) Is morality any more natural than immorality?

To the first question Hume's answer is roughly as follows. We quite readily think that what is 'wrong' with the natural virtues as mere inbuilt character-traits inclining us to certain kinds of action is that morally praiseworthy conduct must be done *because* it is morally due or appropriate. It must be self-consciously moral. We are not merely to do our duty but are to do our duty for duty's sake. This is a common view.

But for Hume it is clearly wrong, because 'the first virtuous motive, which bestows a merit on any action, can never be a regard to the virtue of that action, but must be some other natural motive or principle' (T, 478). The passage is much favoured by examiners.

What Hume means, I think, is this. Moral approval is the approval of a certain kind of motivation. The motivation has to be specifiable independently of the approval. To say that this motivation might in turn be based on moral approval (the agent's own approval of his projected action) is to slip into a regress. How could an action be done or proposed, at the beginning of moral time (as it were), because of its moral goodness? Moral approval is an emotion which supervenes judgementally on something already done or proposed. But in that case, what is done or proposed must first come up for choice before the emotion of approval can supervene.

I think Hume is exactly right on his own terms. And I definitely reject the standard criticism that his argument relies on taking the spectator's rather than the agent's standpoint. The argument can still go through if spectator and agent are identical. Its real vulnerability, if so one regards it, is Hume's emotivism. It is on the emotivist approach to moral judgement that the argument depends; and that is not our topic here. For indeed if moral judgement is a matter of emotional reaction to action done or proposed, the start of the whole process (what leads one to do or propose an action) cannot be that emotional reaction. Hence it cannot be a moral judgement.

To take up now the second question: if the artificial virtues serve self-interest, wherein lies our moral approval? I might reply with a counter-question: why should they not receive moral approval, given Hume's account of the nature of moral judgement?

The relevant *objects* of moral judgement exist. There is the character-trait e.g. of being reliable in paying one's debts. Here is a quality useful to others. The *conditions* can also be met. We can be adequately informed about the typical operation of the institution of property and about the fact of the agreement a debtor has made. Equally we can take a *general view*, detaching ourselves from personal involvements. In these conditions, directed on these objects, the specific emotion of moral approval arises. See further, D. Miller, 1981: 64.

Now for our third question. What of the point that there are people whose exercise of the natural virtues is slight or non-existent? Baldly put, there are bad people as well as good. So how is morality any more natural than immorality?

Hume could, I think, reply along two lines. In the first place, natural virtue has a reinforcement that natural vice lacks: it attracts unfavourable moral judgements which, directed onto offenders, can cause uneasiness and consequent alteration in motivation and behaviour. Put another way, the complete phenomenon of morality includes not only direct inclinations to certain types of motivation and conduct but a tendency to judgement which, within limits but effectively, reinforces such motivation and conduct in others. Secondly, the agent who is immune to moral considerations, the amoralist, is a recognizable figure for any ethical theory. Hume might say that the immoralist presents no more a problem for his ethical theory than a three-legged tiger presents for a theory of animal classification. The *lusus naturae*, the stray specimen, is a fact of life for any scientific theory: why not for his?

For a subtle and deep defence of Hume against the charge that if we lack a direct inclination to act or if we fail to approve morally of the artificial virtues, there the matter simply ends, see Wiggins, 1991.

Humean projectivism

Hume does not face the metaphysical and epistemological problems of moral realism. There are no moral properties; a fortiori we have no knowledge of them. So the problems associated with supervenience and with the intuitive or other sources of our moral knowledge do not arise on Hume's account. Where the moral realist assumes supervenience, Hume assumes projection. Humean projectivism is an extreme, with moral realism as its opposite extreme and semi-realism in-between.

Simon Blackburn offers a useful characterization of projectivism as follows:

> Suppose we say we *project* an attitude or habit or other commitment which is not descriptive on to the world when we speak or think as though there were a property of things which our sayings describe, which we can reason about, know about, be wrong about, and so on (Blackburn, 1984: 107f.)

For 'attitude' and the rest we may read Hume's 'certain peculiar sentiments of pain or pleasure'. The term 'projectivism' is not Hume's but his language makes the notion appropriate to his theory. He talks, for instance, of 'Gilding or staining all natural objects with colours, borrowed from internal sentiment' (EPM, 294). We can take rough hold of the notion in terms of an aesthetic example. Tasting a seven-week-old pie I might exclaim, 'That's disgusting', or, since there is no accounting for tastes, 'That's wonderful.' I use the language of properties as if the pie had a property of disgustingness along with its other properties of solidity, shape and so on. But in fact I am disgusted and I say the *pie* is disgusting; I project my disgust on to the wretched object, where of course 'wretched' marks another projection.

Likewise what we call or even think of as moral properties are, for Hume, really only projections on to actions and character-traits of particular emotional reactions.

We need to know more about this notion of projection, however. A critic might suggest that something like the problem of supervenience, duly adjusted, reappears for Hume. Moral properties supervene on descriptive properties; and emotional reactions are projected on to actions and character-traits. But we agree that moral properties cannot vary independently of descriptive properties: two situations cannot be precisely alike in all their descriptive properties but differ in their moral ones. Hume assumes that there is a similarly lawlike relation between projections and the world. Human beings are such that under the conditions of moral judgement, with their attention directed on certain objects, there will be a common emotional reaction to qualities useful to others or oneself and qualities immediately agreeable to oneself or others. But what secures this lawlikeness of emotional reaction? What yields this subjective counterpart to lawlike supervenience?

Hume's answer is clear. It is no accident or chance convenience of publishing that he included a statement of his ethical theory in a booked entitled, *A Treatise of Human Nature*. We need to be creatures of a certain kind in order to experience the emotional reactions he describes; and, rare exceptions aside, we are (he thinks) creatures of that kind. There is a common human nature.

Whether there is a common human nature and whether, if so, it is as Hume characterizes it, are questions of immense significance to ethics. But I cannot see that the assumption of such a common nature is absurd (on the contrary). Nor can I see that, given that assumption, agreement in projections is a sharp problem for Hume.

For useful discussions of projectivism, see A.W. Price, 1986 and Wright, 1985: 314ff.

A standardless ethics

Aristotle, Kant, and the utilitarians can all be seen, in their different ways, as trying to give a rational agent good reasons for acting morally. The major thrust of a naturalist ethics is not to provide a recommendatory rationale for morality but to ground morality in human nature.

But in doing so, the criticism runs, it tells us neither what to do nor what to be. The justifications of morality offered by theorists such as Aristotle, Kant and the utilitarians lock on to theories of the moral standard. These theorists define a moral standard and then seek to justify it. Hume offers an account of, but cannot justify, morality; and he provides, and seemingly can provide, no moral standard.

There are, I think, two lines of reply. In the first place, an account of morality cannot be properly criticized for failing to provide a moral standard when it does not set out to do so. Hume wants to explain the fact of morality in terms of 'the necessary and uniform principles of human nature' (T, 402). This is part of a larger enterprise of 'introducing the experimental method' into psychology and the social sciences (15.1.3). Explanation, not prescription, is his aim. The only justification available, or Humeanly appropriate to look for, is that, in thus grounding morality in human nature, Hume is undercutting the kind of sceptical challenge put by Mandeville.

Secondly, a moral standard is internal to moral judgement as Hume explains it. What are the objects of moral judgement? Qualities useful or agreeable to oneself or others. Hume even goes so far as to say:

It appears to be matter of fact, that the circumstance of *utility*, in all subjects, is a source of praise and approbation; That it is constantly appealed to in all moral decisions concerning the merit and demerit of actions; That it is the *sole* source of that high regard paid to justice, fidelity, honour, allegiance, and chastity; That is it inseparable from all the other social virtues, humanity, generosity, charity, affability, lenity, mercy, and moderation; And, in a word, that it is a foundation of the chief part of morals (EPM, 231).

For more general approaches to the difficulties of Hume's ethical theory, see Harrison, 1976 and 1981; Kydd, 1946; Norton, 1982 and 1989; and Sidgwick, 1967: 204-12.

28.2.1. Naturalism: sociobiology

Recent sociobiology, under the impact of writers such as Edward Wilson, is in some respects a striking vindication of Humean naturalism. It has a scientific basis which Hume's 18th-century speculative anthropology lacks, but the results are closely similar. Sociology is the use of biological theory to describe and explain human social phenomena. Then how does it explain morality? I can only sketch rough possibilities without doing full justice to the exponents of sociobiological ethics.

Among human beings we can see two types of altruistic behaviour, which Wilson calls hard-core and soft-core altruism. In hard-core altruism relatives are helped non-instrumentally to our own self-interest; and in soft-core altruism non-relatives are helped non-accidentally to self-interest. The congruence between hard-core altruism and Hume's natural virtues, and between soft-core altruism and the artificial virtues, is almost complete.

Soft-core altruism has a basis of reciprocity. In one way or another, taking one occasion with another, there is a reward or return. Its workings are convincingly illustrated in the following example. If I am at home and find a £20 note, I return it to its owner; there is no question of my keeping it. If I find a £20 note in the office I probably try to discover its owner. But if I find a £20 note in the street I pocket it at once. Conversely, no one at random can be relied on to return my £20 note if I lose it in the street; others will only probably return it if they find it in the office; other members of the family will certainly return it if they find the note at home. Hard-core altruism covers the family part of the example; soft-core altruism the remainder. The example illustrates the adjustment of soft-core altruism to anticipated return. This anticipation need not be explicitly present to consciousness, but (within the limits of this kind of instant example) who can doubt its explanatory power?

That is a dangerous question to ask rhetorically. For many critics sociobiology presents, not a deep explanation but a caricature of the moral life. Take the following style of objection, which is by no means uncommon:

I have a Dutch lady friend of Calvinist persuasion, who in 1940 thought it her duty to hide ten Jews on her farm. She will be surprised to learn that she was really quite selfishly acting in behalf of her own DNA, subconsciously trying to maximize it, against all others. Wilson probably explains her unusual behavior as 'reciprocal or soft-core' altruism, which operates in anticipation of future reward. My Dutch friend will find this argument hard to swallow. She will claim that, being of sound mind then, the only thing she had a right to anticipate was getting caught by the Gestapo (Hamburgh, 1981: 49).

The sociobiologist might best reply, I think, that soft-core altruism is a biologically functional policy to which we have an evolutionarily inbuilt disposition. Its advantageousness precisely requires that we do *not* consult advantage on every occasion when we exercise the policy; and that our having the relevant inbuilt disposition makes this possible. Nor, he might add, does the policy's advantageousness and biological rationale require reward or return on all occasions. The moral life is a biological 'trick' that works (in part) because we do not realize that it is a trick; and it would be an ironic paradox if that trick were to begin to fail through sociobiology's account of its biological rationale.

The biological underpinning to this would be that hard-core and soft-core altruism are evolutionarily functional. Creatures that display such behaviour tend to survive; their gene-transmission is safeguarded, and along with it the recurrence of such behaviour in their successors. This is the world of the 'selfish gene' selecting behaviour that secures its preservation and reproduction. But that particular phrase casts more heat than light.

28.2.2. Assessment of sociobiology

This line of thought, this attempt to supply morality with a biological foundation, can be refined and amplified to any extent. The basic objection it encounters is that, according to our normal idea, a person is morally responsible for what he has done only if he could have done otherwise. But if moral conduct is genetically programmed in the way that sociobiology appears to suggest, and governed by causal biological laws, the morally good person's conduct was necessary all along. It lacks any merit. Cf. Rodd, 1987.

I have two responses to this objection. In the first place, determinism is one of the oldest chestnuts in the philosophical fire and its handling is a delicate matter. We cannot assume, in advance of looking into the topic properly, that moral responsibility and determinism are incompatible. Secondly, biological determinism constrains morality within broad limits that allow a degree of autonomy to the moral life.

That is to say that a reasonably sophisticated evolutionary ethics will provide a biological foundation not simply for certain types of behaviour but for something like Hutchinson's 'moral sense' – for our capacity to conceptualize situations morally through ideas of justice, rights, obligation and the rest. That moral sense will yield, within wide biological limits, an autonomous domain.

Wilson writes:

> Can the cultural evolution of higher ethical values gain a direction and momentum of its own and completely replace genetic evolution? I think not. The genes hold culture on a leash. The leash is very long, but inevitably values will be constrained in accordance with their effects on the human gene pool (Wilson, 1978: 167).

But if Wilson here emphasizes the existence of the leash, one might equally stress its length. Take a parallel with mathematics: presumably (as has often been pointed out) our mathematical capacity has a similar biological functionality which explains its existence. But no biologist will attempt on that basis to adjudicate between Euclidean and Riemannian geometry. Why should the biological basis of morality be any more threatening to moral creativity than to mathematical imagination? There is no reason in principle why the play of moral thinking cannot (by the operation of, say, analogical reasoning and imaginative projection) lead us to consider the interests of others, even genetically quite distant others and those from whom no rewards or return can come. Biology delivers a moral capacity; its exercise is another matter.

For an excellent introduction to sociobiological ethics, sympathetic but discerning, see Ruse, 1984. Also of real value are Mackie, 1978; P. Singer, 1981; and Tennant, 1983.

Variations on approaches to the justification of moral judgement explored in this chapter can be found in: Brennan, 1977; N. Cooper, 1981; Finnis, 1980; Gewirth, 1978; Griffin, 1986; J. Jackson, 1978; Kavka, 1986; Lee, 1985; Lonergan, 1978: ch. 18; Lovibond, 1983 (reviewed in Arrington, 1985); MacIntyre, 1981; McDowell, 1979; Nozick, 1981: ch. 5 (reviewed in Goldman, 1983); Paton, 1927; R. Putnam, 1985; Raz, 1986; D.A.J. Richards, 1971; and Wellman, 1971.

CHAPTER 5

Logic, Reasoning and Moral Judgement

29.1. INTRODUCTION

Here we take up our fourth ethical problem, that of the logic and reasoning connected with moral judgements. There are seven topics, split across logic and reasoning as follows.

Under logic:

- the is-ought gap
- 'ought' implies 'can'
- the naturalistic fallacy

Under reasoning:

- the role of principles in moral reasoning
- the practical syllogism and weakness of will
- action explanation: the belief-desire theory
- action explanation: the cognitive model

30.1. PROBLEMS OF LOGIC

30.1.1. The is-ought gap

In a masterpiece of understatement Hume closes *Treatise* III.1.1 with a passage that has all the air of an aside. 'I cannot forbear adding ... an observation', he says:

> which may, perhaps, be found of some importance. In every system of morality, which I have hitherto met with, I have always remark'd, that the author proceeds for some time in the ordinary way of reasoning, and establishes the being of a God, or makes observations concerning human affairs; when of a sudden I am surpriz'd to find, that instead of the usual copulations of propositions, *is*, and *is not*, I meet with no proposition that is not connected with an *ought*, or an *ought not*. This change is imperceptible; but is, however, of the last consequence. For as this *ought*, or *ought not*, expresses some new relation or affirmation, 'tis necessary that it shou'd be observ'd and explain'd; and at the same time that a reason should be given, for what seems altogether inconceivable, how this new relation can be a deduction from others, which are entirely different from it. But as authors do not commonly use this precaution, I shall presume

to recommend it to the readers; and am persuaded, that this small attention wou'd subvert all the vulgar systems of morality (T, 469-70).

It is hard even to estimate how much criticism and commentary these few lines have attracted. Their standard interpretation is that Hume is telling us that descriptive or factual statements do not imply normative judgements. On these lines there are frequent references to 'Hume's Law' that no set of descriptive or factual statements can ever imply a normative statement. 'You can't derive an "ought" from an "is" ', as the catchphrase goes. The 'normative', broadly construed, is whatever expresses approval, commendation or endorsement or embodies a pro-attitude – a preference, intrinsic or instrumental, for one (or one kind of) action, event, state of affairs, etc., to another. Corresponding con-attitudes can be read off for items 'dispreferred'.

'Is' has at least four senses. I follow Hintikka (1984: 35) in distinguishing:

- the 'is' of identity
- the 'is' of predication
- the 'is' of existence
- the 'is' of class-inclusion

Examples are: 'Ricky Nelson *is* the Hollywood Hillbilly', 'Joe *is* a real lazy guy', 'God *is*', and 'A fox *is* a quadruped'. In the passage just quoted Hume has in mind the 'is' of predication, the 'copula' as it is called in traditional logic. What might he mean by 'ought'? In discussing Hare we took a four-way analysis from Harman:

- the 'ought' of expectation
- the 'ought' of evaluation (the ideal 'ought')
- the 'ought' of reasons
- the moral 'ought' (the prescriptive 'ought')

Hume is doing ethics, so it is a fair inference that he has the ideal 'ought' and the prescriptive 'ought' in mind. And his point appears to be that there can be no deductively valid argument in which, from solely 'is'-premises, an 'ought'-conclusion can be derived. This follows, we might say, from the nature of deductive validity. In Dorothy Emmet's witty observation:

deductive logic is concerned with getting pints out of pint pots; in other words no more should appear in the conclusion than can be extracted from the premises taken in conjunction (Emmet, 1966: 37).

The following argument infringes that deductive requirement:

She is old.
She is lonely.

You ought to help her (ideal or prescriptive 'ought').

Hume appears to be saying that any such argument infringes the pint-pot rule; and this is the standard interpretation of the passage. But appearance and reality may not agree. There are two unorthodox interpretations. On the first of these, Hume's language is more fluid than our own; and we have no entitlement to suppose that when he uses the word 'deduction' he has precisely our notion of deductive validity in mind. Our notion has it that an argument is deductively valid if and only if the premises imply or necessitate the conclusion; that is, if and only if the conclusion cannot be false when the premises are true. Hume has such a notion; he calls it 'demonstration' or 'demonstrative inference'. But it is an open question whether he is using 'deduction' in that sense.

On the second unorthodox approach, Hume does not rule out all possibility of deducing an 'ought' from an 'is'. What he actually says is that this operation merely '*seems* altogether inconceivable'; and this leaves open the possibility that it can really be carried through (MacIntyre, 1966: 252).

On the first point, I agree that Hume's language is fluid (MacIntyre, 1966: 253-4). But I think the most natural reading of the passage is to take Hume's 'deduction' in the modern sense. Moreover, I think if we consider Hume's positive ethical theory, his emotivism (15.1.3), we see that he is not remotely interested in a deductive or other logical relation between descriptive or factual premises and normative judgements. Morality, says Hume, 'is more properly felt than judg'd of' (T, 470).

Moral judgements are causal through emotion, not logical through implication. They express a particular emotion that is tied to certain objects and certain conditions. When we attend to certain character-traits and to the motives and actions expressive of them, and when all the facts are in and we take an impartial point of view, a particular emotion arises. This is a story about the causal conditions for moral judgement. Hume never suggests that when all the facts are in they provide premises from which moral conclusions can be deduced or by which moral conclusions can in some other way be logically supported.

For further reading, see Falk, 1976. Falk's paper is one of the best things written on Hume's ethical theory. See also Robertson, 1989-90.

Hume aside, what are we to make of the claim that (to generalize and express the claim at its broadest) no set of descriptive or factual statements can ever imply a normative statement?

An immediate point to get clear is the exact sense of 'implication'. There is one sense of 'implication', that of *material implication*, central to modern logical theory, in which Hume's Law does not appear to be valid.

The premises of an argument materially imply its conclusion if and only if the argument yields a tautology, a schema that can never be false.

Suppose we write:

(1) p

———

p or q

(2) 'p' materially implies 'p or q' if and only if
'If p then (p or q)' yields a tautology.

It does yield a tautology, namely:

(3) 'p → (p v q)' in the propositional calculus.

Now (3) is a tautology because, from 'p' as premise we can always validly deduce '(p v q)' – the 'v' stands for the Latin *vel*, 'or'. To put it informally, it can never be the case that when 'p' is true, '(p or q)' is false. For '(p or q)', a disjunction, is true if at least one of the disjuncts is true; and this precisely must be the case when 'p' is true.

The point of that small excursus is to show a way of using material implication to defeat Hume's Law. I broadly follow Prior, 1960 and Humberstone, 1982.

We need to make just two assumptions, which are independently plausible. (1) We assume that there are at least two statements, one descriptive or factual, call it 'F', and the other normative, to be called 'N'. (2) We assume that the negation of a descriptive statement itself is descriptive.

Now, under material implication, a self-contradictory statement implies any other statement. Suppose we put:

(1A) F and not-F

'F' materially implies '(F or N)' in line with (1) above:

(2A) F

F or N

If Hume's Law is correct, and no set of descriptive statements can ever imply a normative statement, '(F or N)' itself must be descriptive since it is implied by a descriptive statement. But not-F must also be descriptive, since we agreed that the negation of a descriptive statement itself is descriptive. But '(F or N)' and 'not-F' imply 'N':

(3A) F or N
     not-F

N

This is a valid deduction which violates Hume's Law.

There are ways of resisting material implication, but the logical cost of doing so is considerable; for a first look at the issues, see Makinson, 1973: ch. 2. If we accept the validity of material implication, we might try excluding 'N' as non-truth-functional. That is to say that, if we regarded normative statements non-cognitively as (say) imperatives or expressions of emotion, which cannot be true or false, then we might see them as having no proper place in a deductive argument. Vital to deductive validity is the condition that the conclusion cannot be false when the premises are true: so what role can a normative statement play when it cannot be true or false?

The issue is a complex one. But it seems clear that non-truth functional statements can stand in logical relations with one another. Commands cannot be true or false but 'Shut every door' and 'Shut no door' are logical contraries. And 'Shut every door', 'This is a door', 'Shut this door' do appear to be deductively linkable. Moreover, not everyone accepts that normative statements cannot be true or false. A moral realist holds that some moral judgements are literally true; and Mackie holds that all moral judgements are false since there is nothing for them to be true of.

The most innocent and natural response to the above use of material implication is to stress the need for a relevance logic (Meyer, 1974). There is, after all, an air of sleight of hand about the idea that one statement, 'p', implies just any other statement at random, 'q', without any relevance of the antecedent to the consequent. If I said 'Queen Victoria died in 1901' implies 'Queen Victoria died in 1901 or there are fairies at the bottom of the garden' this would be a materially valid implication with a raw irrelevance that looks simply paradoxical.

To work with this response, I shall use the term *entailment* for a set of premises implying a conclusion when the premises are relevant to the conclusion. Sperber and Wilson, 1986 try to make the notion of 'relevance' precise. Here I can only say that what is needed for relevance is that the implication should be informative and address our contextual interests and not merely serve the abstract purposes of logic.

The American philosopher, John Searle, makes just such use of entailment in his attempt, in *Speech Acts*, to deduce a normative conclusion from a set of descriptive premises in defiance of Hume's Law.

First I will explain Searle's distinction between 'brute' and 'institutional' facts. Then I will set out the argument, based on his account of institutional facts, in which he claims that factual or descriptive premises entail a normative conclusion. Next I will make some comments on the deduction; and finally I will assess Searle's result.

Searle's account of 'brute' facts is brief and not over-clear. The key idea is that, in the case of a brute fact, the relevant event or state of affairs is ascertainable through 'simple empirical observations recording sense experiences' (Searle, 1969: 50). In this way I just see that you are sitting opposite me or that there are apples in the garden, or I just feel the pain in my fractured wrist. One hardly knows where to begin in handling critically this account of sense-based knowledge. Are there any brute facts independent of conceptualization? Even 'apple' is a heavily theoretical term. In fairness to Searle, however, he invokes the notion of a brute fact as one used by other philosophers. He is more interested in the notion of an institutional fact. For institutional facts it just is not true that, in whatever sense (if any) I 'just see' that there are apples in the garden, I also 'just see' that the vicar is 'marrying' Matthew and Verity.

'Simple empirical observations recording sense experiences' cannot tell me that a wedding is taking place. For the vicar is doing something within the conceptual context of an institution. Institutions are 'systems of constitutive rules' (Searle, 1969: 51). Perhaps what I see is a dress rehearsal; perhaps the vicar is not authorized to 'marry'; perhaps the couple are already married but to different people and so the ceremony is void. 'Every institutional fact is underlain by a (system of) rule(s) of the form "X counts as Y in context C" ' (Searle, 1969: 51-2). The context is defined by the institution; and you need to know what the institution is, to know if the present context is relevant to it.

The point about the rules of an institution is that they allow normative conclusions to be validly deduced from descriptive premises, 'brute factual' premises if we want to use that notion. We say, for instance, that within the legal system of the United States of America if such-and-such conditions obtain, (say) the President is permanently incapacitated and the Vice-President is in a normal state of health, then the Vice-President 'ought' to assume the President's role. The 'ought' follows from a statement of the (brute) facts.

There is an institution of promising; and within that institution Searle believes that there is an equally valid deduction of the normative from the factual. Here is his argument from Searle, 1969: 177-81:

(1) Jones uttered the words 'I hereby promise to pay you, Smith, five dollars'.
(1a) Under certain conditions C anyone who utters the words (sentence) 'I hereby promise to pay you, Smith, five dollars' promises to pay Smith five dollars.
(1b) Conditions C obtain.
(2) Jones promised to pay Smith five dollars
(2a) All promises are acts of placing oneself under (undertaking) an obligation to do with thing promised.
(3) Jones placed himself under an obligation to pay Smith.
(3a) All those who place themselves under an obligation are (at the time when they so place themselves) under an obligation.
(4) Jones is under an obligation to pay Smith five dollars.
(4a) If one is under an obligation to do something, then, as regards that obligation, one ought to do what one is under an obligation to do.
(5) As regards his obligation to pay Smith five dollars, Jones ought to pay Smith five dollars.

I offer two comments before we check whether the deduction works. In the first place, when Searle says that the relations within his argument are 'not in every case one of entailment' (Searle, 1969: 177) he is referring to a truncated, quick-scan version and not to the argument as set out above. Secondly, Searle is explicit that his argument 'has no necessary connection with morality' (Searle, 1969: 188). But I think that observation is misleading. For one thing, promising is a moral institution. 'Promises ought to be kept' is a classic moral principle. I think Searle's point is to rule out any claim that he is deducing the prescriptive moral 'ought', the 'ought' that claims an overriding requirement on action. Kantian rigorism aside, that kind of 'ought' would not be deducible, from a moral point of view, from the mere fact of someone's having made a promise. For there might be moral considerations that outweigh the promise. But I cannot see that Searle would need to deny that his conclusion contains an ideal 'ought'.

Suppose, however, that we simply observe the institution of promising in the non-participatory way in which I simply observe the American legal system. We just use our understanding, and not our acceptance, of the institution. In that light can we make a valid institutional deduction of the kind that Searle attempts? I do not see that we can.

I accept Perry's view (Perry, 1974) that the crucial error occurs between premises (2a) and (3). As Perry points out, (2a) is ambiguous. 'Placing oneself under an obligation' can mean either (2a1) 'intending (or attempting, or purporting) to acquire an obligation' or (2a2) 'actually acquiring an obligation when intending (or attempting, or purporting) to do so' (Perry, 1974: 136).

Anyone who makes a promise fulfils (2a1). But what if Bill makes a promise under duress? My reaction is to deny that, within the institution of promising, he fulfils (2a2) and actually acquires an obligation. But it is only (2a2) that warrants (3a). If, however, we keep (3a) then it is not true that all promises fulfil this condition.

How might Searle deal with this point? An obvious move is to insert requirements such as non-duress and the absence of fraud into (2a) and to add another premise (Perry, 1974: 138):

(2aa) All promises are acts of placing oneself under (undertaking) an obligation to do the thing promised, unless there has been fraud, duress, mistake or negligence.
(2ab) There has been no fraud, duress, mistake or negligence in this case.

Perry's counter is that this move carries an evaluative commitment that such requirements *ought* to count, with the result that Searle's premises are no longer purely descriptive. My own angle is different. The drawback to Searle's enterprise is that his style of argument presupposes an institution – the institution of promising, a legal system or whatever – which, for those who accept it, embodies at the start a pro-attitude to the behaviour defined by the 'ought' at the end. Premises (1) through (5) are not a deduction but more like a conjunction. At best they are an elucidation, a spelling out item by item in an additive list, of what it is to accept the institution of promising. Or, more accurately, this is true of the shell or schematism of the argument when we have removed the reference to particulars ('Smith', 'Jones', etc.). The schematism may certainly be applied deductively as rule to case, but with a rule itself containing an 'ought'.

If you want to go further into Searle's argument then besides Perry, 1974 you might usefully try Hudson, 1969. Montefiore, 1958: 105-32 contains a good general discussion of the is-ought issue. McNeilly, 1972 is also useful.

Before we end our discussion of the is-ought gap I should point out that the gap could remain even if the fact-value distinction in its unrestricted form were to prove untenable. (In that form, the class of factual statements and the class of evaluative statements are mutually exclusive.) That is, we might find that evaluative statements of the kind marked by an ideal moral 'ought' were true. We should then have evaluative (including moral) facts if 'facts' are what true statements state. But the prescriptive 'ought', signalling an overriding moral requirement on action, might still need to be determined. For several ideal moral 'oughts' may apply to a person's situation. To derive a prescriptive 'ought' we should need a moral criterion for deciding the relative importance of different ideal moral 'oughts'. For a further discussion of the issues here, see Wiggins, 1987: esp. 95-6.

30.1.2. 'Ought' implies 'can'

Our second logical topic concerns the principle, 'ought' implies 'can'. More formally the claim is that:

(1) An agent, A, ought to do an action, x, at time t only if A can do x at t.

I omit, for brevity, the corresponding negative clauses, 'ought not to do x', 'cannot refrain from doing x'. These clauses would complicate our discussion without adding anything of vital substance.

A proper first step is to consider the two crucial terms, 'ought' and 'can'. In discussing the is-ought gap we recalled four senses of 'ought':

- 'ought' of expectation
- 'ought' of evaluation (the ideal 'ought')
- 'ought' of reasons
- the prescriptive 'ought'

One might add Searle's institutional 'ought' or even Price's intellectual-normative 'ought' (H. Price, 1954) – 'You oughtn't to credit Dillon's story on the evidence to hand'. The senses of 'ought' most evidently relevant to the principle are those of the ideal and the prescriptive 'ought'.

What can we do analytically for 'can'? With slight variation of language I follow Canfield (1962: 356) in distinguishing four senses:

- 'can' of ability (physical and psychological)
- 'can' of opportunity
- the rule-consistent 'can'
- the penalty-free 'can'

I can lift a two-pound weight; I can contemplate my own death (physical and psychological 'can'). I can watch 'The Dukes of Hazzard' on television tomorrow; an episode is being screened ('can' of opportunity). In chess I can move my rook in a straight line down the board; the rules allow this (rule-consistent 'can'). I can leave the company; I will not have to repay at 29.75% the loan I secured at 0.5%.

The senses of 'can' of clearest relevance to (1) above are those of ability (physical and psychological) and opportunity. The penalty-free 'can' will reappear when we consider coercion as a moral excuse in chapter 6.

Keeping to the 'can' of ability and opportunity, then, we can amplify (1) to read:

(1a) An agent, A, ideally or prescriptively ought to do an action, x, only if A has the physical and psychological ability and the opportunity to do x.

When I refer to what A can or cannot do, I shall assume the 'can' of ability and opportunity. The first comment that suggests itself is that, intuitively, (1a) does not hold good for the ideal 'ought', which marks merely a desideration. Here it might mean something like, 'from a moral point of view, i.e. by moral standard y, A's doing x is desirable'. That claim might be acceptable whether A can do x or not. I do not have to withdraw the quoted remark if you can persuade me that A cannot do x.

The case is different with the prescriptive 'ought', which marks an overriding requirement on action from the moral point of view. How can it be the case that there is an overriding requirement on an agent to do an action which he has neither the ability nor the opportunity to do? For this type of case (1) is attractive:

(1) An agent, A ought to do an action, x, at time t only if A can do x at t.

But (1) can be read as:

(2) A ought to do x at t

A can do x at t

And by contraposition:

(3) A cannot do x at t

It is not the case that A ought to do x at t

But prima facie (3) derives a normative conclusion from a factual or descriptive premise in violation of Hume's Law. How are we to respond? There are basically three ways in which one might reply.

In the first place, one might deny Hume's Law. You need, therefore, to reconsider the above discussion of the is-ought gap to make up your mind about the present issue.

Secondly, one might deny that the conclusion in (3) is normative. This denial might rest on a general denial that the negation of a normative statement itself is normative. The matter is complex but I offer just the following comment. According to the logical rule of double negation, the double negation of a statement is logically equivalent to the original statement. This means that if 'A ought to do x at t' is normative, which presumably it is, then 'It is not the case that it is not the case that A ought to do x at t' is also normative by double negation. It would be odd, and a matter in need of explanation, if a statement were normative and its double negation normative but its negation ('It is not the case that A ought to do x at t') were not normative. However, I also know that the application to moral judgements of logical operators like double negation is a tricky matter. For more on the present point, see Brown, 1977: 206-7.

Thirdly, one might regard (3) as an enthymeme, an argument with a suppressed premise:

(4) If someone cannot do an action at a time then it is not the case that he ought to do it at that time.

A cannot do action x at t

_____

It is not the case that A ought to do action x at t.

(4)'s first premise is normative, its second premise factual or descriptive; and so there is no attempt to derive a normative conclusion from purely factual or descriptive premises.

For further reading on 'ought' implies 'can' see: Brown, 1977; O'Connor, 1971: 24-6; Tranøy, 1972; and White, 1979.

30.1.3. The naturalistic fallacy

The phrase, 'the naturalistic fallacy', dates from G.E. Moore's *Principia Ethica*, 1903. The concept predates Moore. Moore himself ascribes it to Sidgwick (Moore, 1903: 17); and Arthur Prior finds it in the 17th-century work of Ralph Cudworth (Prior, 1949: ch. 2). But Moore gave the concept its most elaborate and influential exposition. I shall keep to his account of it.

The classification of fallacies is a messy and unsatisfactory business. Aristotle discusses fallacies in his *De Sophisticis Elenchis*, an appendix to the *Topics*; and he has a distinction of fallacies *in dictione* and *extra dictionem*, i.e. between those that depend on the language used and those that are independent of language.

I will put my own view of the matter this way: a *fallacy* is an argument that uses either an invalid logical rule (a formal fallacy) or a valid logical rule which it misapplies though e.g. equivocation (non-formal fallacy, sometimes also called a material fallacy). Take 'If p then q; q, therefore p'. This is a formal fallacy. Put into English: 'If it is raining then the pavements are wet. The pavements are wet, therefore it is raining.' But, clearly, rain is not the only possible explanation for the pavements' being wet. The argument uses a rule on which the premises do not necessitate the conclusion. An example of a non-formal fallacy would be the argument: 'All banks are buildings; all rivers have banks; therefore all rivers have buildings.' The logical rule here, 'All A is B, all C is A, therefore all C is B', is valid but the argument skids on the ambiguity of 'banks' – on the language used, as Aristotle would say.

One's immediate idea is that when Moore talks of the *naturalistic fallacy* he has in mind an argument, or a related set of arguments, that uses an invalid, or misapplies a valid, logical principle. This is the expectation; we must see what he delivers.

Moore's account of the naturalistic fallacy is something of a bane to the beginning student of ethics. I mention two sources of difficulty. One is that Moore uses certain terms, like 'natural property', that are not immediately clear, and others, such as 'definition', which, while reasonably clear, are used in apparently tendentious ways. The other source of difficulty is that presentationally Moore's account of the fallacy – a negative, polemical account which says that a crucial mistake has been widely made in regard to the property of goodness – is run together with his own positive account of what goodness is.

It is no short task, on first facing Moore's text, to see how much of the negative account depends on how much of the positive. The tendency to overrate the dependence is embodied in Frankena, 1967.

How does Moore state the supposed fallacy? He introduces the concept as follows:

> It may be true that all things which are good are *also* something else, just as it is true that all things which are yellow produce a certain kind of vibration in the light. And it is a fact, that Ethics aims at discovering what are those other properties belonging to all things which are good. But far too many philosophers have thought that when they named those other properties they were actually defining good; that these properties, in fact, were simply not 'other', but absolutely and entirely the same with goodness. This view I propose to call the 'naturalistic fallacy' ... (Moore, 1903: 10).

The core idea is that to commit the naturalistic fallacy is to identify two properties, one of which is the moral property of goodness. It is not automatically false quite in general to identify two properties. The property of being a vixen, for instance, is identical to the property of being a female fox. Nor does Moore himself refuse all identity claims with respect even to moral properties. (On property identities, see Achinstein, 1974.) At the time of writing *Principia Ethica* Moore was ready to identify the property of being right with the property of producing good (Moore, 1903: 147), although he later pulled back this claim (Moore, 1912: 25-6).

Moore sometimes gives his statement of the naturalistic fallacy a linguistic twist, as when he tells us that the fallacy 'consists in the contention that good *means* nothing but some simple or complex notion, that can be defined in terms of natural qualities' (Moore, 1903: 73).

But it is the (non-linguistic) identification of properties that really exercises Moore; and what he will not allow is the identification of the moral property of goodness with any other property, natural or supersensible. Then what is a 'natural' or 'supersensible' property?

Natural objects exist in time and are objects of (possible) experience (Moore, 1903: 38, 40). The same is true of natural properties. Examples of such properties are yellowness, being desired, being productive of life or pleasure (Moore, 1903: 40). Metaphysical objects, by contrast, and their properties likewise, are not objects of (possible) experience and 'are only inferred to exist in a supersensible real world' (Moore, 1903: 39). Divine omnipotence is one example of a supersensible or metaphysical property (Moore, 1903: 103). Quick to say, there is a supersensible just as much as a naturalistic fallacy but, for brevity of discussion and because it affects nothing of philosophical substance, I shall concentrate on the identification of goodness with a natural property.

For a closer examination of Moorean natural properties see Cargile, 1989.

There are two main bases to Moore's case against the identification of the moral property of goodness with any natural property:

- the open question argument   • the simplicity of goodness

The open question argument

The open question argument occurs in Moore, 1903: 15-16. Suppose we are offered an identification of goodness with a natural property, say that of being such as we desire to desire. If we accept this identification then to be good just *is* to be such as we desire to desire. But, Moore insists, from that identification it follows that a question is empty or trivial which, on the contrary, is perfectly significant. 'A is such as we desire to desire, but is it *good?*' If the identification of the two properties were correct, then we would be simply and pointlessly asking: 'A is such as we desire to desire but is it such as we desire to desire?'

My reply is brief. The identification of two properties is a *metaphysical* matter; it concerns the count of properties in the world. Questions are *epistemological*; they are requests for information. Quit ethics for a moment. Suppose that propositional knowledge (knowing that p) is justified true belief. Just make that assumption. Then to have the property of knowing something just *is* to have the property of believing with justification something true. The question, 'This is a case of knowledge but is it a case of justified true belief?', remains perfectly significant. There are other views about the nature of knowledge; the question registers that point. The 'significance' of the question does not defeat the identification of the two properties.

The simplicity of goodness

The simplicity of goodness is a matter of its having, like yellowness, no 'parts'. If we see a yellow patch, clearly the patch will have extension and shape; and the yellowness of the patch might be distinguishable by its hue, saturation and brightness. But if we think of the mere yellowness of the patch, Moore's idea is, we cannot distinguish parts in any kind of structural arrangement. Goodness is exactly parallel to yellowness in this respect. If the open question argument rules out (as Moore thinks it does) the identification of goodness with any natural property, simple or complex, this is an extra point against its identification with a complex natural property. If two properties are identical, one cannot be simple and the other complex.

Certainly we can agree that goodness, whatever it is, does not have parts in a structural arrangement. Simplicity, in this sense, prevents definition as Moore understands 'definition'. To define something, for Moore, is to list its parts and to specify their structural arrangement (Moore, 1903: 8). As Butchvarov points out, however, there are other forms of definition: definition by genus and species, for instance (Butchvarov, 1982: 57). In showing that goodness has no parts, we go no way towards showing that it cannot be defined as the genus of a species. This reintroduces complexity into goodness; and so the possibility of identifying goodness with a complex natural property is restored.

I have expressed reservations about Moore's arguments against the identification of the moral property of goodness with a natural property. You should look further into the critical literature for other approaches. This literature will also sensitize you to some of the ambiguities of Moore's discussion, and in particular to his variable statements of the naturalistic fallacy. What I have aimed to provide here is a clear picture which you can proceed to complicate. You will get most help from Baldwin, 1990: ch. 3; and Lewy, 1968.

One clear point is that we are nowhere presented with an attack on a formal or non-formal fallacy of the sort explained at starting. Moore is using 'fallacy' not really in a logician's sense at all; for him a fallacy is in an everyday sense a falsity or sophism. So a topic that we have handled under the heading of logic does not, if I am right, belong there.

Moore's positive account of goodness is that it is an objective, simple, indefinable, non-natural property. It is also a consequential or supervenient property on the natural properties of objects; and one of the tasks of a 'scientific' ethics is to establish lawlike correlations between natural properties and the non-natural property of goodness so that we can say what kinds of thing are good. We had the text earlier: 'Ethics aims at discovering what are those other properties belonging to all things which are good.' But to examine these matters would take us too far afield. It is in any case the polemic against the naturalistic fallacy which has proved most influential in Moore's work.

Many critics who have accepted Moore's strictures on the naturalistic fallacy have been unconvinced by his case for regarding goodness as a property of any kind. Goodness cannot be identified with a natural property, they have agreed; but this is because it cannot be identified with any property. Rather, a projectivist account is to be given of our ascriptions of goodness.

31.1. PROBLEMS OF REASONING

In starting to examine the concept of moral reasoning, we move into the second division of our fourth general ethical problem.

I earlier drew a distinction between logic and reasoning. Logic is concerned with relations between sentences, statements, or propositions in a quite abstract way. If such-and-such is the case then such-and-so follows. Reasoning is more personal. On a standard characterization it is concerned with what to believe or with what to do. In the first case it is theoretical reasoning and in the second, practical.

The relation of theoretical to practical reasoning is a disputed matter. Various asymmetries and similarities, beyond the basic difference, are claimed by different writers (see Darwall, 1976; Hardie, 1980: 222-3; D. Mitchell, 1990; H. Putnam, 1975: 411-12; and Rice, 1988-9). However that may be, one point that immediately arises about practical reasoning can be put in the question: what is the conclusion of a piece of practical reasoning? If theoretical reasoning terminates in belief (or knowledge), what does practical reasoning terminate in? Until we have answered that question we hardly can say exactly what 'the basic difference' is.

I vaguely said just now that practical reasoning is concerned with what to do. More precisely one might suppose that the conclusion of a piece of practical reasoning is (1) a judgement, (2) an intention to act or (3) an action (Rice, 1988-9: 49-50). In the case of moral reasoning the judgement would be a moral judgement, though not all moral judgements centre on what we should do.

I agree with Rice that to terminate practical reasoning at the point of judgement is simply to reduce practical reasoning to a form of theoretical reasoning (Rice, 1988-9: 49): a judgement embodies a belief. However, we should note that many regard the kind of reasoning that issues in a moral judgement as practical reasoning, because of the close connection (closer on some ethical theories than others) between moral judgement and action.

Plainly the issue is coloured by whether one sees moral judgements as embodying beliefs rather than, say, as expressive and elicitory of emotion. So there is no quite neutral way of discussing this matter. The point to underline is that, whether we regard moral reasoning as practical or theoretical, or as both, there is such a thing as deontic inference (Clarke, 1985: 2). This might be represented in an example as follows:

(1) Deontic inference: from 'All promises ought to be kept' and 'I promised

Dillon I'd go out with him' to the moral judgement 'I ought to keep my promise to Dillon to go out with him'.

Now, we can ask about the logical structure of deontic inferences. Is it the case, for instance, that a valid deontic inference will have to deduce the ought-judgement from a major premise citing a moral principle and a minor premise specifying the relevant conditions? Call this the deductivist model of deontic inference. Or are there other possibilities? This defines our first topic:

- the role of principles in moral reasoning

Whether or not moral judgements derive deductively from moral principles in all valid deontic inference, there is another matter connected with moral judgements and practical reasoning. Someone might make a deontic inference and arrive at a moral judgement. How are we to represent someone's reasoning who accepts a moral judgement but, when he believes himself free to act on it, fails to do so, choosing a different intentional action instead? Or is this an impossible situation for which, therefore, we have no need to represent the relevant reasoning?

Aristotle's doctrine of the practical syllogism is one account which accepts that the phenomenon involved here, i.e. *akrasia* or weakness of will, can happen. It attempts to describe how an weak-willed person might reason. So I label our second topic:

- the practical syllogism and weakness of will

But we have not yet done with practical reasoning or with Aristotle. Practical reasoning might, I said, terminate in action. *Pace* Aristotle, *De Motu Animalium*, 701a12-14) I regard action as an unlikely candidate for the conclusion to a piece of practical reasoning. As Rice says, 'we would expect reasoning to consist in a passage of *thought*' (Rice, 1988-9: 51). An action is not a thought, however broadly we construe either 'action' or 'thought'. But an intention or a desire is an attitude with a thought-content, a propositional attitude. (So called because e.g. my desire to eat an ice-cream can be specified in terms of my attitude of desire that I eat an ice-cream, where 'I eat an ice-cream' is a proposition. The expression, 'propositional attitude', came into currency from the discussion in Russell, 1921: ch. 12.)

There can certainly be inference which terminates in desire. Person A wants or desires y. He believes that if he brings about x then this is the (or a) means of bringing about y (or that bringing about x constitutes bringing about y). So he desires to bring about x. Call this practical inference (Clarke, 1985: 3). For simplicity I will keep to cases where one thing is the sole means to another. An example might be:

(2) Practical inference: from 'I want to decorate the house' and 'Only if I buy a tin of paint can I decorate the house' to 'I want to buy a tin of paint'.

Harman favours intention over desire as the end point of practical reasoning. He characterizes practical reasoning in terms of the formation of intention:

> Let us distinguish practical reasoning from theoretical reasoning in the traditional way: practical reasoning is concerned with what to intend, whereas theoretical reasoning is concerned with what to believe (Harman, 1976: 431).

I should rather say that intentions supervene on desires, given the agent's state of character, rather than that they are reasoned to. For instance the practical inference in (2) might lead on to intending to buy a tin of paint. A intends at time t1 to buy a tin of paint at time t2 iff:

(a) A wants at t1 to buy a tin of paint at t2.
(b) A believes at t1 that he will buy a tin of paint at t2.

One way of reading the vague idea of 'leading on to' would be in terms of the practical inference in (2) causally producing the relevant intention, given the agent's state of character.

If this is an account of intending to do, what account are we to give if, subsequently, A intentionally buys a tin of paint? A intentionally buys a tin of paint at t2 iff:

(1) A buys a tin of paint at t2.
(2) A knew (believed, was aware ...) at t2 that he was buying a tin of paint at t2.
(3) A wanted at t2 to buy a tin of paint at t2.

We might see a continuous connection from the practical inference ('I want to decorate the house' and 'Only if I buy a tin of paint can I decorate the house' to 'I want to buy a tin of paint'), through the intention to buy a tin of paint, to the intentional action of buying the tin.

A common idea is that the explanation of intentional action must always be traceable back to an antecedent belief and desire – in our example, my desire to decorate the house and my belief that only if I buy a tin of paint can I decorate the house. A development of the idea is to say that this desire and belief cause my intentional action. The so-called belief-desire theory of action explanation typically involves this *causal* explanation of action through *antecedent* belief and desire.

A dispute over the necessity for antecedent belief and desire to explain intentional action gives us as our final topic the contest between two models of action explanation:

- the belief-desire theory   • the cognitive model

31.1.1. The role of principles in moral reasoning

A full discussion of this topic would run into enormous complexity. What I aim to do is to show the interconnectedness of the present topic with different theories of the moral standard.

Let us start from *ethical monism* in its utilitarian version. This has a 'universal starting point' (Jonsen and Toulmin, 1988: 34). Utilitarianism has a single basic principle, the requirement to maximize the general welfare, and so there can only be one moral major premise. This will read: 'The general welfare ought to be maximized.' A minor premise is needed to specify the particulars of the situation. The conclusion will be a moral judgement. For example, Sasha, a sound utilitarian, contemplates the ethics of a date with Dillon:

(1) The general welfare ought to be maximized.
(2) The general welfare will be maximized if I keep my promise to Dillon to go out with him.

---

(3) I ought to keep my promise to Dillon to go out with him.

To mark out the distinct position of rule-utilitarianism we should need to insert an extra premise between (1) and (2) to the effect that the general welfare will be maximized if promises are kept.

It is clear, by contrast, however, that this kind of deductivist model is completely incongruent with *ethical pluralism* of Ross's sort. Ross's acceptance of an irreducible plurality of moral principles and his notion of prima facie duty makes a defeasibility model more apt:

(1) There is a prima facie duty to keep one's promises.
(2) I have made a promise.

---

(3) Provisionally or conditionally I ought to keep my promise.

The point is that the obligation to keep my promise can be defeated by some other moral principle that is more salient in my situation. There is the complication, of course, that Ross thinks it impossible to provide any principle of moral inference by which to determine the relative saliences of different moral principles in particular situations. This is his intuitionism; and while it involves no crass assumption of infallibility it does rely on a difficult notion of self-evidence.

I might add that the minor premises in both the deductivist and the defeasibility models can present more problems than my simple examples, 'The general welfare will be maximized if I keep my promise to Dillon to go out with him' and 'I have made a promise', suggest. I have already pointed out that for rule-utilitarianism this premise will, while for act-utilitarianism it will not, be mediated by a rule to the effect that the general welfare will be maximized if promises are kept. This is one complexity. But there is also the kind of example in which Aristotle would be interested:

(1) I ought to be courageous (major premise).
(2) Courage in this situation is a matter of doing such-and-such (minor premise).

The situational requirements of courage (minor premise) will not be a matter at all like knowing that I have made a promise. They will require the *aisthesis* of the *phronimos*, the insight of a practically wise man (Woods, 1986).

What model, finally, might an *ethical particularist* use? So far as I can make out, it would have to be a single-premise model. There could be no division between major and minor premise, with the major setting out a moral principle and the minor the particulars of the case. For there are no moral principles for an ethical particularist. It seems then that a particularist ought-judgement would need to be derived purely from a single premise stating the particulars of the case. If these particulars were non-moral, we should need to consider the relation of particularist moral reasoning to Hume's Law. Cf. Dancy, 1992.

There is a final point to be made about the defeasibility model.

When a presumption is defeated, this will lead us to conditionalize it more carefully, perhaps even to reject the presumption altogether. Revisability is the keynote; and for those who accept the defeasibility model of moral reasoning, this process of revision may belong to a coherence approach to moral inquiry, to a pursuit of what Rawls has called reflective equilibrium.

Briefly put, one might (a) sift one's moral judgements to eliminate those that are, by one's own standards, prejudiced, factually suspect, etc. One might then (b) arrive at presumptions consistent with the considered moral judgements that remain. These are the presumptions that figure in the defeasibility model, presumptions subject to continual revision under the impact of moral reasoning. Finally one might (c) test one's moral presumptions against one's total corpus of beliefs. The aim is to arrive at stability, a state of mind in which one's moral judgements are free from the disturbances of stages (a), (b) and (c): reflective equilibrium. Of course, there is no real 'finality' about (c); (a), (b) and (c) are not discrete, consecutive stages but constant, overlapping patterns of reflection. For a further account of reflective equilibrium see Daniels, 1980; Depaul, 1987; and Rawls, 1971: 48-51.

31.1.2. The practical syllogism and weakness of will

Aristotle uses his doctrine of the practical syllogism to explain an agent's reasons for acting. Perhaps 'doctrine' is pitching matters rather high; for really we are presented with a set of ideas expounded piecemeal in NE, VI, EE, II, *De Anima*, III.11, and *De Motu Animalium*, VII.7. Nothing in Aristotle's Greek text precisely matches the expression, 'practical syllogism'. The closest he approaches the phrase is in his reference to *sullogismoi ton prakton*, 'the syllogisms which deal with acts to be done' (NE, VI.12; Ross, 156).

The syllogism's major premise states or presupposes a desire that the agent has or indicates that something is in some respect good: e.g. 'Light meats are wholesome' or 'Sweet things are pleasant'. The minor premise either states the (or some) means by which the desire or good specified in the major premise can be achieved, or applies the major to a particular case. (Hence the labels, 'means/end', 'rule/case', syllogisms.) Thus 'This is sweet' indicates a means by which the desire for sweet things, implicit in the major premise, 'Sweet things are pleasant', can be satisfied. The conclusion is an action:

| (1) Sweet things are pleasant | (major premise) |
| (2) This is sweet | (minor premise) |

| (3) (I taste it) | (conclusion) |

We may, however, part company with Aristotle and say that the conclusion is an intention to act (31.1).

The doctrine is put to work in Aristotle's account of *akrasia* or weakness of will. Recall: *akrasia* or weakness of will occurs when an agent, with a choice between doing x intentionally and doing y intentionally, does y although his moral judgement is in favour of doing x.

Suppose the *phronimos*, who in this case is a father, deliberates as follows:

A. THE GOOD SYLLOGISM

(1) A father should set a good example by not drinking alcohol.
(2) This is alcohol.

(3) Appropriate action of refraining from drinking (intention not to drink).

There are two main interpretative views on how Aristotle explains weak-willed action. On the first view, the akratic man contemplates two syllogisms that share a minor premise. So we may repeat the good syllogism, A, and add B:

B. THE BAD SYLLOGISM

(1) Alcohol is pleasant.
(2) This is alcohol.

(3) Appropriate action of drinking (intention to drink).

The weak-willed person is general accepts the major premise of the good syllogism, 'A father should set a good example by not drinking alcohol.' But under the impact of his desire for pleasure he brings the minor premise, which is common to both syllogisms, under the major premise of the bad syllogism. And so he drinks (or intends to drink).

On a rival view the weak-willed person is prevented, under the impact of his desire for pleasure, from contemplating the good syllogism at all. His acceptance of its major premise, 'A father should set a good example by not drinking alcohol', is dispositional: and the disposition is not activated here. His circumstances activate a different disposition, namely the desire to drink.

On either view the weak-willed person lacks the state of character that enables the *phronimos* to follow the good syllogism.

Following Charlton, I favour the second view. This view enables Aristotle readily to handle the Socratic claim, in effect a denial of *akrasia*, that 'no one does wrong knowingly' (Plato, *Protagoras*, 352A-356C). Aristotle wants to controvert this claim. The weak-willed person 'knows' the major premise of the good syllogism; in general he accepts it. On the second view, in situations of weakness of will, this knowledge is unactivated.

For an acute and textually sensitive discussion, see Charlton, 1988a: 41-9. F.D. Miller, 1984 and Thornton, 1982 are not to be missed. You might also usefully read Strasser, 1983. Wiggins, 1987: 239-67 and Kenny, 1979: 111-65 are very valuable to a reader who is willing to 'chew' his Aristotle. Hardie, 1980: ch. 12 and 13 will also repay study.

Weakness of will is a lively topic of debate: recall our discussion of Hare. An influential modern discussion is that of Donald Davidson (Davidson, 1969).

Davidson takes seriously the question whether there can be any such thing as *akrasia*, weakness of will – or 'incontinence' as it may also be called (with a smile at the ambiguity). The following three principles form apparently an inconsistent set (Davidson, 1969: 95):

(P1) If an agent wants to do x more than he wants to do y and believes himself free to do either x or y, then he will intentionally do x if he does either x or y intentionally.

(P2) If an agent judges that it would be better to do x than to do y, then he wants to do x more than he wants to do y.

(P3) There are incontinent actions, definable as follows (Davidson, 1969: 94):

(D) In doing x an agent acts incontinently iff:

    (a) the agent does x intentionally

    (b) the agent believes there is an alternative action open to him

    (c) the agent judges that, all things considered, it would be better to do y than to do x.

The inconsistency arises in the following way, neatly put by Hurley:

Incontinent action is intentional action contrary to judgement (by defi-nition), judgement leads to wanting more (P2), and wanting more to intentional action (P1). Intentional action contrary to the agent's better judgement appears to be ruled out by P1 and P2, but is necessary for P3 (Hurley, 1992: 11).

Davidson tries to resolve the apparent inconsistency by distinguishing two senses of 'judging'. The judgement in P2 is 'sans phrase'. It marks a preference without regard to any wider context: when the incontinent agent considers x and y just in themselves, one against the other, he prefers x to y. Judgement sans phrase also occurs in P1. P3 then involves no inconsistency with P1 and P2, because the judgement in P3 is judgement 'all things considered'.

One way of applying Davidson's account to ethics would be to identify moral judgements with judgements all things considered. This, you may recall, is exactly what Becker does (17.1).

I do not have any *drastic* reaction to Davidson's analysis. That is, I feel no overwhelming urge to endorse or reject it. It involves no obvious error, so far as I can make out, on condition that the distinction between the two kinds of judgement is psychologically well-founded, which I think it is. However, the analysis presupposes a background which needs to be filled in.

Davidson's picture of incontinent action rather suggests that judgements 'all things considered' explain intentional action – except when they do not. They do not in the case of the incontinent man, who acts on a sans phrase judgement. By the strongest implication, the incontinent man is unusual in this respect. We need to describe the extra features of his case; and we do so through Davidson's analysis. But this only underlines the need for a general account of 'normal', to set against the special features of incontinent, intentional action. Davidson might appeal to his major collection, *Essays on Actions and Events* (Davidson, 1980) as supplying that general account in main outline.

For a more drastic reaction, see Charlton, 1988b: 114-34. Hurley, 1992 argues for the need to revise P2. On the general topic of *akrasia* or weakness of will, Mortimore, 1971 collects a wide range of discussions from Plato onwards. See also Evans, 1975; Gosling, 1990 (reviewed in Politis, 1992); and F. Jackson, 1984. For a corrective to the loose and inaccurate use of 'weakness of will' or 'moral weakness' as a single label for a diversity of phenomena, see Milo, 1984.

31.1.3. Action explanation: the belief-desire theory

The belief-desire theory of action explanation holds that, at some point in the explanation of intentional action, we must cite among the agent's (motivational) reasons for action a belief and a desire: not necessarily only one but at least one of each. If we have to explain, say, A's doing x intentionally, then we have to tell some such story as that A wanted or desired y and believed that if he did x this would achieve or constitute y.

For now I take belief, on A. Phillips Griffiths's characterization, as that state of mind which is appropriate to truth (Griffiths, 1967: 127-43). A desire may also be taken provisionally as a state or continuing condition: a state, for example, of preferring to have to do y rather than not-y, other things being equal.

The belief-desire theory faces two lines of criticism, aside from the obligatory request for more clarity and precision. The first centres on its distinctive claim about the necessity for antecedent belief or, the point on which criticism really fastens, desire. The second fixes on the causal aspect of the theory, which nowadays is usually presented as a causal explanation of intentional action. To continue our example: A's want or desire for y, and his belief that if he did x this would achieve or constitute y, jointly caused him intentionally to do x.

In this section I shall attend mainly to criticism of the theory's causal aspect; the necessity for antecedent belief and desire is best handled when we confront its rival, the cognitive model.

We can quite clearly see how belief and desire might jointly cause action without our agreeing that the resulting action was intentional. Suppose, for instance, that I am driving along and want to turn left for Silver Street, Warminster. I believe that I am approaching the appropriate left turn. However, I get to think about my desire to go to Silver Street. When did I first have that desire? Is it the result of some psychological transference from an infant affection for Long John Silver? And so on and on in a reverie that distracts my attention and causes me to turn left and take the road to Silver Street. Belief and desire enter into the explanation of my action. But, as we may quickly say, they do not enter in the right (non-accidental) way to produce an explanation of intentional action (Davidson, 1973: 151-3; cf. Davidson, 1968).

If the model can be refined, as I am sure in principle it can, to accommodate such problem cases, there remain two serious objections to the causal aspect of the belief-desire theory. The first is the so-called logical connection argument; the second, the claim that since desires are not events they cannot be causes.

The logical connection argument, which traces back to Hume, is most closely associated nowadays with A.I. Melden and Richard Taylor. The essential idea is that in any statement of a causal relationship the cause is specifiable independently of the effect. Madden quotes Taylor exactly on these lines:

> I take it that, whenever there is a genuine cause-effect relationship ..., the cause can be described without any mention of or reference to the effect. For instance, if I know what causes a particular match to ignite at a particular moment, then I can give some description of that cause without mentioning the igniting of the match (Madden, 1975: 7).

The claim is that this condition of independent specifiability is not met in the relationship between desire and action.

If this claim is to be interesting, the connection between desire and action must indeed be logical in some tough sense. 'Logical' has to do some real work in the 'logical connection argument' if any serious argument is to result.

Suppose we explain my crossing the road to buy an ice-cream in terms (a) of my belief that there is a shop on the other side selling ice-cream and (b) of my desire to buy an ice-cream. There is clearly a conceptual connection, as Madden puts it, between the desire and the action (Madden, 1975: 8). In this example, 'to buy an ice-cream' occurs in both the specification of the desire and the description of the action.

But more is required if there to be a cause-defeating logical connection. I should say that a logical connection that would rule out any serious causal claim would be one in which the ascription of the desire and the description of the action were logically equivalent. Under logical equivalence, whenever the ascription were true, the description would be true and vice versa. An informal example of such equivalence in an unrelated matter would be 'All whales are mammals' and 'All non-mammals are non-whales'. But I hardly see how ascription of desire and description of action stand in that logical relationship in our ice-cream example. The ascription of desire might apply and the action not even take place. We have only to keep the ascription and alter the example: I have the desire but, knocked senseless by a speeding 1913 Ford Model T, I never get to cross the road.

So I am not convinced by the logical connection argument. To follow up on the argument, however, see Madden, 1975: 7-10; Melden, 1961: 114; and Otten, 1977.

The other main criticism faced by the belief-desire theory is that since causes are events and desires are not events, desires cannot be causes.

This criticism is open to two replies, I think. In the first place, it is not the case unqualifiedly that causes are events; it depends on your notion of cause. Secondly, it is not the case unqualifiedly that desires are not events. Both these points are put effectively in Madden, 1975: 13-15.

Sometimes when we think of causes we pick out some single factor as 'the' cause of some occurrence or state of affairs, E. It was, we say, Daniel's throwing away carelessly the glowing stub of his Turkish cigarette that caused the fire. This kind of causal explanation runs on events, in this case the event of Daniel's throwing away his glowing stub. At other times we invoke a much larger span of causal explanation: a set of necessary conditions sufficient for E. On these lines we might identify the lack of an adequate security system, the presence of inflammatory material, the presence of oxygen and so on as standing conditions in which the event of Daniel's throwing away the stub had the effect it did.

We might, then, cite factors in a causal explanation that have no plausible appearance of being events – the standing conditions or background factors. To this extent, it is not necessary, if desires are to figure in causal explanations, that they be events.

On the other hand, it is not true without qualification that desires are not events. The onset of a desire or its activation in a situation for action can plainly be events – happenings or changes in states of affairs.

Highly provisionally I want to say that the belief-desire theory survives the two criticisms we have considered. For extra criticisms and replies to them, see Madden, 1975. See also Platts, 1988; Robertson, 1989-90; M. Smith, 1987; R. Jay Wallace, 1990; and S. Williams, 1989-90. Cf. D. Lewis, 1988.

31.1.4. Action explanation: the cognitive model

The cognitive model is a denial of the belief-desire theory's claim that we need to cite antecedent belief and desire in the explanation of intentional action. The main recent representative of the cognitive model is Thomas Nagel in *The Possibility of Altruism*. But just as the belief theory has Hume for its philosophical forebear, so the cognitive model has Kant.

I shall keep mainly to Nagel. This is not because much could not be said about Kant. The point is rather that I doubt whether this part of Kant's ethical theory can contribute a great deal that is of present-day interest. Kant's view is that the mere apprehension that the maxim of one's proposed action fails the test of consistent universalizability suffices to explain one's acting morally. No separate intervention of desire is required. Or, if desire is involved, the desire (triggered by *Achtung*, respect for the moral law) is produced by the apprehension and is not an independent factor in its own right.

The problem is clearly, however, that all too often this apprehension does not suffice to produce action in line with the categorical imperative. Kant himself cannot deny that apprehension suffices only if one has 'elected' to follow the requirements of practical rationality. If we bog ourselves down in this topic, we may be submerged for ever. I shall follow my own judgement: I cannot see any major interest that contemporary ethics takes in this part of Kant's theory. If you want to follow it up, however, you can make a start with O'Neill, 1989.

Nagel's version of the cognitive model, which has attracted sustained attention since 1970, is a different matter. I shall prescind from his full presentation to concentrate on the essentials of his argument.

Cast your mind back to my characterization of intentional action. A intentionally buys a tin of paint at t2 iff:

(1) A buys a tin of paint at t2.
(2) A knows (believes, is aware ..) at t2 that he is buying a tin of paint at t2.
(3) A wants at t2 to buy a tin of paint at t2.

Nagel would comment that the presence of desire in this list of conditions is a purely logical consideration. We cannot say that A buys a tin of paint intentionally unless he wants to buy it, but the ascription of desire follows logically, i.e. trivially, from the description of the intentional action. If the belief that a shop within easy reach sells paint motivates me to go in and buy a tin, then:

That I have the appropriate desire simply *follows* from the fact that these considerations motivate me (Nagel, 1970: 30).

In other words, there is no need to invoke the antecedent belief and desire that we used in setting out the original example: that A wants to decorate his house and believes that only by buying a tin of paint can he do so.

How deep does Nagel cut? I am not myself impressed by his argument. The belief-desire theorist need not deny Nagel's claim about the merely trivial ascription of desire in cases of intentional action. Of course, the belief-desire theorist might counter, we can always specify intentional action in such a way that an ascription of desire follows trivially from the fact that someone was motivated by certain considerations. But the real point at issue is whether, presupposed to every intentional action, is an antecedent desire by virtue of which such considerations have motivational force. Nagel has done nothing, so far as I can see, to dislodge that claim.

Perhaps a deeper problem for the belief-desire theory comes from a different direction. I characterized belief and desire as states. That is a quite common approach but not the only possibility. If we see belief and desire rather as dispositions than as states, the distinction between belief and desire is harder to draw.

Suppose we specify desire or want as Audi does:

S wants p (a state of affairs) if and only if: for any action or activity A which S has the ability and the opportunity to perform, if S believes either (a) that his doing A is necessary for p, or (b) that his doing A would have at least some considerable probability of leading to p, or (c) that his doing A would have at least some considerable probability of constituting an attainment of p, then S has a tendency to do A (Audi, 1979: 230).

Correspondingly for belief we might accept the kind of dispositional account popularized in Ryle, 1949. So that to say S believes that p is to say that if the conditions were such-and-such, X would do or say certain things (cf. Hamlyn, 1970: 87-8).

I cannot trespass too far on the philosophy of mind but clearly if to have a belief is to have a tendency or disposition to do certain things, this is just how we have characterized desire as well. On this basis, why do we need belief and desire as separate factors?

I cannot claim to have done full justice to the belief-desire theory or to the cognitive model, the proper consideration of which would take us far beyond the confines of ethics. But you should now have a fair idea of the contrast between these two theories of action explanation. Their main point of relevance to ethics is that, if the belief-desire theory is correct, then justifying reasons for action must address the agent's desires, else his motivating reasons will not mesh with them. So (to edge the point with an example) moral realism, which holds that some moral judgements are literally true, gives an incomplete justification of moral judgement on the belief-desire theory. I do not desire to act on all things I know or even believe to be true. So why should the truth of moral judgement matter to me in deciding what to do? Why should moral truth not be just another irrelevant category of truth, like the truths of heraldry or etiquette?

CHAPTER 6

Moral Judgement and Moral Responsibility

32.1. INTRODUCTION

In this chapter we take up our final ethical problem, that of moral judgement and moral responsibility. Whether or not Mary Midgley is right in her thought-provoking article (Midgley, 1987) that there is a 'flight from blame', the idea of moral responsibility is still central to ethics. The topics we have to discuss are:

- moral excuses
- free will

Roughly, the division between the topics is that, when we invoke moral excuses, we accept that people can be morally responsible for what they do or fail to do but, in particular cases, not be blameworthy. The issue of free will involves the 'threat' from determinism that no one is morally responsible for their actions or omissions, period.

An obvious point at the outset is that the term 'responsibility' is used in a wide variety of ways, not all of which are equally important to ethics. To bring out this variety, consider this snippet from the *Nixville Gazette*:

Dr Damien Starlight was the physician responsible for the aftercare of Dan 'Dare Devil' Deludo who underwent surgery following an unsuccessful raid on the Nickel Bank. Mavis Moonwalker was responsible for the failure of Dan's raid; she entered the bank and sneezed at a crucial moment, distracting Dan's attention. Swinging round, Dan slipped on the newly polished floor and fractured his skull. Unfortunately for Dan a nurse, at first only dimly remembering him from a previous marriage, soon recovered all her old dislike and injected him with LSD, causing him to leap from his bed and go sailing through the nearest window. Dan's bed was in a luxury suite on the 27th floor of the Safehaven hospital. The nurse responsible for this misdemeanour was later identified by the hospital authorities as Felicity Sunbeam. The porter responsible for 'arranging' Dan's remains when they were found in the parking lot ...

The example is mine but I use it to distinguish the three types of responsibility identified by Dworkin, 1981: 27-8 and Hart, 1968: 211:

- role-responsibility
- causal responsibility
- liability-responsibility

Starlight had a role-responsibility for Dan's aftercare. Mavis had causal responsibility for the failure of Dan's raid. Felicity had both causal and liability-responsibility for Dan's unorthodox exit through the window.

Liability-responsibility is clearly a legal notion without direct relevance to ethics. It is through role- and causal responsibilities that we are morally responsible: liable to praise or blame. (I here pass over the honorific sense of 'responsible' in which we say, for example, that Josh is a responsible person because he carefully considers the consequences of his actions.) My discussion will follow the causal route. For the ethical questions at issue in role-responsibility, see Benson, 1983; Hare, 1972; Hollis, 1975; and Thomas, 1987: 292-5.

The subjects of moral responsibility can vary. Though I fix on the responsibility of individual persons there is clearly such a thing as collective responsibility. This requires not just joint participation but joint contribution:

> Individual participation transfers itself into collective action ... when the entire production is a function of each and every contribution each member makes to the whole project (Fain, 1972: 21-2).

So, for example, if four of us each in succession go into a house and smash a vase, there are four cases of individual responsibility. If four of us go together into a house and combine to smash a vase which is too robust for any of us individually to break, this is a case of collective responsibility.

The objects of moral responsibility may also vary. Perhaps we can be morally responsible for our beliefs (Stocker, 1982; cf. Ammerman, 1964-5 and H. Price, 1954). And might this justify punishment for holding false beliefs? Perhaps we can be morally responsible for our emotions (Schlossberger, 1986). Here I shall concentrate on moral responsibility for actions, to provide a manageable topic.

If someone is (now) to be held morally responsible for an action, either for doing it or for omitting to do it, three conditions appear to be necessary for accountability:

(1) The person did, or omitted to do, the action.
(2) The action falls under a morally significant description.
(3) The person who did or omitted to do the action was, at the time of acting, the same person as now.

(1) appears to be incontrovertible. (2) needs some explanation. The idea is that if someone is to be held morally responsible for doing or omitting an action, there must be some moral viewpoint from which, other things being equal, it would have been better for that action not to have been done or not to have been omitted, whichever the case. That viewpoint plainly derives from a moral standard, which yields the relevant description of the action. This is the first point at which it becomes clear that the two general ethical problems of the moral standard and moral responsibility are closely interlinked.

Condition (3) needs careful handling. You blame me for doing action x.

Condition (1) is defeated if the action, x, is done by A at time t and, at time t, I am not A. But suppose I am A. I did the action: then condition (3) holds that, at time t1, I am not responsible for what I did at time t unless I am the same person. Condition (3) requires continuity of personal identity.

The conditions for this continuity are a matter of extreme complexity. To see the problem: suppose that being the same person requires strict identity. To a first approximation, two things are strictly identical if and only if they have all their properties in common. (Hence Leibniz's principle of the identity of indiscernibles.) But there is no likelihood that my present and any former self have all their properties in common. On 9 December 1969 I remembered many of the events of the previous day; now 8 December 1969 is a total blank. Complete psychological or physical continuity appear to fail. One option is to use a 'closest continuator' criterion for personal identity. At time t1 A is the same person as B at time t if and only if A and B have more physical and psychological properties in common than A has, or B has, with anything else.

The topic is intriguing. The growth-point of modern reflection is Locke's *Essay concerning Human Understanding*, II.27, 'Of Identity and Diversity'. Your best initial guides to Locke are Flew, 1969: esp. 160-3; Mackie, 1976: 179ff.; and Wiggins, 1976. But Wiggins is also of independent interest, as is Parfit, 1984. See also Rorty, 1973.

33.1. MORAL EXCUSES

If conditions (1) to (3) are all met, are they sufficient as well as necessary for moral responsibility? Apparently not: for we can grant that conditions (1) to (3) apply to a person but accept a moral excuse which rules out blameworthiness. (The classic modern discussion of excuses is Austin, 1961: 123-52.) I concentrate on blame for brevity of discussion.

I suggest that there are two types of situation in which moral excuses are offered and accepted. They are not unrelated but they raise different problems. In the first, the person blaming and the person blamed have a common moral standard. They are both, say, utilitarians. In the second, there is not a common moral standard. Typical excuses in the first case are:

- ignorance
- accident
- compulsion
- coercion
- double effect

The normal excuse in the second type of situation is:

- conscientiousness

This is not to say that excuses in the first situation could not occur in the second. But it will be convenient to divide out the excuses between the two types of situation.

33.1.1. Ignorance

'Ignorance' covers broadly two types of situation. In the first it implies 'mistake'; I have a false belief about my action. I believe I am giving you a harmless potion; instead it is a deadly poison. In the second it implies absence of competent belief. I am confronted with the task of taking over the controls of an airplane and I am simply no informed beliefs about what to do. Call this 'blank ignorance'.

If we keep to intentional actions, how might the moral excuse of ignorance apply? Since Anscombe, 1957 is has become customary to say that actions are intentional under a description. One and the same action has, it is claimed, different descriptions. Under one or more of these descriptions the action is intentional; under others, not (see Annas, 1976 and Cody, 1967).

Generalizing from an earlier discussion (31.1) we might try the following formula for doing an action intentionally. A does x intentionally at t iff:

(1) A does x at t.
(2) A knows (believes, is aware ...) at t that he is doing x at t.
(3) A wants at t to do x at t.

An obvious thought is that when ignorance is a moral excuse, condition (2) is not met. On these lines we can think of clear cases in which ignorance – blank ignorance or mistake – would be widely accepted as a valid moral excuse. Here the excuse applies because the action is not intentional under the relevant description.

If, for instance, I have no reasonable grounds for belief that poison has been substituted for the potion – the security procedures are so tight – my mistake is justifiable and I escape blame. Or if I have no idea how to manage the controls of the airplane but am suddenly, without warning or preparation, put into this situation, then again my ignorance excuses me. My action of dangerously pitching the plane is not done under the belief that this is what I am doing.

We can accept such examples in which ignorance is a moral excuse that forestalls blame. The problem is, however, that ignorance may itself be blameworthy. The action is intentional but the ignorance is voluntary. Consider the following three situations:

(1) Reg, a factory worker, operates a machine which is subject to continual modification. He receives updates for each change but has not read the latest update. He flips switches 1, 2 and 3 as usual, with the result this time that the machine drastically overheats and injures a fellow operator. Reg just had not bothered to read the latest update. He was negligent in this respect. This is a case of culpable ignorance; in H. Smith's classification it is a matter of false belief due to deficient investigation (H. Smith, 1983).

(2) Harry, an office worker, has a mass of paperwork on his desk. He quakes at the task of sorting out the important from the trivial, the recent from the up-to-date. So he simply bins the lot on the principle, which he is rather fond

of quoting, that 'if there's anything important, they'll write again'. Unfortunately on this occasion the paperwork contains something very important, namely information that in the following week a major client will break links with the company unless a certain delivery is made. Harry's job is to look after such things. The following week he duly does nothing about the client. He did not know that he was failing to make a vital delivery, but it was his own precipitate action in binning his paperwork indiscriminately that caused this ignorance. So again this is a case of culpable ignorance. H. Smith's term for it is 'prevention of subsequent discovery'.

(3) Bill knows that if Sally calls on Monday he must give her three batteries. He also knows that if he gives the batteries to Sally he must buy replacements on Tuesday. He further knows that if he buys replacements he must fit them in granny's new machine on Wednesday. On Monday he gives the batteries to Sally but on Tuesday he fails to buy replacement batteries. On Wednesday granny is inconvenienced by not having batteries for her machine. Again this is a case of culpable ignorance: 'deficient inference' as H. Smith calls it.

In these examples others may be blameworthy also. Perhaps the management should not leave so much to the sole responsibility of Reg or Harry. Equally there may be further excuses that forestall blame. Perhaps Harry is in the grip of a nervous breakdown. This play of argument fits well, incidentally, with a defeasibility model of moral reasoning (31.1.1). But, if such further excuses are absent, the examples yield cases of culpable ignorance.

On ignorance see further Baldwin, 1979; and Woozley, 1978. Cf. Davies, 1975.

33.1.2. Accident

An example of an accident is as follows. You ask me to pass you a knife. I mean to do so, but when I pick up the knife it slips from my grip and embeds itself, quivering, in your leg. I intended to pass the knife; I actually wounded you. 'I did it by accident', I plead. Is this a valid moral excuse? The answer is an initial 'Yes' followed by a qualification.

The excuse applies because the action was not intentional under the description, 'wounding the person who asked me to pass a knife'. I did not want to wound you. So condition (3) of intentional action is not met:

(1) A does x at t2.
(2) A knows (believes, is aware …) at t2 that he is doing x at t2.
(3) A wants at t2 to do x at t2.

At t2 I did not want to do x at t2.

The qualification is that I can be blameworthy if, for example, I know that I have a physical weakness which renders uncertain my competent handling of objects such as knives. My wounding you was still an accident but a foreseeable risk, given my condition.

33.1.3. Compulsion

'Compulsion' includes at least straight physical control. I am compelled to do something if I am manhandled in such a way that the relevant behaviour results irrespective of my wants and desires antecedently or at the time. Compulsion removes my behaviour from the sphere of intentional behaviour altogether. Neither the agent's beliefs nor his desires, separately or in combination, have any explanatory relevance to what he does.

There will, of course, be complications if the compulsion were foreseeable and the situation avoidable. That aside, there is a question about the extension of compulsion beyond the physical to the psychological. Can I be subject to compulsion, in such a way as to have a valid moral excuse, if I have (say) an addiction or if I have been brainwashed?

If so, one account might be that my alcoholic desire (say) to open another bottle of rum is of a strength or intensity that makes my conduct unamenable to control through other desires that I have (including the desire not to have alcoholic desires), to threats, persuasion, exhortation or advice. The parallel with physical compulsion is incomplete, however, since physical compulsion removes what I do from the sphere of intentional action altogether. Under psychological compulsion my actions can still be fully intentional.

For a finer-grained discussion of psychological compulsion, see Greenspan, 1978.

33.1.4. Coercion

What is coercion? Sir Isaiah Berlin has a characterization ready to hand:

> Coercion implies the deliberate interference of other human beings within the area in which I could otherwise act (Berlin, 1967: 142).

This distinguishes coercion, as human interference, from other forms of obstruction that might have the same effect. But it does not mark off coercion from compulsion. Rather better in this respect is Lloyd Fields's characterization:

> Coercion occurs when a person is threatened with dire consequences unless he does what the coercer wants (Fields, 1987: 16).

This captures the key idea of a threat as central to coercion. Still it is hardly over-precise. How can we spell out adequately the idea of threat? A useful first step is to consider Robert Nozick's account. In a preliminary way Nozick lists five conditions drawn from Hart and Honoré, 1961 and Hart, 1959 (Nozick, 1972: 102). I have changed the schematic letters to fit with the present text and have removed some of Nozick's abbreviations. Person A coerces person B into not doing action x iff:

(1) A threatens to do something if B does x (and A knows that he is making this threat).

(2) This threat renders B's doing x substantially less eligible as a course of conduct than not doing x.

(3) A makes this threat in order to get B not to do x, intending that B realize he has been threatened by A.

(4) B does not do x.

(5) A's words or deeds are part of B's reason for not doing x.

Clearly this account might readily be amended to handle cases where B is coerced into doing an action rather than into not doing it. Nozick's first comment on this set of conditions is that it is not sufficient for coercion. For example, A might make his threat, saying that if B does x a rock will fall and kill him. But B, a superstitious sort, might suppose that A is pointing out to him the effects of a 'strange natural law that holds independently of human action, namely whenever someone performs this action, he gets killed by a falling rock' (Nozick, 1972: 103). To cover the possibility that while A knows that he is making a threat, B does not recognize it as such, we might add a condition:

(6) B knows that A has threatened to do the something mentioned in (1), if he, B does x (or to handle cases of anonymous threats, B knows that someone has threatened to do something mentioned in (1) if he, B, does x).

We have to accommodate cases where A does not threaten B but B misapprehends A's words as a threat. 'I wouldn't do that if I were you', I might say in what (as I suppose) is my blandest, most avuncular tone. But I sound really sinister, and you take fright. Here I do not coerce, but it is just as if I do.

Nozick mounts a pyramid of qualifications to deal with intricate examples. I do not propose to follow the full refinement of his analysis here. One point noticed by Nozick's commentators is that this is a non-normative account. We might accept that coercion has occurred, via conditions (1) – (6) and beyond, without being committed to any view that A was wrong to coerce B. Perhaps B was a bank raider and A an armed policeman threatening B with dire consequences if he, B, did not give himself up. B was coerced into discontinuing the raid. See further Ryan, 1980 and P. Wilson, 1982.

For some purposes, especially those of political theory, this may be a limited account of coercion. But it is serviceable here. For we need to consider whether, if someone is coerced, he or she has a moral excuse. We do not want a concept of coercion that already loads the answer to that question.

The key to coercion is the deliberate restriction of eligible options and alternatives. When I coerce someone he could act differently. I restrict what he can do in Canfield's penalty-free sense of 'can' (30.1.2). He can ignore my threat but his defiance carries a penalty.

So, if under coercion I do an action which, by our shared moral standard, you (my moral assessor) and I agree that, other things equal, it would have been better not to do, can I properly plead coercion as a valid moral excuse?

The answer must, I think, be specific to the relevant moral standard. For, presumably, the same standard that defines the badness of my action will also define the badness of the prospective consequences with which I was threatened and the reasonableness of my bearing them. One can imagine an act-utilitarian account on which the welfare that was decreased by my doing an action under coercion was less than the decrease in welfare that would have resulted (to myself) if I had ignored the threat.

There is, I think, no moral standard-neutral way in which the status of coercion as a moral excuse can be assessed. We may just note, however, that coercion is interestingly different from moral excuses such as ignorance and accident. When ignorance and accident apply the agent escapes blame because the action is not intentional under the relevant description. With coercion, by contrast, the action is intentional under the relevant description but the agent still escapes blame. When the robber says, his blade glinting in the sun, 'Take that man's wallet – or else!', my subsequent action of taking the wallet is intentional under that description. But intentionality is not sufficient for blame if coercion is a valid excuse. In this respect coercion is similar to psychological compulsion, of which indeed it might even be regarded as a special case.

33.1.5. Double effect

Harman gives a brief characterization of the principle of double effect:

> According to this principle, there is an important distinction between what you aim at, either as one of your ends or as a means to one of your ends, and what you merely foresee happening as a consequence of your action. It is much worse, for example, to aim at injury to someone, either as an end or a means, than to aim at something that you know will lead to someone's injury. Doing something that will cause injury to someone is bad enough; but, according to the principle of Double Effect, it is even worse to aim at such injury (Harman, 1977: 58).

Or in Foot's version:

> The doctrine of the double effect is based on a distinction between what a man foresees as a result of his voluntary action and what, in the strict sense, he intends. He intends in the strictest sense both those things that he aims at and those that he aims at as means to his ends. The latter may be regretted in themselves but nevertheless desired for the sake of the end, as we may intend to keep dangerous lunatics confined for the sake of our safety. By contrast a man is said not strictly, or directly, to intend the foreseen consequences of his voluntary actions where these are neither

the end at which he is aiming nor the means to this end (Foot, 1971: 29-30).

To formalize my own understanding of the principle:

(1) I do an action, x, to produce a state of affairs, y.
(2) y is good and is aimed at as such by me.
(3) x is neutral or good considered separately, i.e. independently of its conduciveness to y.
(4) x also produces state of affairs, z.
(4) I foresee that x will produce z.
(5) z is bad and is recognized as such by me.
(6) By the principle of double effect I may escape blame for doing x so long as I do not produce z in order to produce y.

A certain gloss is needed to this sketchy formalization. For one thing, y must be a significant good, not relatively trivial as against the major badness of z. For another, there must be no other possible or likely way of producing y than by doing x and no such way of doing x and avoiding the production of z.

How are we to respond to this principle? The only comment I will make is this. The principle plainly assumes a moral standard. On an act-utilitarian calculation, for instance, if z were used as a means to y, this would make no difference as long as a balance of welfare (y>z) resulted. The principle of double effect could not emerge from such a background. It could be a rule-utilitarian rule; but its natural context is a moral standard for which certain types of action or the intended production of certain states of affairs are forbidden as *malum in se*, intrinsically wrong. The principle then allows the production of those states of affairs as long as this is not the direct aim of our action.

For an account of the principle of double effect from within its original context of Catholic moral theology, the statement in Lehmkuhl, 1914 is probably the most nuanced. Its Latin text is likely however to be the frontier to a closed world. So you might look instead at Cronin, 1939: 687-90 and Kelly, 1955: 20-2. McDonald, 1903: 149-51 gives an interesting critique of the principle from within the Catholic tradition. (Catholic moral theology is the great unworked mine of modern ethics.)

It is perhaps worth noting that where Catholic moral theology has the principle of double effect, act-utilitarianism has the opposite principle of negative responsibility. On the latter principle one is equally responsible for what one directly intends, for what one foresees as a result of what one directly intends, and for what one foresees and fails to prevent. In the case of Jim and the Indians, for example, the principle of double effect might allow Jim to 'bring about' the death of the twenty Indians by refusing to shoot one Indian (21.2.9). For he does not directly intend the death of anyone but merely foresees the twenty deaths as a practically certain outcome of his refusal of the captain's offer. On the principle of negative responsibility, no appeal to what Jim directly intends is relevant as a moral excuse. All that matters is that Jim could have prevented twenty deaths and failed to do so. (I here crudify the act-utilitarian's response simply to point a contrast.) See further Casey, 1971; Bennett, 1971; and Harris, 1974.

33.1.6. Conscientiousness

The excuse of conscientiousness typically applies when moral assessor and morally assessed do not share a moral standard. I have done an action; you disapprove of it morally, yet I escape blame because I acted conscientiously on my own moral standard.

Before we go far into the topic, we need to clear up a possible confusion about the notion of conscientiousness.

A person who acts conscientiously acts, we might say, according to conscience; and there is a traditional view of conscience as a faculty of moral knowledge, a power of moral discernment. This is very much Butler's view of conscience (Butler, 1967). Conscience, the voice of God (Sermon 2), delivers infallible moral principles and also reveals the moral requirements of particular situations unless distorted by 'superstition' (false religion: Sermon 3). (On some differences between conscience and chapter 4's 'moral sense' as faculties, see Alexander, 1899: 153-60. For a sensitive and duly complex view of conscience as a social product, see Mill, U: ch. 3.) I suggest a de-mystified view of conscience. Conscience is not a moral faculty. Rather when we talk of someone acting according to conscience, this is only to say that this person is doing what he thinks he ought to do, what he believes it right to do from the viewpoint of his own moral standard. This is the sense in which 'conscientious' action will be taken here.

C.D. Broad (1969: 75) defines three conditions for conscientious action in this sense. I shall slightly rephrase his exact terms, but essentially a person, A, does an action, x, conscientiously iff:

(1) A has carefully thought out his or her situation and examined the options in order to decide which action would be morally best relative to his or her standard.
(2) A has decided that action x is the morally best option (ignoring here the case of moral parity in which A believes x simply to be morally as good as any other option).
(3) A's belief that x is morally the best action, taken with A's desire to do the morally best action as such, is either (a) the only reason why A does x (in which case the action is 'purely conscientious') or (b) a necessary and sufficient condition of A's doing x (in which case the action is 'predominantly conscientious').

Plainly the terms of this characterization will need to be altered if you think of moral 'beliefs' as 'attitudes' or if you reject the belief-desire model of action explanation. I assume that the characterization can be readily amended accordingly. That said, I accept Broad's account on the whole but draw three points to your attention.

In the first place, Broad's characterization of conscientious action does not appear to take account of habitual action. It focuses sharply on cases where the action is fully deliberate in a reflective way.

Secondly, even in the case of reflective actions Broad pays no particular attention to the element of effort or opposition which (some would say) is a normal accompaniment of conscientious action. He disregards the presence of threats or inducements, more or less strong, not to do what you believe to be morally right as such:

> Conscientiousness includes doing what one thinks right, but it also includes doing the act under a particular sort of condition, namely in the face of obstacles, either internal (such as contrary desires) or external (such as contrary public opinion) (Zink, 1962: 138).

Thirdly, the question arises: how can we ever tell what was necessary or sufficient in a particular situation, let alone that a person had only one reason for what he did? Broad might reply, however, that he is analysing a concept and not telling us how we can know when it applies.

The ground on which conscientiousness is normally accepted as a moral excuse is that, when someone's moral standard differs from one's own, what more can one require of him than that he act in the ways Broad describes?

34.1. FREE WILL

Free will is a topic on which there is a vast range of specific theories of increasing sophistication. I cannot possibly do justice to that variety here. But what is important is to get clear about three broad options which are clearly distinguishable in the literature. The standard labels are:

- hard determinism
- soft determinism
- libertarianism

For the hard determinist, determinism is true and therefore there is no such thing as moral responsibility. For the libertarian, there is such a thing as moral responsibility, therefore determinism is false. The soft determinist or compatibilist holds that moral responsibility is consistent with, or even requires, the truth of determinism.

The labels 'hard' and 'soft' derive from William James's article, 'The Dilemma of Determinism' (James, 1884). The major ethical angle on free will is that the truth of determinism is held by the hard determinist to entail that no one is morally responsible. Provisionally let us take the following as stating a necessary condition for moral responsibility:

A person is morally responsible for what he has done only if he could have done otherwise.

The relative insignificance of this principle in Greek ethics is well brought out in Adkins, 1960. But it is an important starting-point in modern ethics.

34.1.1. Hard determinism and libertarianism

Hard determinism is the following view:

(1) Every event has a cause.
(2) Human actions are events.
(3) For every event, E2, there is a prior event or set of events, E1, which is causally sufficient for E1.
(4) If E1 is causally sufficient for E2 then E1 necessitates E2: E2 cannot but occur.
(5) If (3) and (4) then all human actions have prior events which necessitate them.
(6) If (5) then it is causally impossible for a person to have done any action other than the one he did.
(7) If (6) then no one is morally responsible.

Libertarianism is the view that people are, or can be, morally responsible in some way that involves the falsity of (1) or (2), or both. So the libertarian either denies that every event has a cause or denies that human actions are events.

First, a point needs to be cleared up. The statement of a necessary condition for moral responsibility will not go through without some reservation. Consider the following ingenious counterexample from Blumenfeld:

> Suppose that the presence of a certain atmospheric reaction always causes Smith to decide to attack the person nearest to him and actually to do so. Suppose also that he always flushes a deep red when he considers and decides *against* performing an act of violence and that under certain circumstances the atmospheric reaction is triggered by the appearance of just this shade of red. Now imagine that on a day on which circumstances are favourable to the triggering of the reaction, Smith considers whether or not to strike a person with whom he is conversing, decides in favor of it, and forthwith does so (Blumenfeld, 1971, quoted by Inwagen, 1978: 202).

In the example there is 'no way', a phrase you may have heard before, in which Smith cannot make the attack. If he decides to attack then he attacks; and if he decides not to attack, he still attacks courtesy of the atmospheric reaction.

The relevance of the example is that we should intuitively hold Smith responsible; he did after all decide, 'of his own free will' the libertarian might add, to make the attack. Clearly we need to rephrase the condition in some such way as the following:

A person is morally responsible for what he has done only if he could have chosen or decided otherwise.

The hard determinist argument leading to this will now read:

(1) Every event has a cause.
(2.1) Human actions, and decisions to act, are events.
(3) For every event, E2, there is a prior event or set of events, E1, which is causally sufficient for E1.
(4) If E1 is causally sufficient for E2 then E1 necessitates E2: E2 cannot but occur.
(5.1) If (3) and (4) then all human actions, and decisions to act, have prior events which necessitate them.
(6.1) If (5.1) then it is causally impossible for a person to have done, or decided to do, any action other than the one he did.
(7) If (6.1) then no one is morally responsible.

Two more comments before we proceed. First: must a cause precede its effect? Can there not be backwards causation in which the effect precedes the cause? In this case, every event might be necessitated by a subsequent event or set of events. This may seem counter-intuitive, to put it mildly. But intuitive reactions are not decisive in philosophy. The usual move against backwards causation is to ask how a future event that does not yet exist, namely the effect, can influence a prior event, namely the cause. But the advocate of backwards causation can reply that the same problem applies in 'normal' causation. Causes are past events in relation to their effects, but past events no longer exist. I raise the possibility of backwards causation simply as a conceptual tease. Read Waterlow, 1974 and Forrest, 1985 if you want to look further into the matter. Here I favour the normal; we will keep to forwards causation.

The other comment is that a proper account of causation requires account to be taken of states of affairs as well as events. We saw this in discussing the belief-desire theory of action explanation. I shall, however, omit this complicating factor here. For presumably the occurrence and persistence of states of affairs are themselves explicable in terms of events. We might of course reintroduce states of affairs in relation to the causal efficacy of these events, and so on in an endless loop. For simplicity of exposition I would ask you to make your own allowance for states of affairs in the event-based account of causation used here.

The libertarian attacks (1) or (2.1). How might (1) be attacked? There are two main lines of assault. One move is to point out that (1) is a universal generalization running over all possible events. But we cannot test this generalization against all possible events since our experience is finite. (1) is therefore unverifiable. This is fair comment, but the libertarian has to go beyond this.

For the libertarian is committed to (1)'s actual falsity in respect of (at least a range of) human actions. (1) might be dismissed as false at the quantum level. But how can it be shown to be false at the macro-level of human decisions? The normal libertarian idea along this line is that such decisions are *free causes*: causes which are themselves uncaused. But how do we know our decisions are free in this way?

Appeal may be made to an introspective feeling of freedom. But as Hume pointed out, this feeling (allowing that it occurs) might have any number of explanations. Our actually being free is only one of them.

Then how can the libertarian deny (2.1)? Every event has a cause, he might agree, and causes necessitate their effects, but human actions are not events. Events have causes but actions, at any rate intentional actions, are explainable in terms of reasons. We decide to act; our decisions are based on reasons. Reasons are not causes. So actions are not events. For an account of actions along these lines, see R. Taylor, 1966: 147-52.

In a philosophical discussion outside ethics we should need to attend rather carefully to the notion of an event as a topic in its own right. If we define 'event' as 'occurrence', this is vacuously circular: 'occurrence' is just another term for 'event'. Quine takes 'event' to refer to the content of some discrete portion of space-time, but this will create a problem if (unlike Quine) we think mental events are not spatial. I shall assume here that we have an intuitive grasp of the notion of an event, strong enough to carry the discussion. See Quinton, 1979 and Schlesinger, 1984 for further analysis.

The key to the view that actions are not events, because reasons are not causes, is the debate over the logical connection argument which we examined with reference to the belief-desire theory of action explanation. If we assume that an agent's reasons for action are his beliefs and desires then, according to the logical connection argument, explanation through desires cannot be causal. The only point I would add to our previous discussion is that at most the logical connection argument might show that the *language* of want or desire is inadequate to causal explanation. This would not exempt human actions from causal explanation under a different terminology. See further Bach, 1980.

34.1.2. Soft determinism

For the soft determinist, all actions and decisions to act are causally determined but there is no incompatibility between this fact or assumption and a person's moral responsibility for his actions and decisions. Soft determinism is often called simply 'compatibilism'. Usually, however, the soft determinist goes beyond a claim of compatibility to argue that moral responsibility is not merely consistent with but actually requires the truth of determinism.

How can we map out the soft determinist's position against that of the hard determinist? The major contrast between the positions lies in the notion of cause, which differs between them.

That difference can be spotlighted if we turn to the first soft determinist, Hume, whose main discussions of 'liberty' and 'necessity' occur in T, II.3.1-2 and EHU, VIII.

Hume takes a regularitarian view of causation. Very roughly we might set this view out as follows. For any two events or sets of events, e1 and e2, e1 causes e2 iff:

e1 occurred before e2
e1 is an event of type E1
e2 is an event of type E2
E1 events regularly precede E2 events

There is more to Humean causation than mere regularity and temporal succession, but not much more. In T, I.3.14 Hume defines three conditions for causation. The cause is prior to the effect; cause and effect are contiguous (close in space and time); and the relevant types of event correlate with exceptionless uniformity. Later, in EHU, he dropped the contiguity in space and time condition. There was some consistency in this since in T, I.4.5 he had treated mental events as non-spatial. If causation requires a spatial factor, mental events would be excluded from causal determination. And this is not what Hume wanted to argue.

Why does Hume reject the necessitarian view? The essential point is that he holds not simply that we do not but that we cannot perceive necessary connections between events. As an empiricist he wants to identify clearly what is strictly given in experience; and necessity is not thus given. We cannot see the gas flame making the kettle boil.

There are events, and regularities between types of event. There are different levels of sophistication in the description of events. We can descend from the level of commonsense to that of quantum physics. We will and can at most recognize patterns of repetition between types of event. We cannot see or otherwise perceive one event 'making' another happen. Hume offers an explanation, in terms of his philosophical psychology of the association of ideas, why we think in terms of necessary connections between events. It is our 'custom' or 'habit' to think of necessary connections. But no idea of a cause being a sufficient condition of its effect, such that when the cause occurs the effect cannot but follow, is given in experience. It is therefore 'out'.

From this standpoint, the determinist picture looks very different. If every event has a cause, as Hume accepts, then on a regularitarian notion of cause, this is at bottom only a truth about uniformities of occurrence between types of event. Uniformities do not 'make' anything happen; they are just a matter of what does happen. Any tension between 'every event has a cause' and an agent's being able to do otherwise than he did, abruptly vanishes. Determinism and moral responsibility are reconciled.

Hume explains his positive account of moral responsibility as follows. A person is morally responsible if there is a lawlike correlation between his character and his motives on the one hand, and on the other, his actions. We deny moral responsibility when the correlation fails through external causation – when, for instance, my action is done under your physical compulsion or when under coercion I respond to a threat and so do, with the prospect of dire penalty for non-compliance, an action I have otherwise no desire to do. In the once fashionable slogan, freedom or responsibility is opposed not to causation but to constraint. As long as the causation, the regularity of correlation, runs between character, motive and action without the external compulsion or coercion, I have what Hume calls 'liberty of spontaneity' (T, II.3.2) and may be held responsible for my actions. Compulsion and coercion do not destroy the picture of lawlike correlation; given my character I will respond in a lawlike way to certain threats. But they destroy the kind of correlation on which moral responsibility depends.

Hume holds not only that moral responsibility is consistent in this way with a belief in universal causal determinism; he says that moral responsibility positively requires this belief. For if we withdraw lawlike correlations from the realm of human action, the institution of moral responsibility, the practice of praise and blame, are incoherent. Suppose that we have 'liberty of indifference' (T, II.3.2), which Hume denies. Then an agent's character and motives are irrelevant to what he does. If, irrespective of my character, I might have literally any motive and, irrespective of my motives, I might do literally any action for which I have the physical ability and opportunity, then I am effectively divorced from my actions in a way that would make any praise or blame pointless. I am no more to blame or to be praised for what I did than I am to be complimented on the weather. Neither have anything to do with me. 'Don't blame me', I might say, 'I only did the action; it reflects nothing of my character'. From another angle Hume points out that punishment assumes a lawlike correlation between penalty and character through educability. We take it for granted that there is such a correlation between how we treat the agent now and how he will (or others will, by his example) behave in future.

See Ayer, 1954 or Schlick, 1962: ch. 2 for a more recent defence of this kind of position. R.C. Perry, 1961 is a useful commentary on Ayer.

Hume's version of soft determinism has attracted two main sorts of adverse comment. On the one hand we find a stress on problems within the account; on the other there is a rejection of Hume's entire solution.

Within the account two types of difficulty arise. The first is that Hume's regularitarian notion of cause attracts resistance as inadequate to capture all and only cases of causation. For example the objection is put that, on Hume's account, night is the cause of day: for all three of Hume's causal conditions are met in this case. In his *System of Logic* John Stuart Mill handles this example, within a philosophical perspective broadly similar to Hume's, by correlating the invariable sequence of night and day with the rotation of the earth. So the correlation of night and day becomes just one term in another correlation (Mill,

1872: III.5.8). But the regularitarian notion of cause is certainly not free from difficulty.

The other difficulty within the account concerns Hume's stress on internal versus external causation. It is a small point that there are types of external constraint, hypnosis (say) or brainwashing, of which Hume was not aware. Nor does it greatly matter that he fixes on external compulsion rather than coercion. The real point is that presumably constraint can operate internally in ways that Hume hardly prepares us for when he talks simply of liberty of spontaneity. What of the internal constraint experienced by an addict? The addict has Humean liberty of spontaneity but we do not, or might not, blame him for what he does. I think Hume's response would be that the line between external and internal causation, if hard to specify, is none the less real; and that if the correlation between blame or punishment and alteration in a person's behaviour fails (as well it might for the addict) there would be no point in blaming or punishing that person. (Some complication might be added to account for the deterrent effect on others.)

Beyond such points within the account, however, the major objection to Hume's compatibilism concerns the notion of cause on which it runs. There is a robust response (C.A. Campbell, 1967; cf. Hocutt, 1975) that the real problem about free will and moral responsibility arises on the necessitarian notion of cause, a problem not addressed by redefining the notion of cause in a regularitarian way.

This is a point about the epistemology and metaphysics of causation; and I cannot explore it here except to say that Hume believes himself to be using the only empirically defensible notion of cause. He does not simply assume the regularitarian notion; he argues for it extensively in the *Treatise.* Cf. Hanfling, 1979.

34.1.3. Kant's 'critical' libertarianism

Kant has his own angle on the free will issue, a libertarian angle distinctive enough to be taken separately. He accepts the hard determinist's and the libertarian's notion of cause: causes necessitate their effects. He also takes seriously the hard determinist's challenge. If hard determinism is true, then no one would be morally responsible for any action. So, if there is to be moral responsibility, we must have freedom: the freedom to choose or decide otherwise than we do. Like certain other libertarians he rejects premise (1) of the hard determinist's argument. In conditions of moral action our choices or decisions (the self-prescription of the categorical imperative) are *free causes*: causes which themselves are uncaused.

Kant believes he can show that we have this capacity for free causation. But his account of our knowledge of it varies between the *Foundations* and the *Critique of Practical Reason.* The variation is well expressed by Paton:

In the *Groundwork* [i.e. *Foundations:*] he seems to think that the moral law is both justified and established by an independent and necessary presupposition of freedom. In the *Critique*, on the contrary, it is our consciousness of the moral law which leads to the concept of freedom; and in such consciousness Kant no longer finds difficulty. ... Only on the basis of the moral law can we justify the presupposition that the rational will must be free; and the moral law is even described as a principle for the deduction of freedom (Paton, 1947: 203).

In my view Kant's approach in the *Foundations* is closer in spirit to the *Critique of Pure Reason*, the coping-stone of his whole critical philosophy. I shall keep to that approach here. How, then, is morality's presupposition of freedom to be made good?

As in the earlier discussion of Kant's justification of moral judgement, I shall try to capture the essential play of his ideas. At the end of the section you will find references to discussions which keep closer to Kant's texts.

The heart of Kant's vindication of freedom can, I think, be represented in a five-step argument:

(1) We interpret our experience in a lawlike way.
(2) This interpretation is a product of pure reason, our 'faculty of principles' (*Critique of Pure Reason*, B356; Kemp Smith, 301).
(3) In generating this interpretation pure reason is 'pure spontaneity' (F; Beck, 80), i.e. a free cause, a cause which itself is uncaused.
(4) Pure reason, present also in the moral will, self-prescribes the categorical imperative in the practical sphere.
(5) In self-prescribing the categorical imperative, pure reason is a free cause (from (3) and (4)).

To move through this argument, we need to have a rough picture of Kant's metaphysical and epistemological position. For Kant we have no experience of unconceptualized objects or events; and even to think of objects and events is itself to conceptualize our experience. There is an independently existing real world but our knowledge of it is mediated by a deep structure of conceptualization: our entire construction of the world in terms of space, time, object, event, cause, substance and the rest. If we could subtract from our experience the conceptual contribution of the 'understanding' (*Verstand*) we should know not merely phenomena, the world of appearance, but 'things in themselves', the noumenal world: ultimate reality. There is no point even in trying to imagine what such a world is like, for imagination is no less conceptually infected than any other exercise of the mind.

We interpret this conceptualized experience in various lawlike ways. We think, for example, that every event has a cause (the principle of causality) and that the same cause must produce the same effect (the principle of the uniformity of nature). But these judgements do not record what is given in experience. Rather, they define the framework within which we experience. Kant says:

> Thus the order and regularity in the appearances, which we entitle *nature*, we ourselves introduce. We could never find them in appearances, had not we ourselves, or the nature of our mind, originally set them there (Kant, 1933: Kemp Smith, 147).

The lawlikeness of our experience cannot be a product of the lawlikeness of the world. The world might be lawlike to any degree without our experience registering its regularities. The regularities in our experience are the product of the mind's own activity of 'structuring' and 'frameworking'; and this activity is the 'pure spontaneity' of the noumenal mind, that aspect of our mental life that transcends the phenomenal world. Nothing in our experience explains it; and without it, experience itself would be incoherent and knowledge impossible.

The hard determinist's assumption that every event has a cause looks very different in Kant's hands. Kant does not, like the standard libertarian, assert a breach in causal continuity to admit free will. Rather he collapses the metaphysical depth out of the determinist's assumption about causality by showing it to be a product of pure reason's spontaneous activity in interpreting our experience – an activity in which, contrary to the determinist's view, reason is a free cause.

It is a quick step for Kant to argue to his own satisfaction that the same pure reason (*reinen Vernunft*) which 'introduces' 'order and regularity into the appearances, which we entitle *nature*', is also present in the self-prescribed lawlike activity of the moral will in prescribing to itself the categorical imperative. In morality, pure reason becomes practical. And the 'absolute spontaneity of pure reason' makes the moral will a free cause: a cause which, producing effects, is itself uncaused.

This is only the crude pattern of Kant's epistemological and metaphysical position. (For an elegant statement in compressed compass, see Caird, 1883: 116-18.) Kant is more thorough than I have suggested, even if there are famous lacunas. In the transcendental aesthetic and the transcendental analytic, the *Critique of Pure Reason* examines from a multitude of angles the mind's role in the structuring of experience. (Strawson, 1966 can be seen as a modern reworking of the *Critique*.)

How, then, are we to react? Out of very many possible comments I will select two. In the first place, some critics have queried the equal presence of pure reason in knowledge and morality. The law, 'same cause, same effect', is automatic (we might say) in a way in which the principle of the categorical imperative is not. We do not decide in any self-conscious way to apply the causal principle; we simply see the world in terms of it. But we do not simply prescribe the categorical imperative to ourselves likewise. It is perfectly possible to avoid that self-prescription in the practical sphere.

I think Kant's answer would be that, to the extent to which we do self-prescribe the categorical imperative, we think in terms of the exceptionless and the necessary. Necessarily a rational being acts always on a consistently universalizable maxim; and these ideas of the necessary and exceptionless cannot be, any more than a law like 'same cause, same effect', the product of experience.

The second comment is to ask whether the view of pure reason as 'pure spontaneity' and free cause is really the inference to the best explanation. We can take Kant's point that the lawlikeness of our experience cannot be a product of the world but must rather be the product of our activity of 'structuring' and 'frameworking', without going on to accept that in this activity we are free causes. We can agree that some principles do not derive from experience without having to accept that they do derive from the free play of the noumenal mind beyond the phenomenal realm. Perhaps, we might urge, the mind 'contains' certain ideas or principles *ab initio*, as Plato and Descartes appear to have held. We might appeal, for instance, to genetically-programmed innate ideas, parallel to our innate ability (stressed in Chomskian theoretical linguistics) to learn a natural language.

For further discussion of Kant on free will, see Broad, 1978: ch. 5; Körner, 1967; Rosen, 1988-9; and Scruton, 1982: 58ff., 65ff., 75-7, 84-5.

34.1.4. Other options

I have discussed free will in terms of the relation between moral responsibility and causal determinism. Hard determinism, as presented here, has been the view that actions are causally necessitated in a way that rules out moral responsibility. But there are non-causal versions of determinism, which claim the same result. One of the many merits of Richard Sorabji's discussion of determinism is that he pays full attention to these other versions. Consider fatalism as one possibility. This involves the assumption of a fixed future, nullifying moral responsibility, which has nothing to do with causation.

Suppose that on 1 December 1992, at 17.15 hours British Standard Time, I made a cup of coffee. Philosophers do more exciting things, but autobiographical excess is no part of my brief. Then the following (adapted from O'Connor, 1971: 14) is true:

(S1) On 1 December 1992 at 17.15 hours British Standard Time, GT made a cup of coffee.

(S1) is true now, and will always be true. But equally, the fatalist points out, on 1 December 1900 or at any arbitrary past date, a future tense version of (S1) was also true:

(S2) On 1 December 1992 at 17.15 hours British Standard Time, GT will make a cup of coffee.

So on 1 December 1900 it was true that I would do the relevant action. But if it was true that I would do my action, there was no logical possibility that I would not. It would simply be contradictory to say: 'Even in 1900, it was true that GT would do this action but nevertheless, when the time came, he might have done something different.'

Clearly the argument can be generalized to actions with morally significant descriptions; and if the fatalist argument goes through, its burden is that moral responsibility is nugatory since there is no interesting sense in which anyone can act otherwise than they do.

Now of course philosophical argument is beset with hazards; and the fatalist argument (which is capable of much greater formalization than I have used here) has come under complicated attack. Michael Dummett discusses critically one challenge to the fatalist argument, namely that 'future contingents' (future-tensed statements) are true, in Dummett, 1978: 339-41. I suggest you read O'Connor, 1971: 13-16, 111-19 and Ryle, 1954 first: Ryle and O'Connor are less deep than Dummett, but also less controversial and difficult. Sorabji, 1980 is well worth reading.

For further reading on free will and determinism, Anscombe gives a good handle on the theory of causation in Anscombe, 1975. Probably the two most sophisticated recent works on free will are Honderich, 1988 and Inwagen, 1983.

In a celebrated dovetailing of ethics and the philosophy of mathematics, Lucas, 1970 uses Gödel's Theorem in an attempt to prove that we have free will. For physics, Berry, 1988 is a gentle introduction to the relevance of chaos theory. Frankfurt, 1971 weaves a subtle connection between free will and different levels of desire. O'Connor, 1971 is perhaps the most accessible introduction to traditional debates. Gillet, 1992 is brief but useful. Strawson, 1968 is a minor classic.

Endnote

35.1. FURTHER STUDY

We have now completed the programme set out in 9.1. What next? Your further studies might usefully take five directions.

(1) One is simply to develop and deepen what is sketchy and provisional in the text, taking up the pointers for further reading, joining my loose ends, and reinstating the topics ousted in chapter 1.

(2) Another is to chart the connectedness of problems and topics. For problems touch, topics interpenetrate; and pure division is total fantasy.

(3) A further way is to pick out the conceptual relations of the moral life to other areas of experience: (say) the political, the economic, the religious, and the aesthetic:

Morals and politics

Blanshard, 1966; Croce, 1946; Elster, 1986; Field, 1956: ch. 15; Gallie, 1956; Lloyd Thomas, 1980; Mackinnon, 1957: ch. 6; McKeon, 1962; Nozick, 1974; Sidgwick, 1907: ch. 2; Trépanier, 1963-4; Unger, 1975: ch. 1-3; Wolff, 1990-1 and 1991.

Morals and economics

Buchanan, 1985; Eecke, 1984; Hayek, 1979: ch. 9-10; Kultgen, 1988; Levine, 1988: Part 1; Matthews, 1981; Rawls, 1971: 258-65; Sen, 1987; Varian, 1979.

Morals and religion

Bartley, 1971; Bergson, 1954; Bonhoeffer, 1955; de Burgh, 1935 and 1938; Helm, 1981; Kant, 1956 (Beck, 128-36); Knox, 1968: ch. 12; Lillie, 1955: 303-8; Maclagan, 1961; B. Mitchell, 1967; Paton, 1955: ch. 21; J.A. Smith, 1920-1; Temple, 1912: ch. 2; Vossenkuhl, 1987-8; Ward, 1970; Webb, 1923.

Morals and aesthetics

Beardsmore, 1971; Croce, 1949: ch. 20; Foot, 1970; Hiriyanna, 1954: ch. 7; Kant, 1952: § 59, 'Beauty as the symbol of morality' (see also Neville, 1975); Lesser, 1972; Murdoch, 1970: ch. 3; Plato, R III and X; Scruton, 1974: 24-8, 245-9.

(4) The fourth thing that you might do is to compare and contrast the

philosophical angle on the moral life with other angles of study. What distinguishes a sociologist's or a psychologist's approach to the moral life from that of a philosopher? For examples of how the same subject-matter can be differently treated see, for psychology, Carr, 1987; Ginsberg, 1956: ch. 5; and Kohlberg, 1976; and, for sociology, Ossowska, 1971 and Roubiczek, 1969: ch. 3.

(5) A final way forward is to integrate ethics into the rest of philosophy. Where we have talked e.g. of truth, implication, and belief, here are matters for metaphysics, the philosophy of logic, the theory of knowledge. O'Hear, 1985 and Pateman, 1987 will open some of this territory.

But here we part company. Ethics is now in your charge.

Bibliography

PAS = *Proceedings of the Aristotelian Society*
ASSV = *Aristotelian Society Supplementary Volume*

On a historical note: the Aristotelian Society, the UK's senior philosophical club, has no special connection with the philosophy of Aristotle. It was founded towards the end of the last century to pursue 'the systematic study of Philosophy'. Aristotle seemed the paradigmatic systematic philosopher. There are papers on Aristotle, but the Society, now as always, discusses philosophical problems without regard to any school. The Society, which is open to students as well as professional philosophers, holds an annual conference with the Mind Association; the proceedings are published in Supplementary Volumes.

The journal *Cogito*, to which there are several references below, is particularly helpful for the beginning student in philosophy. The articles are short, clear, scholarly and written specially with starters in mind.

Abbott, E. (1898) 'Aristotle's Conception of the State', *Hellenica*, ed. E. Abbott, London.
Abbott, T.K. (1909) *Kant's Critique of Practical Reason and Other Works on the Theory of Ethics*, 6th ed., London.
Achinstein, P. (1974) 'The Identity of Properties', *American Philosophical Quarterly*, 11.
Ackrill, J.L. (1975) *Aristotle on Eudaimonia*, Oxford.
Acton, H.B. ed. (1969) *The Philosophy of Punishment*, London.
Adkins, A.W.H. (1960) *Merit and Responsibility: A Study in Greek Values*, Oxford.
Alexander, S. (1899) *Moral Order and Progress: An Analysis of Ethical Conceptions*, London.
Allan, D.J. (1970) *The Philosophy of Aristotle*, 2nd ed., Oxford.
Altham, J.E.J. (1983-4) 'Ethics of Risk', *PAS*, 84.
Ammerman, R.R. (1964-5) 'Ethics and Belief', *PAS*, 65.
Annas, J. (1976) 'Davidson and Anscombe on "the same action" ', *Mind*, 85.
Anscombe, G.E.M. (1957) *Intention*, Oxford.
Anscombe, G.E.M. (1970) 'Modern Moral Philosophy', *The Definition of Morality*, ed. G. Wallace and A.D.M. Walker, London.
Anscombe, G.E.M. (1975) 'Causality and Determination', *Causation and Conditionals*, ed. E. Sosa, Oxford.
Anscombe, G.E.M. (1981) *Collected Philosophical Papers*, vol. 3, Oxford.
Aquinas, St Thomas (1892) *Aquinas Ethicus: or, The Moral Teaching of St Thomas*, tr. J. Rickaby, 2 vols, London. Original text: 1265-73.
Aristotle, *Nicomachean Ethics* (1969) tr. W.D. Ross, Oxford. Original text: *c.* 330 BC.
Aristotle, *The Politics* (1981), tr. T.A. Sinclair, rev. T.J. Saunders, Harmondsworth. Original text: *c.* 335-323 BC.
Armstrong, D.M. (1973) *Belief, Truth and Knowledge*, Cambridge.
Arrington, R. (1985) Review of S. Lovibond, *Realism and Imagination in Ethics*, *Mind*, 94.
Attfield, R. (1979) 'How Not To Be A Relativist', *Monist*, 62.
Attfield, R. (1987) *A Theory of Value and Obligation*, London.
Audi, R. (1979) 'Wants and Intentions in the Explanation of Action', *Journal for the Theory of Social Behaviour*, 9.

Austin, J.L. (1961) *Philosophical Papers*, ed. G.J. Warnock, Oxford.
Austin, J.L. (1962) *How To Do Things With Words*, ed. J.O. Urmson, Oxford.
Ayer, A.J. (1936; 2nd ed. 1946) *Language, Truth and Logic*, London.
Ayer, A.J. (1954) 'Freedom and Necessity', *Philosophical Essays*, London.
Babbitt, I. (1931) Contribution to *Living Philosophies*, New York.
Bach, K. (1980) 'Actions are not events', *Mind*, 89.
Baillie, J. (1934) 'The Place of Tradition in the Moral Life', *Philosophy*, 9.
Baldwin, T. (1979) 'Foresight and Responsibility', *Philosophy*, 54.
Baldwin, T. (1990) *G.E. Moore*, London.
Barnes, J. (1980) 'Aristotle and the Methods of Ethics', *Revue Internationale de Philosophie*, Nos. 133-4.
Bartley, W.W. (1971) *Morality and Religion*, London.
Bayles, M.D. (1984) 'Intuitions in Ethics', *Dialogue*, 23.
Beardsmore, R.W. (1971) *Art and Morality*, London.
Becker, L.C. (1973) 'The Finality of Moral Judgments: A Reply to Mrs Foot', *Philosophical Review*, 82.
Becker, L.C. (1986) *Reciprocity*, London.
Beehler, R. (1978) *Moral Life*, New Jersey.
Bennett, J. (1971) 'Whatever the Consequences', *Moral Problems*, ed. J. Rachels, New York.
Benson, J. (1983) 'Who is the Autonomous Man?', *Philosophy*, 58.
Bentham, J. (1967) *An Introduction to the Principles of Morals and Legislation*, ed. W. Harrison, Oxford. Original text: 1780.
Berger, F.R. (1979) 'John Stuart Mill on Justice and Fairness', *New Essays on John Stuart Mill and Utilitarianism*, ed. W.E. Cooper, K. Nielsen and S.C. Patten, *Canadian Journal of Philosophy, Supplementary Volume*, 5.
Bergson, H. (1954) *The Two Sources of Morality and Religion*, tr. R.A. Audra, C. Brereton, W.H. Carter, New York.
Berlin, I. (1967) 'Two Concepts of Liberty', *Political Philosophy*, ed. A. Quinton, Oxford.
Berry, M. (1988) 'Chaos and Order', *Cogito*, 2.
Blackburn, S.W. (1971) 'Moral Realism', *Morality and Moral Reasoning*, ed. J. Casey, London.
Blackburn, S.W. (1984) *Spreading the Word*, Oxford.
Blackburn, S.W. (1992) 'Morality and Thick Concepts', *ASSV*, 66.
Blanshard, B. (1961) *Reason and Goodness*, London.
Blanshard, B. (1966) 'Morality and Politics', *Ethics and Society*, ed. R.T. De George, London.
Blum, L.A. (1980) *Friendship, Altruism and Morality*, London.
Blumenfeld, D. (1971) 'The Principle of Alternate Possibilities', *Journal of Philosophy*, 68.
Blumenfeld, D. (1973) 'About Moral Beliefs', *Philosophical Studies*, 24.
Bodéüs, R. (1982) 'Une interpretation génétiste de l'éthique aristotelicienne', *Revue Philosophique de Louvain*, 80.
Bonhoeffer, D. (1955) *Ethics*, London.
Bosanquet, B. (1888) *Logic*, 1st ed., Oxford.
Bosanquet, B. (1912) *The Principle of Individuality and Value*, London.
Bottomore, T. (1975) *Marxist Sociology*, London.
Bradley, F.H. (1883, 2nd ed. 1922) *The Principles of Logic*, Oxford.
Bradley, F.H. (1927) *Ethical Studies*, 2nd ed., Oxford.
Brennan, J.M. (1977) *The Open-Texture of Moral Concepts*, London.
Bricke, J. (1974) 'Hume's Conception of Character', *Southwestern Journal of Philosophy*, 5.
Broad, C.D. (1969) 'Conscience and Conscientious Action', *Moral Concepts*, ed. J. Feinberg, Oxford.
Broad, C.D. (1978) *Kant*, Cambridge.
Brooks, D.H.M. (1987-8) 'Dogs and Slaves: Genetics, Exploitation and Morality', *PAS*, 88.
Brown, J. (1977) 'Moral Theory and the Ought-Can Principle', *Mind*, 86.

Buchanan, A. (1985) *Ethics, Efficiency, and the Market*, New Jersey.

Burgh, W.G. de (1935) *The Relations of Morality to Religion*, London.

Burgh, W.G. de (1938) *From Morality to Religion*, London.

Burton, S.L. (1992) ' "Thick" Concepts Revised', *Analysis*, 52.

Butchvarov, P. (1982) 'That Simple, Indefinable, Nonnatural Property, Good', *Review of Metaphysics*, 36.

Butler, J. (1967) *Fifteen Sermons*, ed. W.R. Matthews, London. Original text: 1726.

Caird, E. (1883) *Hegel*, Edinburgh and London.

Campbell, C.A. (1967) *In Defence of Free Will*, London.

Campbell, K. (1985) 'Self-Mastery and Stoic Ethics', *Philosophy*, 60.

Canfield, J.V. (1962) 'The Compatibility of Free Will and Determinism', *Philosophical Review*, 71.

Cargile, J. (1989) 'What is a natural property?', *Philosophy*, 64.

Carr, D. (1987) 'Freud and Sexual Ethics', *Philosophy*, 62.

Casey, J. (1971) 'Actions and Consequences', *Morality and Moral Reasoning*, ed. J. Casey, London.

Cashdollar, S. (1973) 'Aristotle's Politics of Morals', *Journal of the History of Philosophy*, 11.

Charlton, W. (1988a) Review of Wiggins (1987), *Philosophy*, 63.

Charlton, W. (1988b) *Weakness of Will*, Oxford.

Chisholm, R.M. (1976) 'Intentional Inexistence', *The Philosophy of Brentano*, ed. L. McAlister, London.

Churchland, P.M. (1981) 'Eliminative Materialism and the Propositional Attitudes', *Journal of Philosophy*, 78.

Clarke, D.S. (1985) *Practical Inferences*, London.

Cody, A.B. (1967) 'Can a Single Action have Many Different Descriptions?', *Inquiry*.

Cooper, J.M. (1975) *Reason and Human Good in Aristotle*, Cambridge, USA.

Cooper, N. (1981) *The Diversity of Moral Thinking*, Oxford.

Cooper, N. (1988) 'The Formula of the End in Itself', *Philosophy*, 63.

Craig, E. (1986-7) 'The Practical Explication of Knowledge', *PAS*, 87.

Crisp, R. (1992) 'Utilitarianism and the Life of Virtue', *Philosophical Quarterly*, 42.

Croce, B. (1946) *Politics and Morals*, London.

Croce, B. (1949) *My Philosophy*, London.

Crombie, I.M. (1962) *An Examination of Plato's Doctrines. I. Plato on Man and Society*, London.

Cronin, M. (1939) *The Science of Ethics*, Dublin.

Dancy, J. (1981) 'On Moral Properties', *Mind*, 90.

Dancy, J. (1983) 'Ethical Particularism and Morally Relevant Properties', *Mind*, 92.

Dancy, J. (1992) 'Can Practical Reasoning Rest on Universal Principles?', *Cogito*, 6.

Daniels, N. (1980) 'Reflective Equilibrium and Archimedean Points', *Canadian Journal of Philosophy*, 10.

Darwall, S.L. (1974) 'Nagel's Argument for Altruism', *Philosophical Studies*, 25.

Darwall, S.L. (1976) 'The Inference to the Best Means', *Canadian Journal of Philosophy*, 6.

Darwall, S.L. (1983) *Impartial Reason*, New York.

Davidson, D. (1968) 'Actions, Reasons, and Causes', *The Philosophy of Action*, ed. A.R. White, Oxford.

Davidson, D. (1969) 'How is Weakness of Will Possible?', *Moral Concepts*, ed. J. Feinberg, Oxford.

Davidson, D. (1973) 'Freedom to Act', *Essays on Freedom of Action*, ed. T. Honderich, London.

Davidson, D. (1980) *Essays on Actions and Events*, Oxford.

Davies, C.A. (1975) 'Morality and Ignorance of Fact', *Philosophy*, 50.

Defourny, P. (1977) 'Contemplation in Aristotle's Ethics', *Articles on Aristotle: 2. Ethics and Politics*, ed. J. Barnes et al., London.

Depaul, M.R. (1987) 'Two Conceptions of Coherence Methods in Ethics', *Mind*, 96.

Depaul, M.R. (1990) Critical notice of Wiggins (1987), *Mind*, 99.

DeWitt, N.W. (1954) *Epicurus and his Philosophy*, Minneapolis.

Donner, W. (1983) 'John Stuart Mill's Concept of Utility', *Dialogue*, 22.

Double, R. (1985) 'The Case Against the Case Against Belief', *Mind*, 94.

Downie, R.S. and Telfer, E. (1969) *Respect for Persons*, London.

Dudley, J. (1982) 'La contemplation (*theoria*) humaine selon Aristote', *Revue Philosophique de Louvain*, 80.

Dummett, M. (1978) *Truth and Other Enigmas*, London.

Dworkin, G. (1981) 'Voluntary Health Risks and Public Policy', *Hastings Centre Report*, 11.

Earle, W.J. (1988) 'Epicurus: "Live Hidden!" ', *Philosophy*, 63.

Eecke, W. Ver (1984) 'The State: Ethics and Economics', *The Georgetown Symposium on Ethics*, ed. R. Porreco, Maryland, USA.

Elinde, M. ed. (1987) *The Encyclopedia of Religion*, NY.

Elster, J. (1986) 'The Market and the Forum: Three Varieties of Political Theory', *Foundations of Social Choice Theory*, ed. E. Elster and A. Hylland, Cambridge.

Emmet, D. (1966) *Rules, Roles and Relations*, London.

Emmons, D.C. (1973) 'Act vs. Rule Utilitarianism', *Mind*, 72.

Engels, F. (1878) *Anti-Dühring*, Eng. tr. (n.d.) E. Burns, London.

Evans, D. (1975) 'Moral Weakness', *Philosophy*, 50.

Fain, H. (1972) 'Some Moral Infirmities of Justice', *Individual and Collective Responsibility*, ed. P.A. French, California.

Falk, W.D. (1975) 'Hume on Practical Reason', *Philosophical Studies*, 27.

Falk, W.D. (1976) 'Hume on Is and Ought', *Canadian Journal of Philosophy*, 6.

Farringdon, B. (1967) *The Faith of Epicurus*, London.

Feinberg, J. (1968) 'Action and Responsibility', *The Philosophy of Action*, ed. A.R. White, Oxford.

Field, G.C. (1932) *Moral Theory*, 2nd ed., London.

Field, G.C. (1956) *Political Theory*, London.

Fields, L.C. (1987) 'Moral and Legal Responsibility', *Cogito*, 1.

Findlay, J.N. (1970) *Axiological Ethics*, London.

Finnis, J. (1980) *Natural Law and Natural Rights*, Oxford.

Flew, A.G.N. (1969) 'Locke and the Problem of Personal Identity', *Locke and Berkeley*, ed. C.B. Martin and D.M. Armstrong, London.

Fodor, J. (1985) 'Fodor's Guide to Mental Representation', *Mind*, 94.

Foot, P.R. (1970) *Morality and Art*, Oxford.

Foot, P.R. (1971) 'The Problem of Abortion and the Doctrine of Double Effect', *Moral Problems*, ed. J. Rachels, New York.

Foot, P.R. (1974) 'Is Morality a System of Hypothetical Imperatives? A Reply to Mr Holmes', *Analysis*, 34.

Foot, P.R. (1978) *Virtues and Vices and Other Essays in Moral Philosophy*, Oxford.

Foot, P.R. (1985) 'Utilitarianism and the Virtues', *Mind*, 94.

Forrest, P. (1985) 'Backward Causation in Defence of Free Will', *Mind*, 94.

Foster, J. (1982) *Idealism*, London.

Foster, J. (1985) *Ayer*, London.

Frankena, W.K. (1967) 'The Naturalistic Fallacy', *Theories of Ethics*, ed. P.R. Foot, Oxford.

Frankena, W.K. (1974a) 'The Philosopher's Attack on Morality', *Philosophy*, 49.

Frankena, W.K. (1974b) 'Sidgwick and the Dualism of Practical Reason', *Monist*, 58.

Frankfurt, H. (1971) 'Freedom of the Will and the Concept of a Person', *Journal of Philosophy*, 68.

Friedman, R.Z. (1981) 'Virtue and Happiness: Kant and Three Critics', *Canadian Journal of Philosophy*, 11.

Gaita, R. ed. (1990), *Value and Understanding: Essays for Peter Winch*, London.

Gaita, R. (1991) *Good and Evil*, London.

Gallie, W.B. (1956) 'Liberal Morality and Socialist Morality', *Philosophy, Politics and Society*, ed. P. Laslett, Oxford.

Galvin, R. (1991) 'Does Kant's Psychology of Morals Need Basic Revision?', *Mind*, 100.

Gauthier, D. (1970) 'Morality and Advantage', *The Definition of Morality*, ed. G. Wallace and A.D.M. Walker, London.

Gauthier, D. (1974) 'The Impossibility of Rational Egoism', *Journal of Philosophy*, 71.

Gauthier, D. (1986) *Morals by Agreement*, Oxford.

Gay, R. (1985) 'Ethical Pluralism: A Reply to Dancy', *Mind*, 94.

Geach, P.T. (1967) 'Good and Evil', *Theories of Ethics*, ed. P.R. Foot, Oxford.

Gewirth, A. (1978) *Reason and Morality*, Chicago.

Gewirth, A. (1981) 'The Future of Ethics', *Nous*, 15.

Gibbard, A. (1992) 'Morality and Thick Concepts', *ASSV*, 62.

Gibbs, B (1986) 'Higher and Lower Pleasures', *Philosophy*, 61.

Gillet, G. (1992) 'A Dialogue on Free Will and Determinism', *Cogito*, 6.

Ginsberg, M. (1956) *On the Diversity of Morals*, London.

Glover, J. (1975) ' "It Makes No Difference Whether or Not I Do It" ', *ASSV*, 49.

Godwin, W. (1971) *Enquiry Concerning Political Justice*, ed. K.C. Carter, Oxford. Original text: 1793.

Gold, H.B. (1977) 'Praxis: Its Conceptual Development in Aristotle's Nicomachean Ethics', *Graduate Faculty Journal of Philosophy* (New School for Social Research, NY), 6.

Goldman, A.I. (1983) Review of Nozick (1981), *Philosophical Review*, 92.

Gomez-Lobo, A. (1989) 'Aristotle', *Ethics in the History of Western Philosophy*, ed. R.J. Cavalier, J. Gouinlock and J.P. Sterba, London, 1989.

Goodman, E. (1975) *A Study of Liberty and Revolution*, London.

Gosling, J. (1990) *Weakness of the Will*, London.

Grant, A. (1898) *Aristotle*, Edinburgh.

Grayling, A.C. (1987) 'Realism', *Cogito*, 1.

Grayling, A.C. (1991-2) 'Epistemology and Realism', *PAS*.

Green, O.H. (1982) 'The Theory of Metaethical Neutrality', *Metaphilosophy*, 13.

Green, T.H. (1899) *Prolegomena to Ethics*, ed. A.C. Bradley, 4th ed., Oxford.

Greenspan, P.S. (1978) 'Behavior Control and Freedom of Action', *Philosophical Review*, 87.

Griffin, J. (1982) 'Modern Utilitarianism', *Revue Internationale de Philosophie*, 141.

Griffin, J. (1986) *Well-Being: Its Meaning, Measurement and Moral Importance*, Oxford.

Griffiths, A.P. (1967) 'On Belief', *Knowledge and Belief*, ed. A.P. Griffiths, Oxford.

Guttenplan, S.D. (1979-80) 'Moral Dilemmas and Moral Realism', *PAS*, 80.

Guttenplan, S.D. (1991) Review of J. Etchemendy, *The Concept of Logical Consequence*, *Mind*, 100.

Haack, R.J. (1975) Review of Rescher, 1973, *Mind*, 84.

Habermas, J. (1972) *Knowledge and Human Interests*, London.

Haezrahi, P. (1968) 'The Concept of Man as End-In-Himself', *Kant: A Collection of Critical Essays*, ed. R.P. Wolff, London.

Hallett, G. (1984) *Reason and Right*, Notre Dame.

Hamburgh, M. (1981) 'Fresh Thoughts on Sociobiology', *Hastings Center Report*, 11.

Hamlyn, D.W. (1970) *The Theory of Knowledge*, London.

Hanfling, O. (1979) 'Hume's Idea of Necessary Connexion', *Philosophy*, 54.

Hardie, W.F.R. (1968) 'The Final Good in Aristotle's Ethics', *Aristotle*, ed. J.M.E. Moravcsik, London.

Hardie, W.F.R. (1980) *Aristotle's Ethical Theory*, 2nd ed., Oxford.

Hare, R.M. (1952) *The Language of Morals*, Oxford.

Hare, R.M. (1963) *Freedom and Reason*, Oxford.

Hare, R.M. (1967) 'Geach: Good and Evil', *Theories of Ethics*, ed. P.R. Foot, Oxford.

Hare, R.M. (1972) 'Can I Be Blamed for Obeying Orders?', *Essays on the Moral Concepts*, London.

Hare, R.M. (1981) *Moral Thinking: Its Levels, Method, and Point*, Oxford.

Hare, R.M. (1987) 'Why Moral Language?', *Metaphysics and Morality*, ed. P. Pettit, R. Sylvan and J. Norman, Oxford.

Harman, G. (1965) 'The Inference to the Best Explanation', *Philosophical Review*, 74.

Harman, G. (1976) 'Practical Reasoning', *Review of Metaphysics*, 29.

Harman, G. (1977) *The Nature of Morality*, Oxford.

Harman, G. (1984) 'Logic and Reasoning', *Synthese*, 60.

Harris, J. (1974) 'Williams on Negative Responsibility and Integrity', *Philosophical Quarterly*, 24.

Harrison, J. (1969) 'Kant's Examples of the First Formulation of the Categorical Imperative', *Kant: Foundations of the Metaphysics of Morals*, tr. L.W. Beck, ed. R.P. Wolff, New York, 1969.

Harrison, J. (1976) *Hume's Moral Epistemology*, Oxford.

Harrison, J. (1981) *Hume's Theory of Justice*, Oxford.

Harrison, J. (1989) 'Logical Positivism', *Cogito*, 3.

Hart, H.L.A. (1959) *The Concept of Law*, Oxford.

Hart, H.L.A. (1968) 'Postscript: Responsibility and Retribution', *Punishment and Responsibility*, Oxford.

Hart, H.L.A. and Honoré, A.M. (1961) *Causation in the Law*, Oxford.

Hayek, F.A. (1979) *Law, Legislation and Liberty*, London.

Helm, P. ed. (1981) *Divine Commands and Morality*, Oxford.

Hintikka, J. (1984) 'A Hundred Years Later: the Rise and Fall of Frege's Influence in Language Theory', *Synthese*, 59.

Hiriyanna, M. (1954) *Art Experience*, Mysore.

Hocutt, M. (1975) 'Freedom and Capacity', *Review of Metaphysics*, 29.

Holland, R.F. (1972) 'Morality and Moral Reasoning', *Philosophy*, 47.

Holland, R.F. (1980) 'Absolute Ethics, Mathematics and the Impossibility of Politics', *Against Empiricism*, Oxford.

Hollis, M. (1975) 'My Role and Its Duties', *Nature and Conduct*, ed. R.S. Peters, London.

Holmes, R.L. (1974) 'Is Morality a System of Hypothetical Imperatives?', *Analysis*, 34.

Honderich, T. (1988) *A Theory of Determinism*, London.

Hooker, B. (1990) 'Rule-Consequentialism', *Mind*, 99.

Huby, P. (1967) *Greek Ethics*, London.

Hudson, W.D. (1967) *Ethical Intuitionism*, London.

Hudson, W.D. (1969) *The Is-Ought Question*, London.

Hudson, W.D. (1980) *A Century of Moral Philosophy*, London.

Hudson, W.D. (1983) *Modern Moral Philosophy*, 2nd ed., London.

Humberstone, I.L. (1982) 'First Steps in Philosophical Taxonomy', *Canadian Journal of Philosophy*, 13.

Hume, D. (1975) *Enquiries concerning the Human Understanding and the Principles of Morals*, ed. L.A. Selby-Bigge, rev. P.H. Nidditch, 3rd ed., Oxford.

Hume, D. (1978) *A Treatise of Human Nature*, ed. L.A. Selby-Bigge, rev. P.H. Nidditch, 2nd ed., Oxford. Original text: 1739-40.

Hume, D. (1987) *Essays Moral, Political and Literary*, ed. E.F. Miller, Indianapolis.

Hurley, P. (1992) 'How Weakness of the Will is Possible', *Mind*, 101.

Hutchinson, D.S. (1982) 'Utilitarianism and Children', *Canadian Journal of Philosophy*, 12.

Hutchinson, D.S. (1986) *The Virtues of Aristotle*, London.

Inwagen, P. van (1978) 'Ability and Responsibility', *Philosophical Review*, 87.

Inwagen, P. van (1983) *An Essay on Free Will*, Oxford.

Irwin, T.H. (1988) 'Disunity in the Aristotelian Virtues, *Oxford Studies in Ancient Philosophy*, Supplementary Volume, ed. J. Annas and R.H. Grimes.

Jackson, F. (1984) 'Weakness of Will', *Mind*, 93.

Jackson, J. (1978) 'Virtues with Reason', *Philosophy*, 53.

James, W. (1884) 'The Dilemma of Determinism', reprinted in *The Will to Believe and Other Essays*, New York, 1903.

Jennings, R.C. (1987) 'Is it True what Haack says about Tarski?', *Philosophy*, 62.

Joachim, H.H. (1906) *The Nature of Truth*, Oxford.

Joachim, H.H. (1955) *The Nicomachean Ethics*, ed. D.A. Rees, Oxford.

Joad, C.E.M. (1938) *Guide to the Philosophy of Morals and Politics*, London.

Joad, C.E.M. (1950) *A Critique of Logical Positivism*, London.

Jonsen, A.R. and Toulmin, S. (1988) *The Abuse of Casuistry: A History of Moral Reasoning*, California.

Joseph, H.W.B. (1935) *Essays in Ancient and Modern Philosophy*, Oxford.

Juhl, P.D. (1980) *Interpretation. An Essay in the Philosophy of Literary Criticism*, Princeton.

Kant, I. (1933) *Critique of Pure Reason*, tr. N. Kemp Smith, London, 1933. Original text: 1st ed. 1781, 2nd ed. 1787.

Kant, I. (1952) *Critique of Judgement*, tr. J.C. Meredith, Oxford. Original text: 1st ed. 1790.

Kant, I. (1956) *Critique of Practical Reason*, tr. L.W. Beck, New York. Original text: 1788.

Kant, I. (1964) *The Doctrine of Virtue, Part II of The Metaphysic of Morals*, tr. M.J. Gregor, New York. Original text: 1797.

Kant, I. (1965) *The Metaphysical Elements of Justice, Part II of The Metaphysic of Morals*, tr. J. Ladd, New York. Original text: 1797.

Kant, I. (1969) *Foundations of the Metaphysics of Morals*, tr. L.W. Beck, New York. Original text: 1785.

Kavka, G.S. (1986) *Hobbesian Moral and Political Theory*, Princeton.

Kavka, G.S. (1987) Review of D. Gauthier, *Morals by Agreement*, *Mind*, 96.

Kekes, J. (1982) 'Happiness', *Mind*, 91.

Kelly, G. (1955) *Medico-Moral Problems*, Dublin.

Kenny, A.J.P. (1979) *Aristotle's Theory of the Will*, London.

Klagge, J.C. (1984) 'An Alleged Difficulty concerning Moral Properties', *Mind*, 93.

Knox, T.M. (1968) *Action*, London.

Kohlberg, L. (1976) 'Moral Stages and Moralization', *Moral Development and Behavior*, ed. T. Lickona, NY.

Kolakowski, L. (1972) *Positivist Philosophy*, Harmondsworth.

Kolenda, K. (1975) 'Moral Conflicts and Universalizability', *Philosophy*, 50.

Körner, S. (1967) 'Kant's Conception of Freedom', *Proceedings of the British Academy*, 53.

Korsgaard, C (1989) 'Kant', *Ethics in the History of Western Philosophy*, ed. R.J. Cavalier, J. Gouinlock and J.P. Sterba, London, 1989.

Krook, D. (1959) *Three Traditions of Moral Thought*, Cambridge.

Kultgen, J. (1988) *Ethics and Professionalism*, Princeton.

Kydd, R.M. (1946) *Reason and Conduct in Hume's Treatise*, Oxford.

Ladd, J (1985) *Ethical Relativism*, Lanham, USA.

Laird, J. (1929) *The Idea of Value*, Cambridge.

Lee, K. (1985) *A New Basis for Moral Philosophy*, London.

Lehmkuhl, A. (1914) *Theologia Moralis*, Freiberg.

Lesser, A.H. (1972) 'Aesthetic Reasons for Acting', *Philosophical Quarterly*, 22.

Levi, A.W. (1961) 'The Trouble With Ethics', *Mind*, 70.

Levine, A. (1988) *Arguing for Socialism*, New York and London.

Lewis, C.I. (1971) *An Analysis of Knowledge and Valuation*, Illinois.

Lewis, D. (1988) 'Desire as Belief', *Mind*, 97.

Lewy, C. (1968) 'G.E. Moore and the Naturalistic Fallacy', *Studies in the Philosophy of Thought and Action*, ed. P.F. Strawson, Oxford.

Leys, W.A.R. (1952) *Ethics for Policy Decisions: The Art of Asking Deliberative Questions*, New Jersey.

Lillie, W. (1955) *An Introduction to Ethics*, London.

Lloyd, G.E.R. (1968) *Aristotle*, Cambridge.

Lloyd Thomas, D.A. (1980) 'Kantian and Utilitarian Democracy', *Canadian Journal of Philosophy*, 10.

Lodge, R.C. (1951) *Applied Philosophy*, London.

Lonergan, B.J.F. (1978) *Insight: A Study of Human Understanding*, San Francisco.

Long, A.A. (1974) *Hellenistic Philosophy*, London.

Lovibond, S. (1983) *Realism and Imagination in Ethics*, Oxford.

Lovibond, S. (1989-90) 'True and False Pleasures', *PAS*, 90.

Lucas, J.R. (1970) *The Freedom of the Will*, Oxford.

Lucas, J.R. (1971) 'Ethical Intuitionism', *Philosophy*, 46.

Lyons, D. (1978) 'Mill's Theory of Justice', *Values and Morals*, ed. A.I. Goldman and J. Kim, Dordrecht.

Macdonald, G. and Pettit, P. (1981) *Semantics and Social Science*, London.

McDonald, W. (1903) *The Principles of Moral Science*, Dublin.

McDowell, J. (1979) 'Virtue and Reason', *Monist*, 62.

McDowell, J. (1988) 'Values and Secondary Qualities', *Essays on Moral Realism*, ed. G. Sayre-McCord, Cornell.

McFetridge, I.G (1985) 'Supervenience, Realism, Necessity', *Philosophical Quarterly*, 35.

MacIntyre, A.C. (1966) 'Hume on "Is" and "Ought" ', *Hume*, ed. V.C. Chappell, New York.

MacIntyre, A.C. (1981) *After Virtue*, London.

McKeon, R. (1962) 'Ethics and Politics', *Ethics and Bigness*, ed. H. Cleveland and H.D. Lasswell, New York.

Mackie, J.L. (1973) 'The Disutility of Act-Utilitarianism', *Philosophical Quarterly*, 23.

Mackie, J.L. (1976) *Problems from Locke*, Oxford.

Mackie, J.L. (1977) *Ethics: Inventing Right and Wrong*, Harmondsworth. (Rev. ed. 1990.)

Mackie, J.L. (1978) 'The Law of the Jungle', *Philosophy*, 53.

Mackie, J.L. (1980) *Hume's Moral Theory*, London.

Mackie, J.L. (1984) 'Can There Be a Right-Based Moral Theory?', *Theories of Rights*, ed. J. Waldron, Oxford.

Mackinnon, D.M. (1957) *A Study in Ethical Theory*, London.

Mackinnon, D.M. (1972) 'The Euthyphro Dilemma', *ASSV*, 46.

Maclagan, W.G. (1960) 'Respect for Persons as a Moral Principle I and II', *Philosophy*, 35.

Maclagan, W.G. (1961) *The Theological Frontier of Ethics*, London.

McNeilly, F.S. (1972) 'Promises De-Moralized', *Philosophical Review*, 81.

Madden, E.H. (1975) 'Human Action, Reasons or Causes?', *Journal for the Theory of Social Behaviour*, 5.

Makinson, D.C. (1973) *Topics in Modern Logic*, London.

Mandeville, B. de (1988) *The Fable of the Bees; or Private Vices, Publick Virtues*, 2 vols, Indianapolis. Original text: Part I, 1725, Part II, 1729.

Martin, R (1972) 'A Defence of Mill's Qualitative Hedonism', *Philosophy*, 47.

Marx, K. (1976) *Preface and Introduction to the Critique of Political Economy*, Peking. Original text: 1857-8.

Mattern, R. (1980) 'Moral Science and the Concept of Persons in Locke', *Philosophical Review*, 89.

Matthews, R.C.O. (1981) 'Morality, Competition and Efficiency', *Manchester School of Economic and Social Studies*, 4.

Melden, A.I. (1961) *Free Action*, London.

Mellor, D.H. (1976) 'Probable Explanation', *Australasian Journal of Philosophy*, 54.

Meyer, R.K. (1974) 'Entailment is not Strict Implication', *Australasian Journal of Philosophy*, 52.

Midgley, M. (1987) 'The Flight from Blame', *Philosophy*, 62.

Mill, J.S. (1872) *A System of Logic*, 8th ed., London.

Mill, J.S. (1962) *Mill on Bentham and Coleridge*, ed. F.R. Leavis, London. Original texts: 'Bentham', 1838; 'Coleridge', 1840.

Mill, J.S. (1971) *Essential Works of John Stuart Mill*, ed. M. Lerner, New York. Original text of *Utilitarianism*: *Fraser's Magazine*, 1861; book form, 1863.

Miller, D (1981) *Hume's Political Thought*, Oxford.

Miller, F.D. (1984) 'Aristotle on Rationality in Action', *Review of Metaphysics*, 38.

Milo, R.D. (1984) *Immorality*, Princeton.

Mitchell, B. (1967) *Law, Morality and Religion in a Secular Society*, Oxford.
Mitchell, D. (1990) 'Validity and Practical Reasoning', *Philosophy*, 65.
Monro, D.H. (1953) *Godwin's Moral Philosophy*, Oxford.
Montague, R. (1974) 'Winch on Agents' Judgements', *Analysis*, 34.
Montefiore, A. (1958) *A Modern Introduction to Moral Philosophy*, London.
Moore, G.E. (1903) *Principia Ethica*, Cambridge.
Moore, G.E. (1912) *Ethics*, Oxford.
Morrall, J.B. (1977) *Aristotle*, London.
Mortimore, G.W. ed. (1971) *Weakness of Will*, London.
Mueller-Vollmer, K. ed. (1986) *The Hermeneutics Reader*, Oxford.
Murdoch, I. (1970) *The Sovereignty of Good*, London.
Mure, G.R.G. (1964) *Aristotle*, New York.
Nagel, T. (1970) *The Possibility of Altruism*, Princeton.
Nathan, D.O. (1979) 'On the Factual Basis of Moral Reasoning', *Australasian Journal of Philosophy*, 57.
Neville, M.R. (1975) 'Kant on Beauty as the Symbol of Morality', *Philosophy Research Archives*, 1, no. 1053.
Nidditch, P.H. (1970) *The Intellectual Virtues*, Sheffield.
Nielsen, K. (1973) 'Some Puzzles about Formulating Utilitarianism', *Ratio*, 15.
Norman, R. (1969) 'Aristotle's philosopher-God', *Phronesis*, 14.
Norman, R. (1971) *A Theory of Reasons for Actions*, Oxford.
Norman, R. (1983) *The Moral Philosophers*, Oxford.
Norton, D.F. (1982) David Hume: *Common-Sense Moralist and Sceptical Metaphysician*, Princeton.
Norton, D.F. (1989) 'Hume', *Ethics in the History of Western Philosophy*, ed. R.J. Cavalier, J. Gouinlock and J.P. Sterba, London, 1989.
Nozick, R. (1972) 'Coercion', *Philosophy, Politics and Society*, 4th series, ed. P. Laslett, W.G. Runciman and Q. Skinner, Oxford.
Nozick, R. (1974) *Anarchy, State and Utopia*, Oxford.
Nozick, R. (1981) *Philosophical Explanations*, Oxford.
Nussbaum, M. (1986) 'The Discernment of Perception: an Aristotelian conception of private and public rationality', *Proceedings of the Boston Area Colloquium in Ancient Philosophy*, I, ed. J.J. Cleary, Lanham, USA.
Nyiri, J.C. (1988) 'Tradition and Practical Knowledge', *Practical Knowledge: Outlines of a Theory of Traditions and Skills*, ed. J.C. Nyiri and B. Smith, London.
Oakeshott, M.J. (1933) *Experience and its Modes*, Cambridge.
Oakeshott, M.J. (1991) *Rationalism in Politics and Other Essays*, 2nd ed., Indianapolis.
O'Connor, D.J. (1971) *Free Will*, London.
O'Connor, D.J. (1975) *The Correspondence Theory of Truth*, London.
O'Hear, A. (1985) *What is Philosophy?*, Harmondsworth.
Olsen, S.H. (1982) 'Text and Meaning', *Inquiry*, 25.
O'Neill, O. (1981) Review of Beehler (1978) *Philosophical Review*, 90.
O'Neill, O. (1986) *Faces of Hunger*, London.
O'Neill, O. (1989) *Constructions of Reason*, Cambridge.
Ossowska, M. (1971) *Social Determinants of Moral Ideas*, London.
Otten, J. (1977) 'Reviving the Logical Connection Argument', *Canadian Journal of Philosophy*, 7.
Parfit, D. (1984) *Reasons and Persons*, Oxford.
Pateman, T. (1987) *What is Philosophy?*, London.
Paton, H.J. (1927) *The Good Will: A Study in the Coherence Theory of Goodness*, London.
Paton, H.J. (1947) *The Categorical Imperative*, London.
Paton, H.J. (1955) *The Modern Predicament*, London.
Peirce, C.S. (1934) 'The Fixation of Belief', *Collected Papers of Charles Sanders Peirce*, ed. C. Hartshorne and P. Weiss, 5, Harvard. Original text: 1877.

Perelman, C. (1963) *The Idea of Justice and the Problem of Argument*, London.
Perry, R.C. (1961) 'Professor Ayer's "Freedom and Necessity" ', *Mind*, 70.
Perry, T.D. (1974) 'A Refutation of Searle's Amended "is-ought" Argument', *Analysis*, 34.
Perry, T.D. (1976) *Moral Reasoning and Truth*, Oxford.
Peters, F.H. (1906) *The Nicomachean Ethics of Aristotle*, 10th ed., London.
Phillips, D.Z. and Mounce, H.D. (1965) 'On Morality's Having a Point', *Philosophy*, 40.
Pigden, C.R. (1990) 'Geach on "Good" ', *Philosophical Quarterly*, 40.
Pivcevic, E. (1986) *The Concept of Reality*, London.
Plamenatz, J.P. (1958) *The English Utilitarians*, Oxford.
Plato (1988) *Republic*, tr. H.D.P. Lee, 2nd ed., Harmondsworth. Original text: *c.* 380 – 370 BC.
Platts, M. (1979) 'Moral Reality', *Ways of Meaning*, London.
Platts, M. (1980) 'Moral Reality and the End of Desire', *Reference, Truth and Reality*, ed. M. Platts, London.
Platts, M. (1988) 'Hume and Morality as Matter of Fact', *Mind*, 97.
Politis, V. (1992) Review of Gosling, 1990, *Cogito*, 6.
Popper, K.R. (1945) *The Open Society and Its Enemies*, 2 vols, London.
Price, A.W. (1986) 'Problems about Projectivism', *Philosophy*, 61.
Price, H.H. (1954) 'Belief and Will', *ASSV*, 28.
Prior, A.N. (1949) *Logic and the Basis of Ethics*, Oxford.
Prior, A.N. (1960) 'The Autonomy of Ethics', *Australasian Journal of Philosophy*, 38.
Putnam, H. (1975) *Mind, Language and Reality*, Cambridge.
Putnam, R.A. (1985) 'Creating Facts and Values', *Philosophy*, 60.
Quine, W.V.O. (1953) *From a Logical Point of View*, New York.
Quinton, A. (1979) 'Objects and Events', *Mind*, 78.
Raphael, D.D. (1969) *British Moralists*, 2 vols, Oxford.
Rashdall, H. (1924) *The Theory of Good and Evil*, 2 vols, 2nd ed., Oxford.
Rawls, J. (1971) *A Theory of Justice*, Oxford.
Raz, J. (1985-6) 'Value Incommensurability', *PAS*, 86.
Raz, J. (1986) *The Morality of Freedom*, Oxford.
Rescher, N. (1973) *The Coherence Theory of Truth*, Oxford.
Rice, H. (1988-9) 'Practical Reasoning as Reasoning', *PAS*, 89.
Richards, D.A.J. (1971) *A Theory of Reasons for Action*, Oxford.
Richards, N. (1978) 'Using People', *Mind*, 87.
Rist, J.M. (1969) *Stoic Philosophy*, Cambridge.
Robertson, J. (1989-90) 'Hume on Practical Reason', *PAS*, 90.
Robinson, N.H.G. (1952) *The Claim of Morality*, London.
Rodd, R. (1987) 'The Challenge of Biological Determinism', *Philosophy*, 62.
Rorty, A.O. (1973) 'The Transformations of Persons', *Philosophy*, 48.
Rorty, A.O. (1978) 'The Place of Contemplation in Aristotle's Nicomachean Ethics', *Mind*, 87.
Rosen, M. (1988-9) 'Kant's Anti-Determinism', *PAS*, 89.
Ross, W.D. (1930) *The Right and the Good*, Oxford.
Ross, W.D. (1939) *Foundations of Ethics*, Oxford.
Ross, W.D. (1964) *Aristotle*, 5th ed., London.
Roubiczek, P. (1969), *Ethical Values in the Age of Science*, Cambridge.
Royce, J. (1908) *The Philosophy of Loyalty*, New York.
Rundle, B. (1972) *Perception, Sensation, and Verification*, Oxford.
Ruse, M (1984) 'The Morality of the Gene', *Monist*, 67.
Russell, B.A.W. (1921) *The Analysis of Mind*, London.
Ryan, C.C. (1980) 'The Normative Concept of Coercion', *Mind*, 79.
Ryle, G. (1949) *The Concept of Mind*, London.
Ryle, G. (1954) 'It Was To Be', *Dilemmas*, Cambridge.
Sartre, J.-P. (1948) *Existentialism and Humanism*, tr. P. Mairet, London.

Sayre-McCord, G. ed. (1988), *Essays on Moral Realism*, Ithaca, USA.

Scaltsas, T. (1989) 'Socratic Moral Realism: An Alternative Justification', *Oxford Studies in Ancient Philosophy*, 7, ed. J. Annas.

Scheffler, S. (1979) 'Moral Scepticism and the Ideals of the Person', *Monist*, 62.

Schlesinger, G.N. (1984) 'Events and Explicative Definitions', *Mind*, 83.

Schlick, M. (1962) *Problems of Ethics*, New York.

Schlossberger, E. (1986) 'Why We are Responsible for Our Emotions', *Mind*, 95.

Scruton, R. (1974) *Art and Imagination*, London.

Scruton, R. (1982) *Kant*, Oxford.

Scruton, R. (1988) '*Rechtsgefühl* and the Rule of Law', *Practical Knowledge: Outlines of a Theory of Traditions and Skills*, ed. J.C. Nyiri and B. Smith, London.

Seanor, D. and Fotion, N. ed. (1988) *Hare and Critics*, Oxford.

Searle, J. (1969) *Speech Acts*, Cambridge.

Sen, A. (1987) *On Ethics and Economics*, Oxford.

Sen, A. and Williams, B. (1982) *Utilitarianism and Beyond*, Cambridge.

Shope, R.K. (1978) 'Rawls, Brandt, and the Definition of Rational Desire', *Canadian Journal of Philosophy*, 8.

Sidgwick, H. (1907) *Methods of Ethics*, 7th ed., London.

Sidgwick, H. (1967) *Outlines of the History of Ethics*, 6th ed., rev. A.J.B. Widgery, London. Original text: 1905.

Silber, J.R. (1982) 'The Moral Good and the Natural Good in Kant's Ethics', *Review of Metaphysics*, 36.

Simon, H.A. (1979) *Models of Thought*, Yale.

Singer, M.G. (1963) *Generalization in Ethics*, London.

Singer, P. (1981) *The Expanding Circle: Ethics and Sociobiology*, Oxford.

Smart, J.J.C. and Williams, B. (1973) *Utilitarianism For and Against*, Cambridge.

Smart, R.N. (1958) 'Negative Utilitarianism', *Mind*, 67.

Smith, B. (1988) 'Knowing How vs. Knowing That', *Practical Knowledge: Outlines of a Theory of Traditions and Skills*, ed. J.C. Nyiri and B. Smith, London.

Smith, J.A. (1911) 'Introduction', *The Nicomachean Ethics of Aristotle*, tr. D.P. Chase, London.

Smith, J.A. (1920-1) 'Morals and Religion', *Hibbert Journal*, 19.

Smith, J.A. (1935) 'Aristotle', Parts I & II, *Philosophy*, 9 & 10.

Smith, H. (1983) 'Culpable Ignorance', *Philosophical Review*, 92.

Smith, M (1986) 'Should We Believe in Emotivism?', *Fact, Science and Morality*, ed. G. Macdonald and C. Wright, Oxford.

Smith, M. (1987) 'The Humean Theory of Motivation', *Mind*, 96.

Snare, F. (1974) 'The Definition of Prima Facie Duties', *Philosophical Quarterly*, 24.

Snare, F. (1975) 'The Argument from Motivation', *Mind*, 84.

Sorabji, R. (1980) *Necessity, Cause and Blame*, London.

Sorley, W.R. (1930) *The Moral Life*, Cambridge.

Sperber, D. and Wilson, D. (1986) *Relevance*, Oxford.

Stephenson, W. (1988) 'Winch on Universalizability', *Philosophical Papers*, 17.

Stevenson, C.L. (1944) *Ethics and Language*, Yale.

Stevenson, C.L. (1963) *Facts and Values*, Yale.

Stich, S. (1983) *From Folk Psychology to Cognitive Science*, Cambridge, USA.

Stock, St George (1908) *Stoicism*, London.

Stocker, M. (1982) 'Responsibility Especially For Beliefs', *Mind*, 81.

Strasser, S. (1983) 'Le syllogisme pratique et son importance pour les sciences humaines', *Revue Philosophique de Louvain*, 81.

Strawson, P.F. (1966) *The Bounds of Sense*, London.

Strawson, P.F. (1968) 'Freedom and Resentment', *Studies in the Philosophy of Thought and Action*, ed. P.F. Strawson, Oxford.

Stubbs, A. (1981) 'The Pros and Cons of Consequentialism', *Philosophy*, 56.

Sturgeon, N.L. (1974) 'Altruism, Solipsism, and the Objectivity of Reasons', *Philosophical Review*, 83.

Sturgeon, N.L. (1976) 'Nature and Conscience in Butler's Ethics', *Philosophical Review*, 85.

Swindler, J.K. (1975) 'Subjects: A Consideration of the Ethics of Aristotle and Kant', *Auslegung*, 3.

Taylor, C.C.W. (1980) 'Plato, Hare and Davidson on Akrasia', *Mind*, 89.

Taylor, R. (1966) *Action and Purpose*, New Jersey.

Telfer, E. (1989-90) 'The Unity of the Moral Virtues in Aristotle's *Nicomachean Ethics*', *PAS*, 90.

Temple, W. (1912) *The Kingdom of God*, London.

Tennant, N. (1983) 'Evolutionary versus Evolved Ethics', *Philosophy*, 58.

Thomas, G.L. (1986) 'Strange Days for Philosophers', *Radical Philosophy*, 44.

Thomas, G.L. (1987) *The Moral Philosophy of T.H. Green*, Oxford.

Thomson, G. (1987) *Needs*, London.

Thornton, M.T. (1982) 'Aristotelian Practical Reasoning', *Mind*, 91.

Tranøy, K.E. (1972) ' "Ought" Implies "Can": A Bridge from Fact to Norm', *Ratio*, 14.

Trépanier, E. (1963-4) 'La politique comme philosophie morale chez Aristote', *Dialogue*, 2.

Unger, R.M. (1975) *Knowledge and Politics*, New York.

Urmson, J.O. (1958) 'Saints and Heroes', *Essays in Moral Philosophy*, ed. A.I. Melden, Seattle.

Urmson, J.O. (1968) *The Emotive Theory of Ethics*, London.

Valberg, E. (1977) 'Philippa Foot on Etiquette and Morality', *Southern Journal of Philosophy*, 15.

Varian, H.R. (1979) 'Distributive Justice, Welfare Economics, and the Theory of Fairness', *Philosophy and Economic Theory*, ed. F. Hahn and M. Hollis, Oxford.

Vlastos, G. (1970) 'On Heraclitus', *Studies in Presocratic Philosophy*, ed. D.J. Furley and R.E. Allen, London.

Vossenkuhl, W. (1987-8) 'The Paradox in Kant's Rational Religion', *PAS*, 88.

Walker, R.C.S. (1988) 'The Rational Imperative: Kant Against Hume', *Proceedings of the British Academy*, 74.

Wallace, D. (1983) Critical Notice of Foot (1978), *Canadian Journal of Philosophy*, 13.

Wallace, R. Jay (1990) 'How to Argue about Practical Reason', *Mind*, 89.

Ward, K. (1970) *Ethics and Christianity*, London.

Ward, K. (1971) 'Kant's Teleological Ethics', *Philosophical Quarterly*, 21.

Ward, K. (1972) *The Development of Kant's View of Ethics*, Oxford.

Warnock, G.J. (1968) 'The Primacy of Practical Reason', *Studies in the Philosophy of Thought and Action*, ed. P.F. Strawson, Oxford.

Warnock, G.J. (1971) *The Object of Morality*, London.

Waterlow, S. (1974) 'Backwards Causation and Continuing', *Mind*, 83.

Watt, J. (1988) 'John Rawls and Human Welfare', *Radical Philosophy*, 49.

Webb, C.C.J. (1923) 'Morality and Religion', *A Century of Anglican Theology and Other Lectures*, Oxford.

Wellman, C. (1971) *Challenge and Response: Justification in Ethics*, S. Illinois.

West, H.R. (1976) 'Mill's Qualitative Hedonism', *Philosophy*, 51.

White, M. (1979) 'Oughts and Cans', *The Idea of Freedom*, ed. A. Ryan, Oxford.

Wiggins, D. (1976) 'Locke, Butler and the Stream of Consciousness: and Men as a Natural Kind', *Philosophy*, 51.

Wiggins, D. (1980) *Sameness and Substance*, Oxford.

Wiggins, D. (1987) *Needs, Values, Truth: Essays in the Philosophy of Value*, Oxford.

Wiggins, D. (1991) 'Categorical Imperatives: Kant and Hume on the Idea of Duty', *Monist*, 74.

Wilkes, K.V. (1978a) 'The Good Man and the Good for Man in Aristotle's Ethics', *Mind*, 87.

Wilkes, K.V. (1978b) *Physicalism*, London.

Williams, B. (1965) 'Ethical Consistency', *ASSV*, 39.

Williams, B. (1971) 'Morality and the Emotions', *Morality and Moral Reasoning*, ed. J. Casey,

London.

Williams, B. (1985) *Ethics and the Limits of Philosophy*, London.

Williams, S. (1989-90) 'Belief, Desire and the Praxis of Reasoning', *PAS*, 90.

Wilson, E.O. (1978) *On Human Nature*, Cambridge, USA.

Wilson, P. (1982) 'Ryan on Coercion', *Mind*, 91.

Winch, P. (1972) 'The Universalizability of Moral Judgements', *Ethics and Action*, London.

Windelband, W. (1893) *A History of Philosophy*, New York and London.

Wittgenstein, L. (1958) *Philosophical Investigations*, tr. G.E.M. Anscombe, 2nd ed., Oxford.

Wolff, J. (1990-1) 'What is the Problem of Political Obligation?', *PAS*, 91.

Wolff, J. (1991) *Robert Nozick*, Oxford.

Wood, A.W. (1976) 'Kant on the Rationality of Morals', *Proceedings of the Ottawa Kant Conference*, Ottawa.

Woods, M. (1986) 'Intuition and Perception in Aristotle's Ethics', *Oxford Studies in Ancient Philosophy*, 4, ed. J. Annas.

Woozley, A.D. (1978) 'Negligence and Ignorance', *Philosophy*, 53.

Wright, C. (1985) Review of S. Blackburn, *Spreading the Word*, *Mind*, 94.

Wright, C. (1988) 'Moral Values, Projection and Secondary Qualities', *ASSV*, 62.

Zink, S. (1962) *The Concepts of Ethics*, London.

Index

Index